DIGITAL PERFORMER FOR ENGINEERS AND PRODUCERS

quick**PRO**
guides

DIGITAL PERFORMER FOR ENGINEERS AND PRODUCERS

David E. Roberts

Hal Leonard Books
An Imprint of Hal Leonard Corporation

Published in 2013 by Hal Leonard Books
An Imprint of Hal Leonard Corporation
7777 West Bluemound Road
Milwaukee, WI 53213

Trade Book Division Editorial Offices
33 Plymouth St., Montclair, NJ 07042

Printed in the United States of America

Book design by Adam Fulrath
Book composition by Kristina Rolander

Library of Congress Cataloging-in-Publication Data

Roberts, David E.
 Digital Performer for engineers and producers : music production, mixing, film scoring, and live performance / David E. Roberts.
     pages cm. -- (Quick pro guides)
 Includes bibliographical references and index.
 1. Digital Performer (Computer file) 2. Digital audio editors. I. Title.
 ML74.4.D54R63 2013
 781.3'4536--dc23
                                   2013021718

ISBN 978-1-4584-0224-0

www.halleonardbooks.com

To my wife, Lisa

CONTENTS

Chapter 3

Chapter 4

INTRODUCTION

Digital Performer (DP) is digital audio workstation software for a Mac or Windows computer. It has been used by professionals for many years as a sophisticated production tool. *Digital Performer for Engineers and Producers*: *Music Production, Mixing, Film Scoring, and Live Performance* focuses on three typical uses of the software: live performance, sound for picture, and studio production. Although each section deals with specialized uses of the software, there are tips and techniques described throughout the book that will be helpful for any DP user.

This book assumes that the reader has a basic understanding of how to create a session file in DP and how to navigate within that file. *Digital Performer for Engineers and Producers* is designed to be intermediate to advanced in its descriptions of the functions of the software.

This book is not designed to be a replacement for the *Digital Performer User Guide*, which ships with DP as a printed reference text, and is also available in PDF format from the Help menu. The user guide works as a companion and reference volume to *Digital Performer for Engineers and Producers*.

Each section of this book explores the tips and tricks used by top professionals to get the most out of DP. *Digital Performer for Engineers and Producers: Music Production, Mixing, Film Scoring, and Live Performance* will turn the reader into a DP Power User.

A General Description of Digital Performer

Digital Performer is software. It has the following basic functions:
- Import and recording of audio and MIDI data
- Import of video files
- Import of additional file formats, including OMF, AAF, and XML formats
- Playback of audio, MIDI, and video

- Use as a music composition tool
- Creation, editing, and output of music notation
- Transmission and reception of time code synchronization
- Live processing of audio and MIDI signals
- Editing and production of audio and MIDI
- Mixing and mastering
- Export of various file and data formats

These capabilities allow DP to be used in many different ways for a wide variety of purposes.

Three Typical Uses of Digital Performer

Historically, Digital Performer has been used by musicians and audio engineers for three general functions:

- Recording, playback, and processing in live performance
- Music composition, scoring, and post-production for picture
- Music composition and production in the studio

Digital Performer for Engineers and Producers is divided into four sections. The first section deals with general requirements for setting up a DP-based system. This includes essential configuration information, regardless of the intended use of DP.

There are sections for Live Performance, Film Scoring, and Music Production. These sections describe specific requirements and techniques for using DP in those situations.

The Included DVD

In addition to text and illustrations, a DVD is included that contains DP example files and tutorial movies. The example files are set up to show off specific functions and templates for various uses of DP. The movies are tutorials for specific functions that are discussed in the book.

The example files on the DVD are the same files that are used in the tutorial movies. This allows the reader to open the example files in DP and work along with the tutorial movies.

The files and movies on the DVD are described in detail in the appendix.

Chapter 1
DESIGNING A DP SYSTEM

The following section will describe the general hardware requirements to set up an efficient and reliable system for working with Digital Performer. In later sections, there will be additional information that describes more detailed requirements for specific tasks. Because DP can be used for many types of jobs, there can be many different configurations of hardware and software. Some tasks have minimal requirements. Other tasks require more resources and more complex configurations.

The Computer

Digital Performer is software that runs on a Mac or Windows computer. There are minimal computer hardware and software requirements to run DP efficiently. Computer specifications include hardware and software. Minimum requirements for DP include CPU type and speed, operating system version, amount of installed RAM, and hard drive configuration.

Operating System

DP8 will install and run under Mac OS 10.6.8 or later, or Windows 7 or later. Therefore the first requirement to run DP is a computer that is running a compatible version of Mac or Windows OS.

Digital Performer is written and designed to be the same program on both platforms. There is no "better" platform to run DP. In most cases, the DP user will choose to run on Mac or Windows based on a computer they may already own, or a familiarity with either the Mac or Windows OS in general.

There are inevitable differences between DP on Mac and Windows. For example, the Audio Unit plug-in standard is a Mac protocol that does not exist under Windows. ASIO audio interface drivers are a Windows OS standard protocol, but are not a Mac OS protocol. The good news is that the basic functionality of DP is the same under Mac and Windows, and it is possible to move files and entire projects between the two platforms if that is ever required. The VST instruments and effects plug-in protocol is native to Mac and Windows OS, and is supported by DP on both platforms.

Computer Specifications

When selecting a computer to run Digital Performer, the critical components of the computer include:

- CPU type and speed (including multi-core processors): Any current generation Mac or Windows computer is at least powerful enough to run DP. The faster the CPU, the more performance DP will be able to provide. CPU speed affects how many tracks can be recorded or played back, how many effect plug-ins can run, and how many simultaneous virtual instruments can be used. CPU speed also makes a difference to video playback efficiency. Digital Performer takes full advantage of multiple CPU cores and hyper-threading.
- Installed RAM: Minimum RAM to run DP is 4 GB. More RAM will improve performance, especially with virtual instruments. DP runs as a 64-bit application on both Mac and Windows, which means it can take advantage of as much RAM as is available in the computer.
- Hard drive configuration: Digital Performer can use the stock internal hard drive for recording and playback. As with other aspects of the computer, more power means greater performance. A faster hard drive will allow a greater number of simultaneous record/playback of audio tracks. Video playback can be demanding on a hard drive. Therefore using separate drives for audio recording/playback, video playback, and virtual instrument sample streaming will improve overall performance.
- Available connection formats on the computer (USB, Firewire, PCI, Thunderbolt, etc.): Connection formats on a computer have to do with moving data in and out of the computer. In some cases the only connection required on the computer may be a built-in headphone jack. Audio interfaces and MIDI interfaces connect via a variety of protocols. Specific requirements for audio and MIDI interface connection will be discussed in later sections.

Monitors

Digital Performer can be run on a simple laptop configuration, or as part of an elaborate system with two or more video monitors. The only requirement for video monitors is that the operator is comfortable looking at the screen or screens.

The DP user interface provides many options for customizing how the software looks on the computer monitor. The entire program can be viewed in a single consolidated window. Any combination of windows can be displayed on any combination of monitors. Window sets can be saved and recalled, and assigned to hot keys.

Audio Interfaces

An audio interface is a hardware device that provides audio input and output to a computer. Audio interfaces can be rack devices, tabletop boxes, or cables with specific built-in connections. An audio interface may provide analog and/or digital audio connections. An audio interface may have a single channel of input or output, or it may be a sophisticated system with many channels of input and output. Most computers have some sort of onboard audio input and output connections. Although these connections are built in to the computer, they are still considered an audio interface.

Digital Performer uses standard drivers to communicate with the audio interface. DP will work on Mac OS with any audio interface that supports Apple Core Audio drivers. DP will work on Windows OS with any audio interface that supports WDM or ASIO drivers. This includes the built-in audio jacks of the computer.

Many currently available audio interfaces have some sort of built-in mixer for direct input to output monitoring. Some audio interfaces also have DSP processing, such as EQ, dynamics, or reverb.

Audio interfaces may have additional features such as the ability to receive or generate time code. Some models of audio interfaces also have MIDI inputs and outputs, foot switch inputs, and remote control capabilities.

Choosing the appropriate audio interface is a process of identifying the requirements of the task at hand, and then finding the model of interface that has the features needed to get that job done.

MIDI Interfaces

A MIDI interface is a hardware device or connection that provides MIDI input and output to the computer. Digital Performer will work with any MIDI interface that is supported under Mac or Windows OS. A dedicated MIDI interface hardware box typically connects to the computer via USB and provides from one to eight MIDI input and output connections. MIDI input and output ports may also be found on some models of audio interfaces.

An external MIDI device such as a keyboard controller may have a built-in USB port for direct connection to the computer. That means the device has its own built-in MIDI interface. If the USB keyboard (for example) is the only MIDI device that needs to be connected to the computer, no additional MIDI interface is required.

A MIDI interface is required in order to connect external MIDI devices to the computer. Therefore, to select an appropriate MIDI interface, the system designer needs to know how many MIDI devices need to be connected. It is desirable to have a dedicated MIDI port connection for each hardware device. For large systems it is possible to use a USB hub to connect several multiport USB MIDI interfaces.

Some models of MIDI interfaces can also function as MIDI patch bays. A MIDI patch bay provides the the capability to directly connect MIDI input ports to MIDI output ports. A MIDI patch bay may function as a stand-alone MIDI router when disconnected from the computer. A typical use of a MIDI patch bay is to provide MIDI routing capabilities for MIDI hardware in a live performance, when no computer is in use. When external MIDI hardware is used with a software MIDI sequencer such as DP, typically all input to output routing is done by the software, and through the computer.

A MIDI interface may have the capability to filter different types of MIDI data. This is also a function that is typically used in a live performance configuration, as opposed to when the interface is connected to a computer and communicating with DP.

If the MIDI interface has patch bay or filtering capabilities, there is usually some sort of software utility that is used to make those settings. For example, Clockworks software is used to configure MOTU MIDI interfaces that have patch bay functions.

Video Interfaces

By definition, a video interface is a device that provides video input and output to the computer. Digital Performer does not record video, so it has no use for video input. However, DP can play back a digital video file, and that picture can be displayed on the computer screen, as well as on a dedicated external video monitor. For live performance, it is even possible for DP to play back video that is sent to projectors to be viewed by an audience.

To play back video to an external monitor or projector, DP can use a dedicated video interface. Video interfaces can connect to the computer via Firewire, PCI, ExpressCard, or Thunderbolt.

Digital Performer supports video and audio playback through the MOTU V4HD, HD Express, and HDX-SDI interfaces. DP also supports video playback through general firewire video converters such as the Grass Valley ADVC110. For more information, visit: http://www.grassvalley.com/products/advc110.

Figure 1.1

Third-Party Plug-Ins and Applications

Digital Performer provides support for common plug-in formats on Mac and Windows OS. On Mac, DP supports MAS, AudioUnit, VST, and Rewire protocols. On Windows, DP supports MAS, VST, and ReWire. This allows DP to run internal effects and instruments developed by other companies. Rewire also allows DP to synchronize with external software applications.

Effect plug-ins

Third-party plug-ins work the same way as stock plug-ins in DP. Effect plug-ins are instantiated on inserts for audio tracks, aux tracks, master faders, and effects inserts on instrument tracks. Third-party plug-ins are managed the same way as stock DP plug-ins. All installed plug-ins can be enabled or disabled in the Preferences window. All loaded plug-ins will be available in the Effects Chooser window. A powerful feature of the Effects Chooser window is that it can sort and display plug-ins by manufacturer.

The capabilities of the plug-in are up to the designer. For example, some plug-ins may support more than two channels of input and output, and can work as surround-sound plug-ins. Other plug-ins may not support multi-channel formats. Some plug-ins support external MIDI control. Others do not. Some third-party effect plug-ins have their own preset management system. The third-party presets will work in DP. Digital Performer still also supports its own internal preset system, which will work with third-party plug-ins.

The various plug-in protocols are designed to provide a standardized method of programming. The idea is that no matter who develops the host software or the plug-in, they will work together. However, the reality is that standards continually change, along with updates to both plug-ins and host applications, as well as to the operating systems. Therefore, incompatibility between plug-ins and host applications can happen. It is always a good idea to check that the latest versions are installed.

Instrument Plug-Ins

Third-party instrument plug-ins work the same way as the stock instrument plug-ins in DP. Virtual instruments are instantiated on instrument tracks. Instrument tracks are created via the Project menu>Add Track>Instrument Track.

Third-party virtual instruments can support multiple channels of MIDI input and audio output within DP. Digital Performer supports pre-rendering and automatic delay compensation with third-party instrument plug-ins.

Running virtual instruments can be one of the most taxing jobs for a computer DAW. If the computer is underpowered or does not have enough RAM, large virtual instruments can cause audio problems or crashes. A slow hard drive can cause problems with virtual instruments that use sample disk streaming. This type of problem may not be the fault of the instrument, host application, or OS. There are two effective ways to check whether a virtual instrument is overwhelming the available computer resources: If a large sampled instrument is loaded, or if many instruments, audio tracks, and effects are running, cutting back on that load will indicate whether a lesser load makes a difference to system performance. Also, some virtual instruments have the capability to run as stand-alone applications. This allows the instrument to be tested by itself, with no other software running. As with any software, it is always a good idea to make sure the latest updates are installed.

ReWire

ReWire is a protocol developed by the Propellerheads Software company. ReWire is supported by DP on both Mac and Windows. ReWire allows DP to synchronize with another software application, running on the same computer, that also supports the ReWire protocol. Examples of other programs that support ReWire are Plogue Bidule, Reason, and Ableton Live.

When two software programs communicate via ReWire, one program is the master and the other program is the slave. Digital Performer functions as a ReWire master. That means DP must be launched first, and the ReWire slave application must be launched second. If the ReWire slave application is launched before DP is launched, the two applications will not communicate.

ReWire provides for synchronization, MIDI, and audio transfer between DP and the slave program. Digital Performer can use a ReWire application as an external sequencer or rack of virtual instruments. MIDI and audio communication is done via inputs and outputs to tracks in DP.

To set upDigital Performer with Reason:

- Launch DP and create or open a session file.
- Launch Reason. Reason can be configured to open to an existing file, or to open to an empty rack.
- In order for DP and Reason to properly communicate, there must be an audio return from Reason into DP. In DP, create either an aux or audio track.
- Assign the output of the DP aux or audio track to the main monitor outputs.
- Click on the input assignment for the aux or audio track and choose either New Mono or New Stereo Bundle. The resulting menu will include all the ReWire audio return channels that are available from Reason.

Figure 1.2

- In Reason,create at least one virtual instrument and load a patch. Reason provides sophisticated internal routing options, including mixers and effects. Make sure the output of the instrument is ultimately routed to an output on the Reason audio interface. That Reason output should be what is selected as the input to the DP aux or audio track.

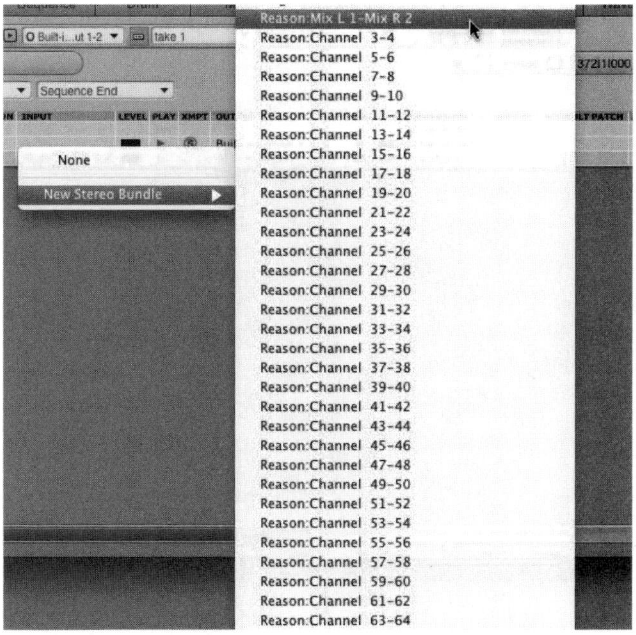

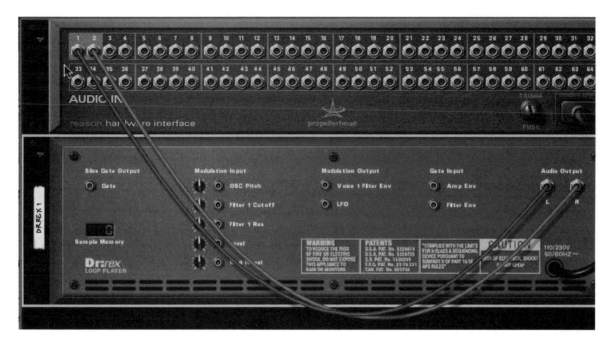

Figure 1.3

- In DP, create a MIDI track. If all previous steps have been followed correctly, all devices currently installed in the Reason rack that can receive MIDI will now be available as output assignment choices to DP MIDI tracks. Select the Reason virtual instrument as the output assignment for the DP MIDI track.

Figure 1.4

- Record-enable the DP MIDI track. This will provide MIDI Patch Thru from an external MIDI controller to the Reason instrument. At this point, if an external controller generates a MIDI note, that MIDI note should pass through the DP MIDI track and out to the Reason virtual instrument. The Reason virtual instrument should then generate audio, which is routed back into DP to the aux or audio track. The aux or audio track can then pass the live audio signal to the main monitor outputs.
- The audio output of the Reason instrument can be recorded into the audio track.
- Additional effect plug-ins can be applied to the Reason aux or audio tracks in DP.

- Reason has its own internal sequencer and some tempo-based effects. The transport and tempo or Reason are locked to DP. That means Reason will follow the transport commands and tempo of DP.

If a ReWire application is not working correctly with Digital Performer, here is a trouble-shooting checklist:

- Make sure DP is launched before the ReWire software. The ReWire software must be in slave mode. The ReWire application may have some sort of indication of its mode. For example, in Reason, the audio interface at the top of the rack shows whether Reason is in master mode or ReWire slave mode.

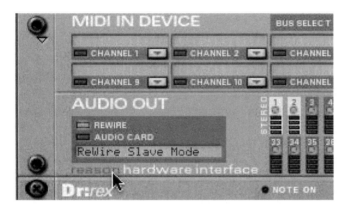

Figure 1.5

- Make sure there is a working audio return from the ReWire program into DP. In DP, there must be at least one aux or audio track that has a ReWire input assignment and a working audio output assignment. If the input or output assignment of the DP aux or audio track is displayed in italics, that means it must be reassigned.

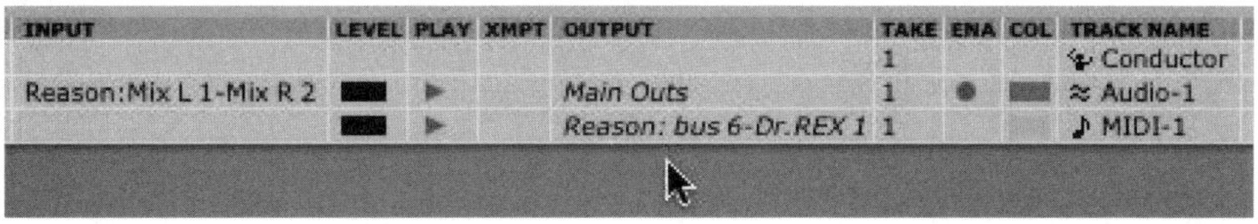

INPUT	LEVEL	PLAY	XMPT	OUTPUT	TAKE	ENA	COL	TRACK NAME
					1			Conductor
Reason:Mix L 1-Mix R 2	▮	►		Main Outs	1	●	▮	≈ Audio-1
	▮	►		Reason: bus 6-Dr.REX 1	1			♪ MIDI-1

Figure 1.6

- In order to trigger a ReWire virtual instrument from DP, there must be a MIDI track in DP that is assigned to the ReWire instrument. If the ReWire output of the MIDI track is displayed in italics, it must be reassigned. If the ReWire instrument is not available as an output assignment for a DP MIDI track, that means one of two things: There is no virtual instrument set up and available within a ReWire slave program, or there is no audio return set up from the ReWire program back to DP.
- In order to trigger a ReWire virtual instrument through DP, the DP MIDI track must be record-enabled. Make sure that MIDI Patch Thru is set to Auto-Channelize. Check to make sure that external MIDI does record into the MIDI track. Also check playback of recorded MIDI to the ReWire instrument.
- If a ReWire instrument can be triggered by an external controller when there is no record-enabled MIDI track in DP, that means the ReWire program is configured to receive direct external MIDI input, as well as ReWire MIDI input.

- If there is no audio signal from the ReWire program back into DP, check the audio routing in the ReWire program. Make sure the same ReWire audio channels are being used for output from the ReWire program and as inputs into DP. Make sure the aux or audio track in DP is routed to a working monitor output. If an audio track is used for the ReWire audio return, make sure that DP is set to monitor through record-enabled tracks, and make sure Audio Patch Thru is enabled both in DP and for the specific audio track.

Additional Software Programs

Digital Performer can interact directly with other stand-alone software programs. This can include other programs running on the same computer as DP or on remote computers.

DP can send and receive MIDI via interapplication drivers and network drivers. DP can send and receive audio via utilities such as Soundflower, see http://cycling74.com/soundflower-landing-page/.

Figure 1.7

and Audio HiJack at http://www.rogueamoeba.com/audiohijackpro/.

Figure 1.8

DP can transmit or receive MIDI clock and MIDI Time Code.

Digital Performer supports a wide range of standardized file formats for audio, MIDI, video, graphics, and sophisticated session import and export. These formats are discussed in later chapters.

Reliability and Troubleshooting

Part of of the goal of creating and using a DP-based system is to have everything working as expected, and working reliably. The design of a DP system can be based on a realistic expectation of the hardware and software requirements for a specific task. A properly designed DP-based system will be efficient and reliable.

If any part of the system doesn't work as expected, or malfunctions in any way, there is always a way to test the system to isolate and diagnose the problem. Most troubleshooting can be a simple process of elimination. If the operator has a basic understanding of how the system works, it should not be a problem to isolate and work around any "unexpected event."

Building and Maintaining a Reliable DP System

Any software or hardware component can break or malfunction. A single malfunction within a system can cause the entire system to work poorly, or not at all. If there is a problem, it can usually be isolated and fixed. A better idea is to avoid problems in the first place.

A practical approach to building and using a DP-based system is to understand the job to be done, and its requirements. A DP-based system can be designed and optimized for specific uses. Once the system is up and running, basic maintenance can keep that system working at optimum efficiency.

In a critical situation, such as playback or recording in a live performance situation, a malfunction of the computer could be a disaster. It is possible to have multiple backup systems to ensure that if one system stops working, another setup is ready to automatically kick in and take over. Even in a less critical environment, the artist or engineer should have an assurance that the various hardware and software components work together efficiently. Contingency and backup plans can be created when appropriate.

Reliability comes from having a system that is properly configured and tested. As the system is being designed, care should be taken to understand the software and hardware requirements of the specific tasks.

If a computer is running at the limits of its capabilities, it is more vulnerable to crashes and other problems. Different tasks in a DAW system use different computer resources. It's a good idea to understand what type of load is being placed on the computer, depending on how the computer is being used. In some cases, more RAM will improve performance. In other cases, a faster CPU or hard drive may make the critical difference. It is possible to test different parts of the system to see where there is more or less load and activity.

Headroom always makes a system more reliable. More CPU power, more RAM, and faster hard drives almost always make an improvement to computer-related functions.

A computer is a complex device that interacts with software and hardware that come from many different sources. All the various components need to be compatible with each other. If a hardware or software component doesn't work in some way, it can affect the reliability and performance of the entire system. As a DP-based system is being built, attention should be paid to each additional software and hardware component that is in use. It is always a good idea to check that software or hardware is listed by the manufacturer as compatible with the computer OS.

How to Diagnose and Solve Problems

When something doesn't work as expected, there is a two-step procedure to solve the problem. The cause of the problem must be isolated, and then either fixed or worked around.

Troubleshooting is usually a process of elimination. Change one variable at a time and test. If changing a variable makes no difference to symptoms, move to the next variable. If changing something about the system does change the problem symptom, that may point in the direction of the cause.

The causes of system problems fall into several basic categories:

- All components are working, but a parameter setting or connection is incorrect somewhere in the system: Within DP, it is possible to reset the preferences to factory defaults. The MIDI Monitor window is useful to check for MIDI input. The Meter Bridge window is useful to check for audio input and output. Tracing the signal path for audio or MIDI can be helpful. Does MIDI or audio record into a track? Does it play back? What are the clock settings for the audio interface?

- There is some sort of problem with a specific file: If there is a problem within a file, that problem will likely not exist in a new, empty file. Creating a new file in DP is a good way to test whether a problem is file-specific, or general to any DP file. If a problem appears to be specific to a DP session file, it may be possible to isolate that problem and rescue the rest of the file. One technique is to create a new empty DP session file, and use the Load command to try to import data from the problem file. The Load command allows individual sequences and other specific parts of a DP session file to be imported.

- There is a flaw or malfunction in a piece of software or hardware: If something is wrong with a piece of hardware or software, the solution may be to isolate the problem and work around it until the software is updated or the hardware is repaired. In most cases, if there is a software bug or broken hardware, the problem will be repeatable, and will happen with a newly created file.

- There is a compatibility or environmental problem for the software or hardware: This can be a common type of problem in a DAW system. A computer recording system is complex combination of software and hardware components. These components must all be compatible with the computer, and with each other.

Chapter 2
LIVE
PERFORMANCE

Digital Performer has multiple uses in a live performance situation:

- Digital Performer can be used for live recording. This can include audio and MIDI tracks. DP can record while referenced to external time code. DP can record while generating time code. DP can record while playing back pre-recorded tracks. The number of audio and MIDI tracks that can be recorded in DP is limited only by the power of the computer and the number of available inputs on the audio and MIDI interfaces.

- Digital Performer can be used for onstage playback. This can include audio, MIDI, and video. Playback tracks can sent to independent outputs for routing to musicians' monitors, front of house, or any other required destination. DP can play back while referenced to external time code or while generating time code. DP provides powerful tools for set list management. DP has complete remote control accessibility. It is possible to set up synchronized redundant backup systems for absolute performance reliability.

- Digital Performer can be used as a live host for virtual instruments. DP can provide powerful signal routing and effects processing for virtual instruments. Live setups can be programmed to change sounds, routing, and effects on the fly.

- Digital Performer can be used for MIDI and audio routing control for external instruments and sounds. DP can process external audio and MIDI signals in real time, allowing for sophisticated software plug-in setups and mixing control for live sound. Live mixes can be automated and synchronized to other aspects of the live performance.

- Digital Performer can do all these tasks at the same time on the same computer. It is also possible to use multiple computers in a live setting and to distribute different jobs to dedicated, synchronized workstations.

The number one consideration for a live setup should always be reliability. Artists and engineers need to know that their tools will not fail at a critical moment. Reliability comes from having a properly configured system, and rigorously testing that system before it is used on stage.

The following sections will discuss how to build and optimize a Digital Performer system for live use.

Recording

Multitrack recording is a basic operation for DP. In order to set up a working system, the following hardware is required:

- Computer
- Hard drive
- Audio and/or MIDI interface

Computer Requirements

Any current generation Mac or Windows computer is powerful enough to record at least 24 simultaneous tracks of audio at 24-bit, 44.1/48 kHz resolution. To record more than 24 simultaneous tracks, and for higher sample rates, a more powerful computer may be required. The computer needs to have at least 4 GB of installed RAM. For longer recordings (an hour or more), more RAM is desirable. For the most robust multitrack recording system, 8-12 GB RAM is adequate.

Hard Drive Requirements

The hard drive must be fast enough to record the data, and must have enough space to store the recorded data. In many cases the stock internal drive of the computer may be adequate for multitrack recording. There are different advantages to using internal or external drives for recording. For a portable recording system, it may be most convenient to record to the internal drive of a laptop computer. The advantage of dedicated internal or external record drives is that they can be configured for maximum efficiency, and external drives are easily moved between different computer systems.

If an external hard drive is used for recording, there are a number of ways that drive can connect to the computer. USB2.0 and Firewire 400 have roughly the same performance. USB3.0 and Firewire 800 are faster protocols. External drives may also connect via expansion cards with eSata connections. The newest connection protocol is Thunderbolt. ESata and Thunderbolt are the fastest available connections for external drives.

Drives are available with different rotation speeds. Solid State Drives (SSD) are also available. The faster the drive, the more simultaneous tracks the drive can record.

It is possible to use multiple hard drives simultaneously for recording and playback of audio. This may significantly increase the number of tracks that can be recorded or played back in the session. In DP, it is possible to assign audio record tracks to any available hard drives. Recording to, or playing from multiple drives can distribute the load and increase overall track count.

Different sample rates and different bit depth use different amounts of hard drive space. It is possible to calculate how much space is needed for recording:

- 16-bit/44.1 kHz audio uses 5 MB per mono minute
- 24-bit/44.1 kHz audio uses 7.5 MB per mono minute
- 24-bit/96 kHz audio uses 16.5 MB per mono minute
- 24-bit/192 kHz audio uses 34 MB per mono minute

Therefore, a one-hour recording of 24 tracks of audio recorded at 24-bit/44.1 kHz resolution will require 10.8 GB of hard drive space.

In general, it's a good idea to always have more drive space than is required. Try to keep at least 10 GB of free space on any recording drive. This will help with long-term drive performance.

Audio Interface Requirements

The audio interface provides channels of audio input and output to the computer. There must be an individual input on the interface for each separate track that is to be recorded in a single recording pass. In other words, in order to record 24 tracks of simultaneous audio, there must be 24 available inputs on the audio interface.

Audio interfaces connect to a computer via USB, Firewire, PCI, or Thunderbolt protocols. USB and Firewire have enough bandwidth to pass a reliable 24 channels of audio at 44.1/48 kHz sample rate. PCI and Thunderbolt connections can pass a great deal more data. For example, a PCI-based MOTU 24i/o audio interface system can pass up to 96 channels of 24-bit input and output at 96 kHz sampling rate.

Most modern computer audio interfaces also have some sort of direct monitoring capabilities. This allows input signals to be routed directly to outputs of the audio interface. Direct input monitoring has zero CPU latency delay, and does not place any load on the computer.

Some models of audio interfaces have built-in effects processing. For example, the MOTU 896mk3 Hybrid interface has eight channels of mic line analog inputs, as well as optical, S/PDIF, and AES/EBU digital inputs. Each input can have a seven band EQ, and two types of dynamics compressor. These effects are applied inside the interface, before the input signal reaches the computer. This allows for EQ and dynamics conditioning of the signal before it is recorded.

MIDI Interface Requirements

In order to record MIDI from an external source into DP, there must be a path for that MIDI signal. Some external MIDI controllers have direct USB connections to the computer. If the external device does not have a USB port, or if multiple MIDI devices need to be connected, a MIDI interface is required.

Some models of audio interface also have MIDI ports. If additional ports are still required, a dedicated MIDI interface will do the job. The interface should have enough MIDI ports to connect all external devices.

File Formats

Uncompressed digital audio is typically stored in a WAV or AIFF file. WAV and AIFF are similar formats and are recognized on Mac or Windows computers.

AAC and MP3 are examples of compressed digital audio formats. Digital Performer does not directly record or play compressed audio. DP can import and export compressed audio formats.

To set the format of the audio files to be recorded, go to the Preferences window>General>Audio Files. At the top of the window are settings for the default audio file format, as well as settings specific to the currently open DP session file.

The choices for sample format include 16-bit, 24-bit, and 32-bit. For most musical applications, 24 is the typical default bit depth. 16-bit is used for output to audio CDs. 32-bit float is a special file format that uses a floating decimal point to describe an extremely wide dynamic range.

The interleave option describes whether multichannel audio will be recorded into a single stereo or surround audio file, or whether individual channels of an audio signal will be recorded into separate single-channel audio files.

Monitoring

In a live recording situation, there is typically a separate audio monitoring system for the musicians. The front of house mix engineer listens to the PA system. The recording engineer typically monitors the signals going into or out of the recording system.

At the very least, it's a good idea to have a pair of headphones available to check signals. If each input signal is recorded to its own track, the engineer only needs to check that the signal is present, and is a proper level. If signals are to be submixed together before recording, then it is important that signals can be properly monitored to ensure that the inputs are properly balanced in the submix.

There are two ways to monitor input signals with a DP system. Input signals can be monitored independently of the computer. In a live recording situation, external mixers may be used for stage monitors and front of house speakers. Monitoring may take place long before the signals reach the recording system. Another possibility for external monitoring is that the audio interface may have direct monitoring capabilities. This means the input signals are passed directly to output on the audio interface, and monitored from there.

Figure 2.1

It is also possible to monitor through DP. Monitoring through DP allows monitoring through plug-in effects. The trade off of monitoring through DP is that the computer introduces latency delay to the monitored signal. In order to reduce that CPU delay, a setting in the audio hardware driver called Buffer Size can be adjusted. The faster the patch through, the greater the load on the computer. This load is compounded by the number of channels being patched through, and by any plug-in effects that may be running.

To enable monitoring through effects in DP, go to the Setup menu>Configure Audio System>Input Monitoring Mode. In this window, select Monitor record-enabled tracks through effects.

Now go to the Studio Menu>Audio Patch Thru, and select Auto.

To reduce monitoring latency delay, go to the Setup menu>Configure Audio System>Configure Hardware Driver. Adjust the Buffer Size setting. Typically settings of 128 or 64 will provide a fast enough patch through that musicians do not notice any delay on the monitored signal.

Patch through monitoring latency delay may not be a concern in all recording situations. For example the recording system may be in a remote location, or the recording engineer may be setting levels based only on input VU meters. If the recording engineer does not need to hear the input signals in real time, monitoring latency becomes irrelevant. If monitoring latency is not a concern, leave the Buffer Size at its highest available setting in order to conserve CPU power.

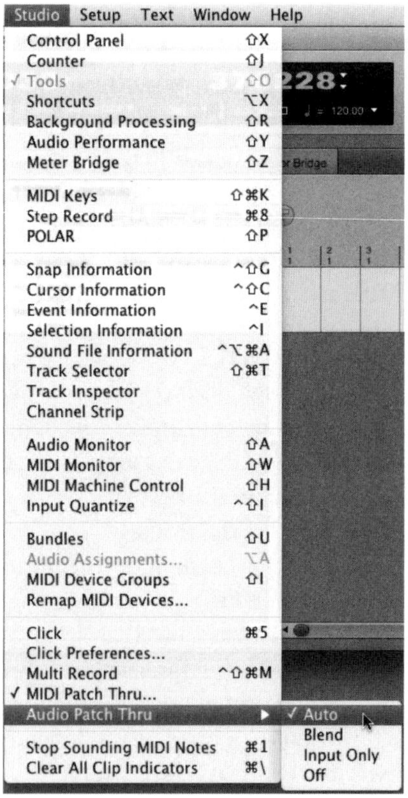

Figure 2.2

Setting Up the DP Session File

Audio and MIDI tracks are required in order to record audio and MIDI data. It is possible to add multiple tracks to a DP session with a single operation. Hold down the Option/Alt key and click on the Project menu>Add Track. The Option/Alt key will cause the Add Track function to show Add Multiple MIDI Tracks, and Add Multiple Mono or Add Multiple Stereo Audio Tracks.

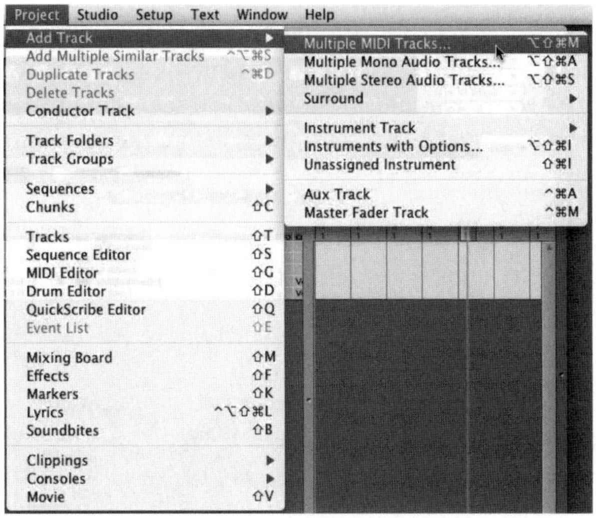

Figure 2.3

When one of these options is selected, a window opens that allows the DP operator to specify the number of tracks to be added.

If any track is currently selected in an edit window, newly added tracks will appear below the selected track. If no track is selected, the new tracks will be added at the bottom of the track list.

When new audio tracks are added, the outputs of those tracks are all assigned to the first available stereo output in the Bundles window. Inputs of newly added tracks are assigned to consecutive available input bundles. This means that if multiple input bundles are created before the audio tracks are added, the newly added audio tracks will automatically be assigned to the available bundles.

It is possible to assign inputs and outputs to multiple existing tracks with a single command. Select the tracks and go to the Studio menu>Audio Assignments... This window provides a range of options for assigning track inputs and outputs to available bundles.

If there are multiple MIDI sources that need to be recorded to different MIDI tracks, go to the Studio menu and select Multi-Record. When DP is in multirecord mode, it is possible to record-enable more than one MIDI track at a time. In multirecord mode, the input for each MIDI track must be specified.

Figure 2.4

Figure 2.5

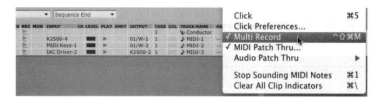

Figure 2.6

It may be desirable to create a DP recording template ahead of time. This will save time in the session, and provide an organized recording environment.

Track colors and folders can be used to easily identify specific tracks and groups of tracks. Inputs, outputs, and subgroups can be preconfigured before the recording session.

In the following graphic, DP is set up for a 24-track recording session with four additional tracks set up for MIDI recording. Notice that the Audio Monitor window is displayed to show record levels. Notice that DP is in multirecord mode and each of the MIDI tracks has a separate input assignment.

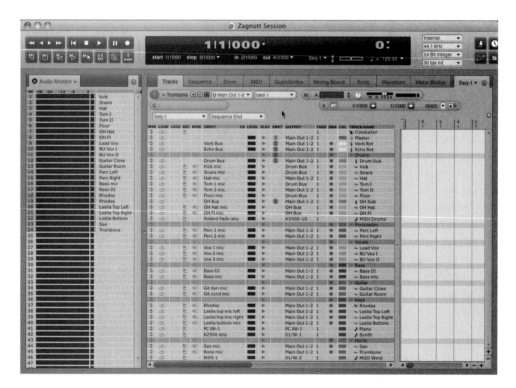

Figure 2.7

Subgroups, Master Faders, and Recording Through Effects

Digital Performer provides buses aux tracks, which can be used to create subgroups. Subgroups are typically used at mixdown to group playback tracks together, and to create effects returns. Playback subgroups and effects returns are not a requirement during the recording process. It is possible to have playback subgroups and effects return in a recording template, but that part of the signal path is after the recording stage, and therefore has no effect on the recorded signals.

If any type of mixdown is done in DP, it's always a good idea to run the final mix through a master fader. The master fader provides a single volume control point for the mix. The master fader provides a way to monitor the sum total of the mix gain. It's also possible to put effect plug-ins on the master fader that will affect the entire mix.

If an effect plug-in is placed on an audio track, the plug-in is on playback only. It is possible to monitor a live input signal through a plug-in effect. If an effect is placed on an audio track, the signal can be recorded while monitoring its output through the effect. The recorded signal will be "dry," meaning that the effect was not printed as part of the recording process. Because the effect is on playback only, it can be adjusted or tuned off at any time in the mix process.

It is possible to place plug-in effects in the signal chain before the record stage. It is also possible to submix multiple input signals in DP before they are recorded to audio tracks. This is done by creating aux tracks and buses, and passing the input signal through the aux track and bus, and then into an audio track. If a plug-in is placed on the aux track, it will affect the input signal before it is recorded. If multiple aux tracks are set to different inputs and then their outputs are assigned to a common bus, the bus can pass the submixed signals to an audio track for recording. Submixing and adding effects can increase the overall gain of the signal, so it is important to check the level of the signal going into the audio track for recording, so that it does not overload and clip.

In the following graphic, a live guitar signal is routed into DP through an aux track. The aux track is bussed to an audio track for recording. There is a plug-in effect on the aux track, which means the audio track will record the signal with the effect.

Figure 2.8

Tempo and Clicks

It is not a requirement to use a click, or any kind of tempo reference, when recording with DP. If required, it is possible to record without a click track, and then create a tempo map around the musical performance at a later time. This will be discussed in the chapter on studio production techniques.

If a click track is to be used for the recording, DP can generate that click. It is possible to preprogram a tempo map with tempo changes. For example, if DP is used to compose music for picture, it is a common technique to do the initial composition with MIDI instruments and programmed tempo maps. Then, a live orchestra can play along with the click that is generated by the DP sequence, and the live performance will synchronize with the original score.

Digital Performer can generate a MIDI click, audio click, or video click. A MIDI click signal can be assigned to an internal virtual instrument or an external MIDI sound module. An audio click can be routed to any audio output on the audio interface. A video click is a punch that is superimposed over a movie playing within DP.

To set click preferences, Double+Click on the Click button in the Control Panel, or open the Preferences window.

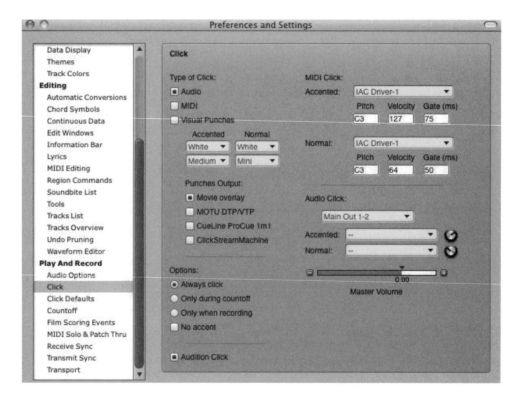

Figure 2.9

To set up an audio click, a click sound must be selected, and an audio output must be selected. If either of these pop-up menus appear in italics, they must be reassigned. Digital Performer installs a number of available click sounds. Any WAV or AIFF audio file can also be assigned as the click sound. The output assignment for the audio click can be assigned directly to an audio interface output. The audio click can also be assigned to a bus, which allows the click to be routed as an audio signal within DP. For example, the click audio output could be assigned to a bus, which is then assigned to the input of an audio track. This would allow the audio click to be recorded and printed to an audio file.

Figure 2.10

Single or Multiple Sequence Chunks

In DP, the word "chunk" is used to describe a sequence timeline. A sequence chunk can contain an unlimited number of audio and MIDI tracks. Each sequence chunk has its own mixing board. A single DP session file can contain one or more sequence chunks.

A new DP session file initially contains a single sequence chunk. The sequence chunk can be thought of as similar to a reel of tape. A sequence chunk can be used to record a single take, or an entire recording session. New sequence chunks can be added at any time. Sequence chunks can be renamed by Option/Alt+Clicking on the name in the Chunks window.

When doing a recording session, it is possible to record separate takes into different sequence chunks inside a single DP session file. If multiple sequence chunks are to be used, it may be desirable to set up a template for the first sequence, and then duplicate that track layout for successive sequences. To do this, set up the first sequence for recording, then choose that sequence in the Chunks window, and select Duplicate Track Layout from the Chunks window mini menu.

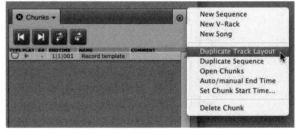

Figure 2.11

Recording individual compositions into separate sequence chunks is a good idea if the recording is to be done to a click track. This way, each sequence chunk starts at bar 1, and has its own independent tempo settings.

It may also be desirable to set up a single sequence chunk for recording, and record all takes and performances into that single sequence. The individual takes and performances can be split into separate sequences later. This technique is similar to the old-school style of recording to a reel of tape. Each take is on the time line in sequential order. This technique also means that a single starting mix can be set up for the entire recording session.

When recording multiple takes into a single sequence chunk, it's a good idea to use markers to designate and name the start of each new recording take. Markers can also be used within a sequence to designate verses, choruses, solos, and other rehearsal points. Control-M is the factory default command to create a marker at the current timeline location.

The disadvantage of recording multiple takes to a single sequence is that only the first take starts at bar one. If the recording is to be done with click tracks, tempo information would need to be embedded in the conductor track for each take that used a different tempo. For sessions where a click is used, it may be more efficient to record different takes into separate sequence chunks. In the Chunks window, select the initial record template sequence and choose Duplicate Sequence from the Chunks window mini menu.

If multiple takes are recorded into a single sequence, it is possible to select the separate takes later and turn them into independent sequence chunks.

- Display the sequence in the Tracks window.
- Click and drag in the time ruler to select the individual sequence.

- Choose Copy Selection to New Sequence... from the pop-up menu in the upper left-hand corner of the Tracks window.

Figure 2.12

- A window will open that allows the new sequence chunk to be named, as well as setting up start and end times for the sequence.

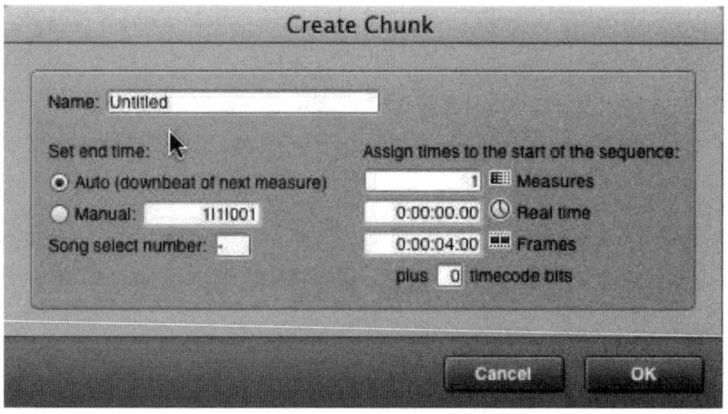

Figure 2.13

- The newly created sequence chunk will now be available in the Chunks window.

Working with Track Takes

Digital Performer allows any track to contain multiple takes. A take is the entire content of the track, including audio or MIDI data and automation. There can even be multiple takes for the conductor track. This allows for different sets of markers, different configurations of click playback, and even different sequence tempos.

During a recording session, it may be desirable to record multiple passes of the same piece of music. After the initial recording session, the separate takes may get edited together for a final "comp" take.

There are two general approaches to recording multiple takes of a performance. The recordings can be made one after the other, either into a single long sequence chunk, or into separate sequence chunks. The other technique is to use a single sequence chunk, and record into multiple takes within that sequence. The latter technique is most likely to be used for overdubs.

In a new DP file, all tracks are initially set to Take 1. Takes can be created and managed via pop-up menus in the Tracks window or Sequence Editor window.

Figure 2.14

Figure 2.15

It is possible to switch between or create new takes for multiple tracks with a single operation. Tracks can be assigned to a track group, and the track group can be set to control take behavior for all included tracks.

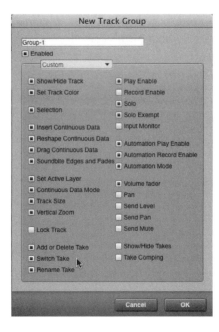

Figure 2.16

It is also possible to use key commands to control take behavior. The key command will affect takes for all currently selected tracks.

Figure 2.17

It is possible to copy and paste between takes. Take comping and editing is further described in the section on music production.

Take File Naming and Record Destination

When recording audio on a computer, it is possible to generate many files. File management is always an important part of using a computer. One important aspect of audio file management is the naming of the audio files. By default, DP records audio to the Audio Files folder that is created within the initial Project folder. In this context, recorded audio files are referred to as Take Files.

When DP records audio, the names of the resulting take files can be based on the name of the track, the name of the input to the track, or a customized name. The default behavior is that newly recorded take files are based on the track name. Therefore, audio tracks should be named before any recording takes place. Take file naming can be set via the Audio Monitor window mini menu.

Figure 2.18

If Custom is selected for take file names, Option/Alt+Click on the take file name to rename.

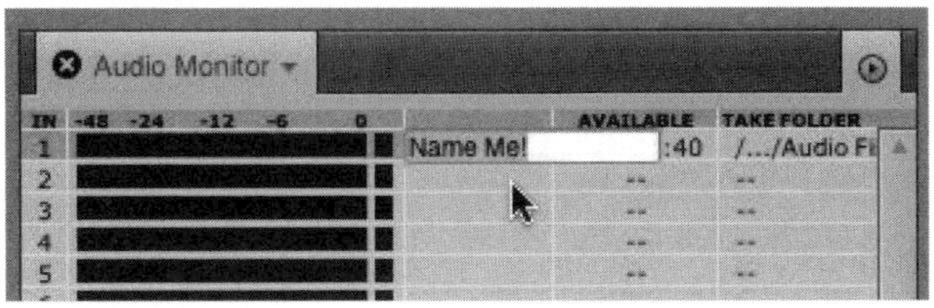

Figure 2.19

In DP, it is possible to assign audio record tracks to any available hard drives. This can distribute the load and increase record track count. By default, the DP session file assigns take file record destinations to the Audio Files folder in the project folder. Take file record destinations can be reset. This is done in the Audio Monitor window. In the Audio Monitor window, record-enabled tracks are highlighted. The Audio Monitor window displays the VU level of the incoming signal, the name of the take file that will be created when recording, available record space on the drive, and file path to the record destination.

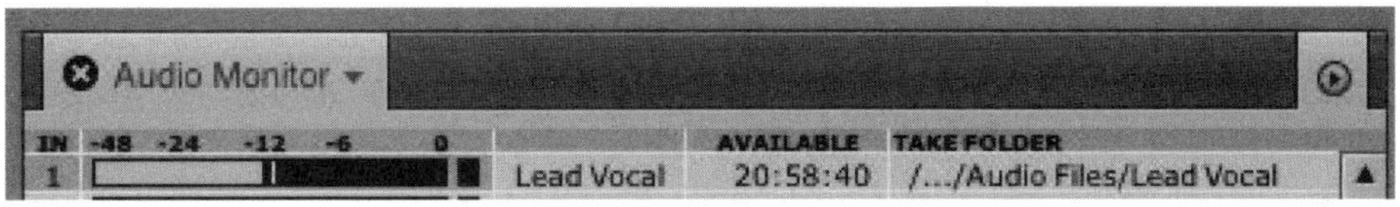

Figure 2.20

Double+Click on the name of the take file to get a window that will allow the take file destination to be re-selected. Alternately select a single or multiple record-enabled take files and reassign as a batch via the Audio Monitor window mini menu.

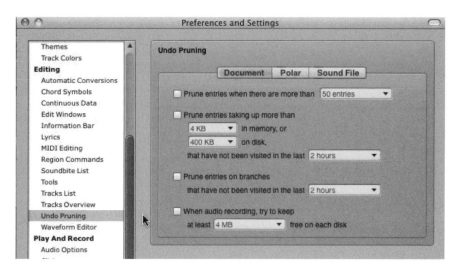

Figure 2.21

Undo Record Take

During the course of a recording session, there may be audio files that are not ultimately used in the project. A common situation is that DP is put into record mode, then stopped because a musician made a mistake, etc. The engineer then has the choice to undo the record take, which will remove the audio from the tracks. When a record pass is undone, the audio files are not automatically deleted from the hard drive. Undone record take files are moved from their record destination to the Undo folder in the Project folder.

To clear audio files in the Undo folder from the hard drive, go to the Edit menu>Undo History. From the Undo History window mini menu, choose Flush All Undo Entries...

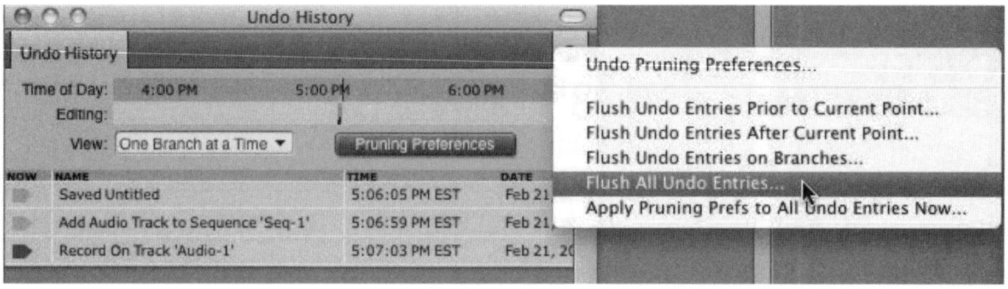

Figure 2.22

Alternately, the files can manually be moved from the Undo folder to the Trash.

It is possible to automatically manage the undo history so that large amounts of unused audio files do not build up. To set the undo history preferences, go to the Preferences window>Editing>Undo Pruning.

Figure 2.23

If audio was recorded and then the DP session file is closed without saving, DP will put up a prompt:

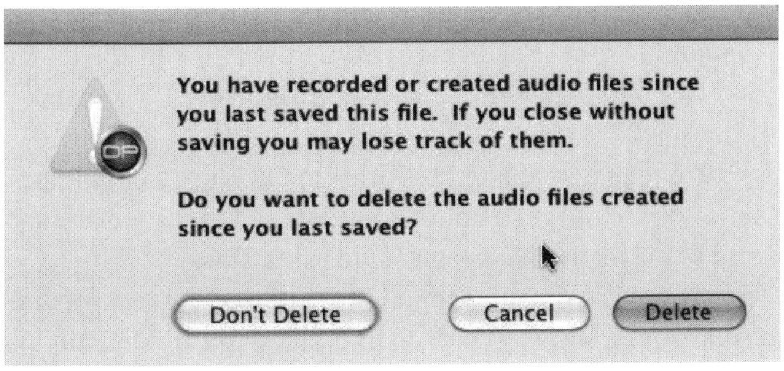

You have recorded or created audio files since you last saved this file. If you close without saving you may lose track of them.

Do you want to delete the audio files created since you last saved?

[Don't Delete]   [Cancel]   [Delete]

Figure 2.24

File Backup

A simple way to back up a DP session is to drag the entire project folder to a second hard drive, or to some sort of recordable format such a DVD. If audio has been recorded to multiple drives, don't forget to back up the additional audio file folders.

It is also possible to create back-up files that contain only specific portions of the session. For example, perhaps multiple sequence chunks were created during a recording session, but the goal is to make an archive of just one of those sequence chunks.

- In the Chunks window, select the chunks that do not need to be backed up.
- From the Chunks window mini menu, delete the unused chunks.
- Open the Soundbites window.
- From the Soundbites window mini menu, Select Unused Soundbites.
- From the Soundbites window mini menu, select Remove From List (This will remove the references of the Soundbites from the DP session file, but will not delete the audio files from the hard drive).
- Go to the File menu and choose Save As.
- In the Save As window, select a new destination and change the file name. Select the option to Duplicate Audio Data.
- Press Save. Digital Performer will create a new project folder. The new DP session file will be created in this folder. All referenced audio will be copied to an Audio Files folder within the project folder.
- The new project folder now contains only the selected sequence chunks and reference audio. The project folder can now be backed up with the assurance that all referenced audio, and no extra audio, is included.

Playback

Digital Performer has become a standard playback tool for many live performing acts. Common playback functions include:

- Playback of clicks.
- Playback of audio tracks. This can include tracks for front of house, tracks for musicians' monitors, or tracks for any other discrete destinations that require audio playback.
- Playback of MIDI data, which can be used to trigger sound modules, effects devices, lighting, pyrotechnics, and even staging changes.

- Playback of video.
- Generation of time code, which can also be used to control lighting, staging, video, pyrotechnics, and other external playback and recording systems.

A DP playback system can be simple or complex. It can be used to generate pre-programmed clicks to start songs. Digital Performer can be used to run the entire show, including music, lights, video, pyrotechnics, and staging. How DP is used is based on the requirements of the show.

The Chunks function in DP provides a sophisticated way to organize live set lists. V-Racks are useful for live setup of virtual instruments and audio signal processing. Chunks are a key part of using DP for many live performance situations.

A DP playback system can be controlled by musicians onstage, or technicians offstage. This includes song selection, transport control, and mix control. Virtually all functions of DP can be set up for customized remote control. A DP playback system can synchronize to external time code, or can generate time code to other slave devices.

DP playback may include audio tracks that are used as onstage cues to musicians and technicians. DP can provide automation for keyboard patches, guitar effect preset changes, and all sorts of other live performance control.

In many cases, the entire playback of a live performance may depend on DP. In such a critical situation, it is possible to set up one or more backup systems that can automatically take over if a computer fails.

Audio Tracks

Digital Performer can be used to play some or all of the audio that an audience hears. Individual playback tracks can be muted or enabled depending on whether live musicians are playing the parts. DP may be used in a playback situation where no prerecorded audio tracks are heard by the audience. For example, DP may be used to provide click tracks and slate tracks to musicians for the sole purpose of keeping the musicians in sync with lighting, video, etc.

Audio tracks in DP can be assigned directly to output ports on the connected audio interface. Some tracks may grouped together into "stems" for submixed outputs. The entire audio mix could be sent to a simple mono or stereo output. If multiple audio tracks are routed to the same outputs, it's a good idea to use a master fader to make sure the summed playback tracks do not clip.

Individual audio tracks can also be routed to separate outputs. For example, it may be desirable to route a click track to a dedicated output on the audio interface. Typically, a click track would not be sent to the front of house PA, but may be sent to the drummer or other musicians on stage.

Besides playback of music, audio tracks can be used for onstage cues. For example, an audio track could be created that provided count-offs for the musicians. Instead of a simple click, a voice could be recorded to track that says something like: "Bridge coming up... One, two, three, four!"

MIDI Tracks

MIDI is a flexible control protocol. Here is a partial list of what can be controlled via MIDI messages:

- Internal virtual instruments
- External sound modules
- Patch changes on internal and external sound modules and effect devices
- Parameter control and automation of internal and external sound modules and effects devices

- Triggering and control of lighting and visual effects
- Control of mechanized staging
- Triggering of pyrotechnics devices
- Triggering and control of specialized systems such as fountain displays and animatronics systems

Because these types of functions can be precisely controlled from DP, that means a performing act can have a show with complete synchronization of lights, video, music, and stage production effects. Changing any aspect of the performance is as simple as editing events on the DP sequence timeline.

Video

There are two ways to control video playback with DP in a live performance environment. Movie files can be loaded into DP sequence chunks, and played back through an external video converter. For more information on direct video playback from DP, check the section on film scoring later in this book.

The other technique is for DP to generate time code, which is then used to trigger video playback on a secondary system. Large-scale productions may use a combination of live video and sequenced video. Time code generated by DP is then used to lock the synchronized portions of the video playback with the rest of the show.

Time Code and Synchronization

Digital Performer can generate time code, or can lock to time code. Inside the computer, DP generates MTC and/or MIDI clock. These signals can be routed to other MIDI applications, or to external MIDI devices. To generate MTC or MIDI clock from DP, go to the Setup menu>Transmit Sync.

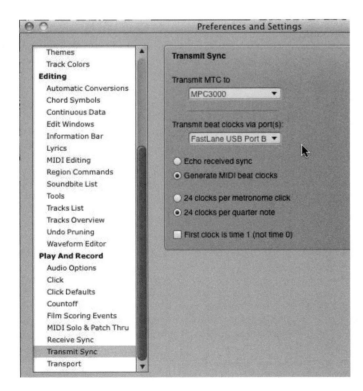

Figure 2.25

If DP is used in combination with a MOTU audio interface, the audio interface can be used to generate LTC SMPTE that is referenced to the DP sequence location. All MOTU audio interfaces, with the exceptions of the MicroBook and MicroBook II can be used to generate LTC SMPTE.

Launch the MOTU SMPTE Setup. Designate the SMPTE output destination. Select the option to Generate from Sequencer.

Figure 2.26

Now when DP plays, the interface will generate LTC SMPTE based on the current sequence timeline location. It is possible to set any SMPTE start time for the sequence. Choose Set Chunk Start Time... from the mini menu in the Control Panel window.

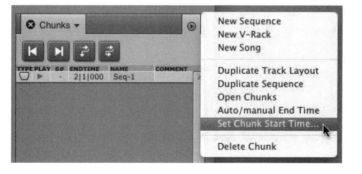

Figure 2.27

Set Chunk Start Time... Can also be set from the Chunks window mini menu.

Figure 2.28

In Set Chunk Start Time, the start of the sequence can be referenced to any SMPTE time code location.

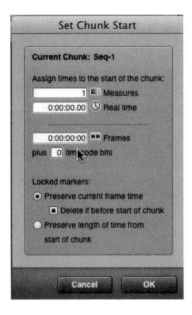

Figure 2.29

Clicks

Digital Performer can generate audio, MIDI, or video click tracks based on the sequence tempo. In a live playback situation, clicks are typically sent to musicians' monitor systems, but not to the front of house speakers. Check the sections on live recording and film scoring for additional click track setup information.

Sequence Chunks

A key function of DP is a live playback system with the ability to have separate sequence chunks in a single DP session file. This is a unique and powerful feature in DP. Although the chunks feature was originally designed for scoring multiple film cues, it has become an indispensable function for live playback.

- Each sequence chunk is completely independent, with its own track list, mixer, and SMPTE start times.
- The Chunks window can function as a set list. There is no limit to how many sequence chunks can exist in a DP session file, so that means the session can have not just the separate songs for the set, but any variations of those songs that may be required.
- Sequence chunks can be used to send MIDI messages to external hardware to reconfigure that hardware for each song in the set.
- Chunks can be selected via remote control.
- Chunks can be chained together in two different modes for sequential playback of the set list.
- Each sequence chunk can reference a separate movie, or different start points for the same movie.

If the Cue Chunks button is engaged, the current sequence will play to its end, then the next sequence in the list will be play-enabled and ready to trigger. This allows the Chunks window to be set up as a set list. The only command needed to start each song in the set is a simple start command.

Figure 2.30

The Chain Chunks button puts DP into a continuous play mode. Each chunk will be cued up and automatically played. After the last chunk in the list plays, the first chunk will be cued up and played again.

Figure 2.31

The end time of a sequence is preset based on the content of the sequence. It is possible to override the preset sequence end time. Select the sequence in the Chunks window and choose Auto/Manual End Time. The sequence end time will now be an editable field.

It is possible to cue up sequence chunks via remote MIDI messages. This is configured in the Commands window.

Figure 2.32

Digital Performer can automatically configure key commands and MIDI remote controls for newly added sequence chunks. Enable this function from the Commands window mini menu.

Figure 2.33

If a remote MIDI command is sent to cue a sequence chunk while another sequence is currently playing, the first sequence will finish playing, then the new sequence will be cued up to play. The remote chunk selection allows sequences to be called up in the set, regardless of their order in the Chunks window.

A sequence chunk does not need to contain MIDI notes or audio files. A sequence chunk could contain MIDI tracks that play back controller data and patch change messages. A sequence chunk could contain aux tracks that had specific input and output assignments and effect plug-ins.

Triggering on the Fly

In some live performance situations, music or sound effects may have to be triggered "on the fly." For example, in a theatrical presentation, sound and music may be cued by the action on the stage. In this case, the DP operator may need to be able to trigger sounds or sequences with little or no notice.

When DP plays back an audio track, the audio is streamed from a hard drive. When track playback is initiated, DP uses buffers to hold the audio from the hard drive before it needs to play back. Because the audio must be streamed from the drive, it can take time between when the play button is pressed, and when audio playback actually starts. One way to get faster playback response is to press the pause button, and then the play button. This fills the track buffers. When DP is un-paused, playback will start immediately.

Besides triggering sequence playback, it is also possible to load audio samples into a sampler for live triggering. Digital Performer includes the Nanosampler virtual instrument, which can be used to load "one shot" mono or stereo samples. For more elaborate triggering setups, a more sophisticated sampler such as the MOTU MachFive 3 may be the right tool for the job. MachFive 3 streams samples from disk, so there is no limit to the length of the triggered sample. MachFive 3 allows multiple samples to be spread over a MIDI keymap. MachFive 3 can play back mono, stereo, or surround format samples.

Redundant Backup Systems

In a live record or playback situation, it may be critical that the computer does not stop for any reason. The system should be a robust design and should be tested thoroughly for reliability. It is also possible to design redundant backup systems so that if the primary record/playback machine stops, there is another system ready to take its place.

Multiple Computers

It is possible to set up multiple computers that each have the same DP session running. The computers can be controlled and run simultaneously. If computer "A" fails for any reason, it is then possible to switch playback to the "B" system.

To set up a backup system, there needs to be a way for the two systems to run simultaneously, but with no direct connection to each other. There also needs to be a way to switch between the outputs of the two systems.

Output Switching

If there are two computer systems playing back at the same time, only one set of signals should be monitored. If one computer stops playing for any reason, there needs to be a way to switch playback to the second system. One simple way to do this is to send all the audio signals from both systems into a mixer. One set of inputs can be muted and the other set of inputs can be live.

A more sophisticated way to switch outputs is to use a device designed for this specific job. One commonly used device for system switching is the Radial SW8 Auto-Switcher. See http://www.radialeng.com/r2011/sw8.php.

Figure 2.34

This device accepts eight channels of audio input from two separate sources. There are eight channels of audio output, and the inputs can be switched either automatically or manually. For automatic switching, a tone is sent from a dedicated track in DP to the switcher. If the tone stops, the switcher automatically switches from the A system to the inputs from the B system. When the A system resumes playing, the switcher will switch back to those inputs.

Simultaneous Control

If simultaneous control signals are sent to multiple computers, the computers will respond together, even though they are not directly connected to each other. This means that if one computer stops playback for any reason, other computers will not be affected.

Simultaneous control is easily set up via MIDI remote control. Any device that generates MIDI notes can be used to control DP. The output of the MIDI controller is then split to two MIDI outputs. This can be done with a device such as the Thru box from MIDI Solutions. For more information, go to http://www.midisolutions.com/prodthr.htm.

Figure 2.35

The two MIDI outputs are then sent to MIDI interfaces on the two computers. When the controller generates a MIDI command, the command is sent simultaneously to both computers. Both computers respond together, but they are not actually connected to each other. Therefore if one computer stops for any reason, it will not affect the other.

Some MIDI and audio interfaces include a foot switch input. Typically, the foot switch input on the interface is set up to emulate a computer keyboard command. For simple simultaneous control, it is possible to set up a foot switch that is connected to a Y-jack which then passes signal to the foot switch inputs on the audio interfaces of each computer. An example of an audio interface with a foot switch input is the MOTU 828mk3 Hybrid. For more information, go to http://www.motu.com/products/motuaudio/828mk3.

Figure 2.36

A foot switch setup would typically be used to initiate play for each cued sequence chunk.

Sync

It is possible to lock two computers together with time code. The problem with this for a backup system is that if the time code stops, any computer slaving to that code will also stop. One way to use time code in a redundant playback system is to use a device that will "jam sync" if time code stops. Jam sync is a function built into some audio and MIDI interfaces. LTC SMPTE time code is sent into the interface, and the interface is set to jam sync. As long as time code comes into the interface, it is passed through to output. If incoming time code stops, the interface will continue to internally generate sync from that point. Therefore the slave computer will continue to run. The problem with this setup is that at the end of each song when the master computer stops, the interface will go into jam sync mode. The interface will continue to generate time code until is it given a command to stop. So that means at the end of each song, the operator needs to send a stop command to the interface.

Virtual Instruments

Virtual instruments can be used in the composition process to build up tracks. VIs can also be used in a live performance setting. In many situations, software musical instruments are replacing physical musical instruments on stage. VIs generally use synthesis, sampling, or some combination of both technologies to generate audio. VIs are triggered by MIDI controllers, such as keyboards, drum pads, or guitar to MIDI converters.

Some VIs can run as stand-alone applications on the computer. Virtual instruments can also run as plug-ins within DP. There are a number of advantages to using DP to host live VIs.

- Complex audio routing setups can be created. Some VIs provide the capability to route signals to separate audio outputs, which can then be routed to audio or aux tracks in DP. For example, a sampler instrument that plays a drum sound may provide the ability to route the individual drum sounds to separate outputs for additional processing.
- Multiple instruments can be triggered simultaneously.
- MIDI and audio can be processed in real time.
- Digital Performer can provide comprehensive metering and level control.
- VIs can be integrated into sequence playback. Automation can be used to control VI patches and effects within a song.

Instrument Tracks and MIDI Routing

The input to an instrument track is a MIDI signal. MIDI is routed to an instrument track from the output of one or more MIDI tracks. No specific assignment is made at the input of the instrument track. Assignments are made at the output of the MIDI tracks.

In order for an instrument track to be available as a destination for MIDI track outputs, there must be a virtual instrument assigned within the instrument track, and the output of the instrument track must be set to a working audio destination. If the outputs of the instrument track are displayed in italics, that means the output must be reassigned to a working location.

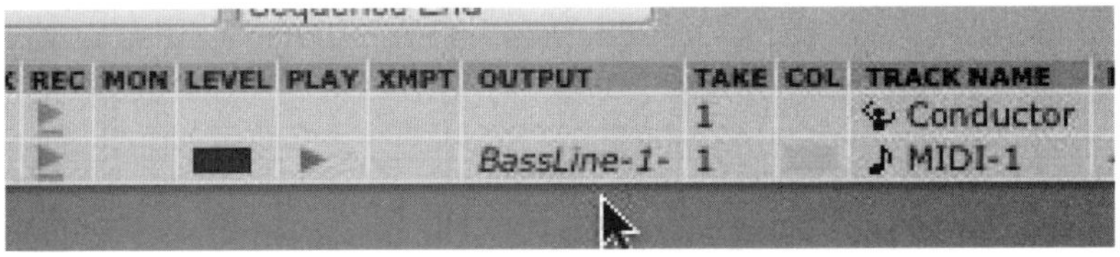

Figure 2.37

If the instrument track is assigned to a working audio output, and a virtual instrument has been set up within the instrument track, the instrument will now be available as an output destination for MIDI tracks.

REC	MON	INPUT	LEVEL	PLAY	XMPT	OUTPUT	TAKE	ENA	COL	TRACK NAME
▶							1			🎼 Conductor
▶			■■	▶		BassLine-1-in	1			♪ MIDI-1
			■■	▶	Ⓢ	Built-in Outpu 1-2	1	●	■■	▭ BassLine-1

Figure 2.38

Multiple MIDI tracks in DP can be assigned to the same virtual instrument. Some virtual instruments are multitimbral, and can receive MIDI on more than one channel at a time. The following graphic shows 16 available MIDI channel assignments for the MOTU MachFive 3 virtual instrument.

In order to pass live MIDI information from an external controller to a virtual instrument, there must be an assigned MIDI track, and the MIDI track must be record-enabled. Record-enabling the MIDI track will pass the incoming MIDI data from the controller to the virtual instrument.

By default, DP is set to autochannelize incoming MIDI. That means it doesn't matter what channel the MIDI uses on input. The MIDI data will be rechannelized by the output assignment of the MIDI track. This preference can be changed so that the incoming MIDI channel is preserved on output through the MIDI track. Live MIDI patch through can also be disabled. These parameters can be changed in the MIDI Solo and Patch Thru preferences.

PT	OUTPUT	TAKE	ENA	COL	TRACK NAME	
		1			🎼 Conductor	
	MachFive3-1-1	1			♪ MIDI-1	
	MachFive3-1-2	1			♪ MIDI-2	
	MachFive3-1-3	1			♪ MIDI-3	
	MachFive3-1-4	1			♪ MIDI-4	
	MachFive3-1-5	1			♪ MIDI-5	
	MachFive3-1-6	1			♪ MIDI-6	
	MachFive3-1-7	1			♪ MIDI-7	
	MachFive3-1-8	1			♪ MIDI-8	
	MachFive3-1-9	1			♪ MIDI-9	
	MachFive3-1-10	1			♪ MIDI-10	
	MachFive3-1-11	1			♪ MIDI-11	
	MachFive3-1-12	1			♪ MIDI-12	
	MachFive3-1-13	1			♪ MIDI-13	
	MachFive3-1-14	1			♪ MIDI-14	
	MachFive3-1-15	1			♪ MIDI-15	
	MachFive3-1-16	1			♪ MIDI-16	
	Built-in Output 1-2	1	●	■■	▭ MachFive3-1	

Figure 2.39

Audio Routing and Processing

In DP, virtual instruments are instantiated on instrument tracks. To add a VI, go to the Project menu>Add Track>Instrument Track. A list of currently available instrument plug-ins will be displayed. Choose the desired instrument.

An instrument track will be created, and the selected instrument window will open. Typically a patch or sample instrument is then loaded into the instrument.

The output of the instrument track is an audio signal, and therefore must be routed to an audio output. Typically the output of the instrument track is routed to the main monitor outputs. Some instruments provide for multiple channels of output. These additional outputs can be returned into DP using aux tracks or audio tracks.

For example, perhaps DP is being used to host a drum VI, and the mix engineer has asked for separate signals from the kick, snare, and remainder of the kit. For this example, the Model 12 drum VI that is included with DP is used. The main output of Model 12 is routed to analog outputs 1-2 on the audio interface. The kick is routed separately to an aux track, and the aux track is

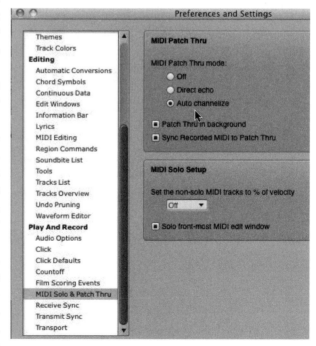

Figure 2.40

assigned to analog output 3 on the interface. The snare is routed to analog out 4 on the interface.

Figure 2.41

It is possible to place effect plug-ins after the instrument in the track effect inserts. In this example a reverb plug-in is placed on the aux track that is returning the snare signal, and EQ has been placed on the general output of the drum kit.

Figure 2.42

VIs are capable of producing audio signals that will clip the output of DP. This can be especially true if effect plug-ins are added to the VI signals. Therefore it is a good idea to monitor the VU output of the instrument signals from DP. If multiple instruments are routed to share the same outputs, a master fader can be created to monitor and manage that summed output.

Trigger Latency

When a virtual instrument receives MIDI, it generates an audio signal. There is a delay between when the virtual instrument generates the audio, and when that audio actually reaches the output of the audio interface. This delay is referred to as "latency." It is important to understand that latency delay only applies to live triggering of virtual instruments from an external source. When DP plays back recorded MIDI to a virtual instrument plug-in, it plays the MIDI slightly early to compensate for the latency delay. Because of the automatic delay compensation, there is no latency when triggering virtual instruments from pre-recorded MIDI.

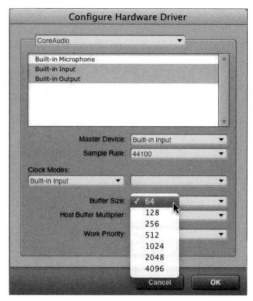

The amount of audio delay for live triggering of virtual instruments is determined by the Buffer Size in the Audio Hardware Driver window: Setup menu>Configure Audio System>Configure Hardware Driver.

In general, any Buffer Size setting over 128 will produce a noticeable delay when triggering virtual instruments from an external MIDI controller. In many cases a Buffer Size setting of 128 will produce no noticeable trigger delay. If there is a perceived delay with a Buffer Size setting of 128, changing the Buffer Size

Figure 2.43

to 32 will lower the delay further. At a Buffer Size of 64, MIDI trigger input to audio output will be around 3-4 ms, which is generally undetectable to the human ear. A lower Buffer Size places a greater load on the computer CPU. Therefore if a Buffer Size setting of 128 provides no detectable delay for virtual instrument triggering, lowering that setting to 32 will place a greater load on the CPU with no additional benefit.

Remote Parameter Control

Besides being triggered by MIDI notes, most virtual instruments also respond to various MIDI continuous controller data and pitch bend data. Some, but not all virtual instruments respond to MIDI patch change messages.

All external MIDI data is routed to virtual instruments through record-enabled MIDI tracks.

It is up to the specific virtual instrument as to which parameters can be controlled via remote MIDI data. Some virtual instruments have set controller assignments. For example, MIDI CC#7 is almost always used for volume control. Some virtual instruments have a MIDI learn function that allows easy assignment of external MIDI to internal parameters.

V-Racks

A V-Rack is a specific type of chunk. V-racks are used to host instrument tracks, aux tracks, and master faders. A V-Rack can remain enabled while switching between other sequence tracks. The purpose of the V-Rack is to have a common set of instruments or audio processing channels when also using multiple sequences within the session for recording or playback.

To create a V-Rack, go to the Chunks window and choose New V-Rack from the mini menu. A new icon will appear in the Chunks window.

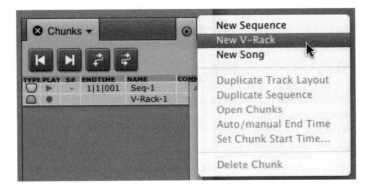

Figure 2.44

The V-Rack can be named by Option/Alt+Clicking on the name. V-Racks can be enabled or disabled. There can be multiple V-Racks in a single session file.

The V-Rack is essentially a mixing board. Double+Click on the V-Rack in the Chunks window to open the V-Rack window. V-Rack tracks are also available to display in any sequence chunk mixer via the track selector.

A new V-Rack will contain a single, unassigned instrument track. To add more instrument tracks or aux tracks, go to the Project menu>Add Track. The new track will appear in the V-Rack.

V-Rack aux tracks, instrument tracks, and master faders have the same available input and output assignment as if they existed in sequence chunks. Virtual instruments assigned to instrument tracks are available as output destinations for MIDI tracks from any sequence chunk. In order for a MIDI track in a sequence chunk to send MIDI to an instrument track in a V-Rack, the sequence chunk must be play-enabled. Aux tracks and master faders in V-Racks can use any available audio input or output or internal bus.

V-Rack track instrument track outputs, and aux and master fader inputs and outputs, are selected at the bottom of the V-Rack fader strips. V-Rack tracks can also be deleted via the menu at the bottom of the fader strip.

V-Racks do not record or play back MIDI or audio. V-Racks are not capable of automation (although MIDI tracks and audio tracks in sequence chunks that make use of V-Rack tracks can be automated).

In a live performance situation, a V-Rack can be useful for providing a consistent set of audio processing channels as well as live virtual instruments, while multiple sequence chunks are used for recording and playback.

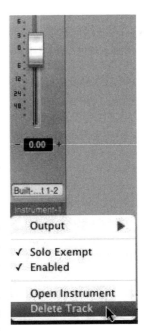

Figure 2.45

Live Processing

Digital Performer can be used as a mixer and signal processor for MIDI and audio signals. The DP mix can be controlled and automated from the computer screen or from a remote device. DP can store and switch between mix presets. Live mix automation in DP can be synchronized to external time code. DP can function as a mixer and signal processor while also recording and playing back audio and MIDI data.

Patch Through Latency

When MIDI is sent from an external MIDI controller, through DP, and out to an external MIDI device, the MIDI transmission is so fast that any delay to the signal is usually negligible. MIDI in, through, and out of the computer typically happens within 2-3 ms. Therefore patch through latency of MIDI is rarely a concern.

When audio is patched through a computer system, there is a great deal of data and processing to be handled along the way. This is multiplied by the number of separate channels of audio. The processing takes time, and causes patch through latency delay. All digital audio processing devices have some amount of internal latency delay. As long as the delay is small enough to not be noticeable to the human ear, it will generally not be a problem on stage. As computers get more powerful, the ability to patch audio through faster, and with more channels and processing, will continue to increase.

Audio patch through latency in DP is determined by the Buffer Size setting in the Configure Hardware Driver window (Setup menu>Configure Audio System>Configure Hardware Driver). For live audio processing, a low Buffer Size setting means less patch through latency delay.

MIDI Routing and Processing with MIDI Tracks

There are two ways to route MIDI through DP. MIDI data can be routed through a record-enabled MIDI track. MIDI data can also be used to control elements within a Custom Console, which in turn can generate MIDI data to external MIDI devices as well as internal MIDI destinations.

To route external MIDI through a MIDI track, the MIDI track must be record-enabled, and MIDI Patch Thru must be enabled in the Studio menu. There are three available preferences for MIDI Patch Thru. MIDI Patch Thru can be disabled, regardless of whether a MIDI track is record-enabled or not. MIDI Patch Thru can be set to Direct echo, which will patch MIDI through the record-enabled track using the same MIDI channel that is being used for input. Auto channelize will patch MIDI through a record-enabled MIDI track, and will rechannelize the MIDI according to the MIDI track output assignment.

By default, DP is in omni-record mode for MIDI. That means only one MIDI track at a time can be record-enabled, and any live external MIDI signal will be patched into the MIDI track. If separate external MIDI inputs are to be processed independently in DP, go to the Studio menu and check Multi-Record. When DP is in multirecord mode, more than one MIDI track at a time can be record-enabled. Also, in multirecord mode, the input for each MIDI track must be specified. The MIDI track will not accept incoming data from any source other than what is specified for the track input.

MIDI track outputs can be assigned to instrument tracks, external MIDI devices, or device groups. A device group is a way to route a MIDI track to multiple destinations. To create a MIDI device group, click on the output assignment of the MIDI track and choose New Device Group... from the menu. A Device Group window will open. Click the icon on the left to display all currently available MIDI destinations. Check the boxes for the desired outputs for this device group. Option/Alt+Click on the name of the device group to rename. MIDI Device Groups can be edited via the Studio menu.

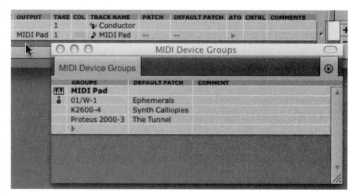

Figure 2.46

MIDI Plug-Ins

MIDI tracks in DP have effects inserts that work in a similar way to audio track inserts. MIDI track inserts are available in the Mixing Board window. MIDI track inserts follow the same controls as audio track inserts. They can be shown or hidden via the Mixing Board window mini menu. There can be up to 20 available inserts for each audio and MIDI track.

MIDI track plug-ins process the output of prerecorded MIDI. Some, but not all MIDI track plug-ins can also be used to process incoming MIDI data in real time. MIDI track plug-ins include:

- Arpeggiator: This plug-in can work on live MIDI and prerecorded MIDI.
- Change Duration: This plug-in works only on prerecorded MIDI.
- Change Velocity: This plug-in works on live MIDI input and prerecorded MIDI. Change Velocity can be useful as a MIDI "compressor" to control and limit MIDI note velocities.
- DeFlam: This is a playback only plug-in. DeFlam will move notes together onto the same timeline location if they are within the specified distance from each other. This is a form of quantization used to tighten up a live MIDI performance.
- Echo: This plug-in works on live and prerecorded MIDI.
- Groove Quantize/Humanize/Quantize: All three plug-ins work by moving MIDI data based on the plug-in parameters and the sequence grid. These are playback-only effects. It can be useful to change quantize parameters on the fly during playback to check for optimum settings.
- Invert Pitch: This is a playback process that inverts pitches chromatically based on a selected axis pitch.
- Reassign Continuous Data: This is a powerful plug-in that works in real time or on playback. The plug-in can translate pitch bend, controller, or aftertouch information. One type of data can be translated to another. The plug-in also supports reassignment to NRPNs, a specialized form of MIDI control.
- Remove Duplicates: This is a playback only plug-in. Duplicate MIDI notes can be recorded if a controller transmits the same data on multiple channels. This plug-in will remove any duplicate MIDI data in the track.
- Time Shift: This is a playback-only plug-in that shifts recorded MIDI data earlier or later in the track.
- Transpose: Transpose will work in real time or on playback. Custom transposition maps can be created in the Transpose window from the Region menu. These custom maps will then be available in the Transposition plug-in. A transposition map can be used to change a range of notes to a note that is out of the range of the instrument. This effectively masks those notes and can be used to create keyboard splits.

MIDI track plug-ins are nondestructive playback effects and do not change the actual data in the track. MIDI track plug-ins can be printed to the MIDI track. Select a region of MIDI data that includes MIDI track plug-ins. Go to the Region menu and choose Capture Realtime MIDI Effects... A window will open to provide the choices to expand any loops in the selected region, and to bypass the MIDI plug-in after it has been printed.

Custom Consoles

Digital Performer includes the ability to create a custom console. Custom consoles are powerful tools for real-time audio and MIDI control and processing.

To create a new custom console, go to the Project menu>Consoles>New Console. An empty window will open. Next to the window will be a palette of objects.

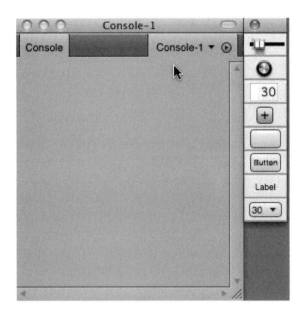

Figure 2.47

The choice of objects includes Slider, Knob, Value box, Increment object, Button, Text button, Label, and Menu. Drag an object from the palette into the custom console window.

If a Label is dragged into the Console window, a simple window to name the label appears.

Figure 2.48

If any other type of object is dragged into the custom console window, a Control Assignment window appears.

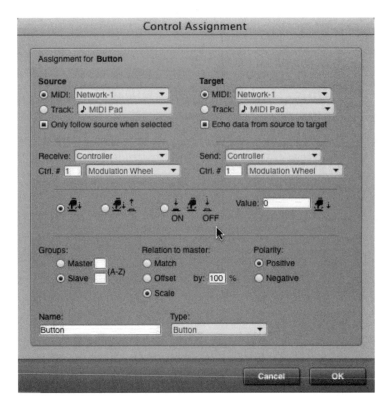

Figure 2.49

Objects created in a custom console have input and output assignments. Input assignments can be either MIDI devices or MIDI tracks. This allows console objects to be controlled in real time via external MIDI devices, or to be controlled by playback from a MIDI track. Console object outputs can be assigned to MIDI devices or to audio or MIDI tracks. This allows console objects to control MIDI devices in real time, or to be recorded into audio or MIDI tracks.

One type of incoming MIDI data can be translated into a different type of MIDI data on output. Console objects can be controlled by MIDI notes, velocities, pitch bend data, continuous controller data, or mono aftertouch data. Console objects can generate MIDI notes, velocities, pitch bend, continuous controller, mono or poly aftertouch, patch change commands, and variable sys ex messages. Console objects can be used to control audio track volume or pan. For example, MIDI notes from an external controller could be used to change the pan position of an audio track. As higher or lower MIDI notes are played, the audio track will pan left or right.

Figure 2.50

There are many options for control. Data ranges can be limited or inverted. Objects can be set so that they only respond to external control when the object is selected in the console window.

Custom console objects can be configured as group masters and slaves. For example, incoming mod wheel data from a single source could be used to control a slider, which is designated as a group master. Additional sliders could then be created that are designated as group slaves. The slave sliders could be set up to control different parameters on different tracks. The initial mod wheel input can now control many different parameters in real time.

Console objects can generate streams of variable data, such as continuous controller or pitch bend data. Console objects can also generate single messages, such as specific continuous controller values, or patch change messages.

Once a console object has been created, it can be resized and positioned within the console window. Many console object parameters can be edited directly from the console window mini menu. To exit the customizing mode of the console, deselect Edit Console from the mini menu.

Figure 2.51

Audio Routing and Processing

Digital Perfomer can be used for real-time audio processing. Record-enabled audio tracks, buses, aux tracks, and master faders can be used for routing external audio input signals through DP and back to external outputs. Plug-ins can be used at any point in the signal path.

Since automation is part of a sequence, the sequence may also contain tracks that are used for playback and recording. The sequence can generate sync or be slaved to external sync. This allows precise automation of a live mix and performance.

A computer takes time to do any processing. When an audio signal is sent through a computer, the signal is delayed. The amount of latency delay is determined by the Buffer Size setting in the audio hardware driver. Best case analog in, through DP, to analog out will be 5-7 ms. How many channels of audio that can be simultaneously processed will be determined by the power of the CPU.

Some plug-ins work within the Buffer Size set in the DP audio hardware driver. Other plug-ins may add additional processing delay. This will be up to the individual plug-in.

Using Sequence Chunks for Scenes

A sequence chunk can contain complex MIDI and audio routing. Patch change messages, continuous controllers and even sys ex can be embedded in tracks. When the sequence chunk is played, the MIDI messages are sent to reconfigure any MIDI devices.

Multiple sequence chunks can be set up as "scenes" for different routing and MIDI setup messages. A sequence chunk could be just a few seconds long, containing only the required setup and routing information for that scene.

Sequence chunks can be used in combination with V-Racks. The V-Rack contains aux tracks, master faders, and instrument tracks that are always active. Sequence chunks can then be used to change mix and setup parameters around the V-Rack tracks.

Remote Control

Digital Performer can be controlled via computer keyboard commands and mouse clicks. DP may also be controlled from a remote location. This can be useful for both recording and playback. For the configuration of a a redundant playback system, simultaneous remote control of two computers is essential.

MIDI Control

Digital Performer can be remotely controlled via MIDI notes, patch changes, or continuous controller messages. DP remote controls are configured via the Setup menu>Commands window. In the Commands window, enable the Master Master to turn on remote MIDI control.

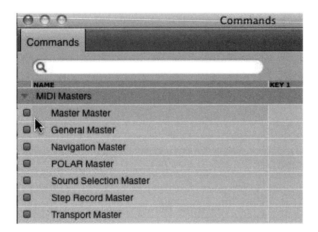

Figure 2.52

To assign a MIDI message to a command, click in the MIDI field of the desired command. The MIDI field will highlight and wait for an incoming patch change message. Generate the MIDI message from the external MIDI controller, and the command will "learn" the MIDI message. Press Return to exit the learn mode.

If MIDI notes are used for commands, be aware that there are MIDI note on and MIDI note off messages. If the command field is highlighted, and a key on an external MIDI keyboard is pressed, the command field will initially show the note on message.

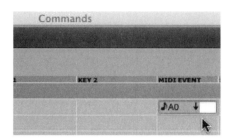

Figure 2.53

When the key is released on the external controller, a note off message is sent and that is reflected in the command field.

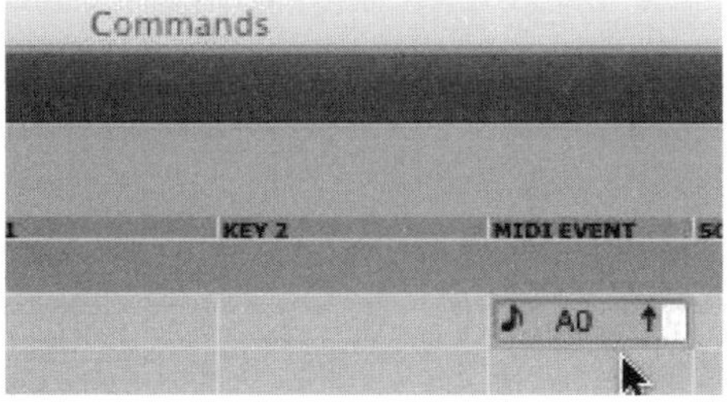

Figure 2.54

This provides the choice to activate the command with either the note on or the note off from the external controller.

Figure 2.55

Faders in the Mixing Board window can also be mapped to MIDI continuous controller messages.

- Go to the Mixing Board window mini menu and select Attach MIDI Controller...
- Click on a fader or panner. The fader or panner will be highlighted with a flashing red border.

Figure 2.56

- Generate a continuous controller message from the external MIDI controller. The highlighted fader or panner will learn the command and the flashing red border will turn green, indicating that the MIDI controller has been assigned.
- Click on the next fader or panner to assign a new remote control, or press the Return button to exit the assignment mode.

Digital Performer Control app

The DP Control app is a free download from the iTunes store:
https://itunes.apple.com/us/app/dp-control/id380483770?mt=8

Figure 2.37

DP Control works over a WiFi network to control the transport mix and basic track functions of DP. DP Control runs on an iPhone, iPad, or third-generation iPod Touch.

Dedicated Control Surfaces

Digital Performer supports Mackie HUI, Mackie Universal Control, EuCon, SAC, and PreSonus FaderPort protocols. Control surface support is described further in the section on Music Production.

OSC Control

OSC is a software-based remote control protocol. A well-known application for generating OSC commands is TouchOSC from hexler.net at http://hexler.net/software/touchosc.

Figure 2.58

OSC control is also further described in the section on Music Production.

Chapter 3
FILM SCORING AND POST PRODUCTION

Digital Performer has become an industry standard tool for creating audio soundtracks for video. This includes television commercials, feature films, corporate promotional videos, web videos, and any other situation where audio production or music composition is required for picture. DP provides options for a variety of file format outputs and delivery. This includes audio, MIDI, video (with embedded soundtrack), and sheet music.

Digital Performer can be used as a powerful composition tool for creating original music for video and can be used as a post-production tool for assembling final soundtracks for video.

The development of DP is driven by user demand. The user base for DP has always consisted of film composers, post-production engineers, mixing engineers, music editors, and other professionals involved in sound for picture. This means that DP has a complete and well-developed set of tools for the composition, editing, mixing, and assembling process.

The following section describes how to work with video in DP, from importing video files to final output. Workflow features that are described include:

- Setting SMPTE time code offsets for the movie and musical cues: A digital movie file can have an assigned SMPTE time code start time. Sequences can then be assigned to start at any time code location referenced within the movie.
- Working with codecs and different formats of digital movie files: Digital video can be stored in a variety of compression formats. Some compression formats (codecs) are more efficient than others. Video files play back at specific frame rates. Digital Performer provides support for all video frame rates.
- Routing movie playback to dedicated video monitors: DP can play a movie file on the computer desktop. The movie window can be displayed within the Consolidated window.
- Importing, playing back, and editing embedded audio from digital movie files.
- Creating and working with EDLs (Edit Decision Lists).
- Creating complex tempo maps that reference hit points within the video.
- Editing music and sound in reference to the movie.

- Creating and working with video overlays for streamers, punches, flutters, and video clicks.
- Mixing in surround-sound formats.
- Exporting a movie file that includes a bounced mixdown of the sequence.

System Requirements

It is possible to use DP for serious composition and production work with a minimal amount of hardware. Some composers work with nothing more than a laptop computer, USB keyboard, and a pair of headphones. Of course, it is also possible to use DP in a large recording studio, set up for full orchestral recording.

As with any application, the hardware requirements match the specific task at hand. The following section will discuss hardware requirements that are specific to using DP for creating and producing sound for picture.

Computer Requirements

Playback of digital video can place significant demands on a computer system. When DP is used to play video files, the computer also has to do the work of playing back audio tracks, virtual instruments, and any effects processing in the sequence. The basic hardware components that affect overall system performance are: CPU speed, amount of RAM, and drive setup. Regardless of how powerful the hardware system, it's always a good idea to understand how to use the available resources to be as efficient as possible.

For example, it is possible to use a single hard drive for playback of a movie, audio tracks, and virtual instrument sample streaming. By comparison, if those three jobs are split up among three different drives, the result will be the ability to play back more audio tracks, larger movie files, and more streamed samples for virtual instruments.

Digital video files can contain uncompressed data, or they can contain audio and video data that has been compressed using one of many available compression codecs. Uncompressed video takes up large amounts of disk space. To play back uncompressed video, a fast hard drive is usually required. Uncompressed video is best played back from an eSata or SSD drive, or RAID setup.

Compressed video takes up less drive space, and can typically be played back from slower drives. However, in order for the computer to play back a compressed video file, it must decompress that data on the fly. Different types of compression codecs require different amounts of relative CPU power.

It is possible to play back video and audio, as well as run virtual instruments, on a laptop computer, using the stock internal drive. Absolute minimum RAM is 4 GB, but at least 8 GB is far more preferable for serious work. A more powerful computer with more RAM and a faster drive setup will allow for smoother video playback, more audio tracks, more effect plug-ins, and more simultaneous virtual instruments.

External Video Hardware

When a movie file is opened in DP, the movie is displayed on a window on the computer desktop. The movie window can be dragged to any connected computer monitor. It is also possible to route video playback out of the computer to a dedicated external video monitor. For example, if DP is playing back an HD format video file, it may be desirable to view that movie on a dedicated flat screen TV monitor.

DP8 is compatible with most Firewire video output converters. One example of a Firewire video converter is the Grass Valley ADVC110, available at http://www. grassvalley.com/products/advc110.

Figure 3.1

It is also possible to use a MOTU video interface, such as the V4HD, HD Express, or HDX-SDI. For more information, see http://www.motu.com/products/body. html?productslider=3.

Figure 3.2

Other Video Editing Software

Digital Performer can open a digital movie file. It can play the movie file while synchronized to the sequence timeline. DP can bounce audio and video to a digital movie file. DP has no other capabilities in terms of editing a digital video file. In many cases, no additional video editing will be required in order for the musician or engineer to do sound for picture work with DP.

In some situations, it may be useful to have video editing software, or at least a software utility program that can convert between digital video file formats. There are many available utility programs for Mac and Windows that do video editing or file format conversion.

File Formats

An understanding of file formats is essential for any type of collaboration. Video, audio, MIDI, and session-specific information can be moved between studios and different software applications. DP can import and export a wide variety of file formats.

Video files

A digital video file is a file that contains video information, and may also contain audio information. A video file is a container. There are different video file formats available for Mac and Windows systems. Examples of common video file container formats include MOV, WMD, AVI, DV, and MP4.

The video and audio contained in the file may be uncompressed, or may be compressed using one of many available compression formats. A video compression format is called a codec. Examples of video codecs include DV, DVCPro, and H.264.

Uncompressed video takes up a great deal of hard drive space, and requires a fast drive setup in order to play back. Compressed video takes up less space and generally can be played back from a slower drive. Compression does affect video quality. However, many codecs are high enough quality to be okay for broadcast work. Also, the video file does not need to be the best possible quality in order for it to be used as a reference for scoring and post-production work.

In some cases, a specific codec may be required. For example, in order to play video through the Grass Valley ADVC110 converter, the video must be encoded in DV format.

Digital Performer can play back any codec that can be played back by the computer. The ideal codec for maximum playback efficiency with DP8 is H.264. If DP has trouble playing back an uncompressed video file, or a video file made with a different codec, converting the file to H.264 format may solve that problem.

Video is based on multiple frames that play back at a specific rate. There are a number of different standardized video frame rates. Knowing the frame rate of video is required for precise location within that video. The sequence time line in DP can be set for any frame rate, which allows for correct identification of frame locations within the video.

When receiving a video file from an outside source, it is always desirable to know the codec and frame rate of the file. That will make it much easier to get the video file working properly in DP.

Audio Files

Digital audio file formats can be divided into two categories – compressed and uncompressed. File compression typically works by discarding some data from the original file. Therefore some audio fidelity is lost when the file is compressed. The trade-off with compressed audio files is a smaller file vs. loss of fidelity.

OMF and AAF

OMF and AAF are general file formats that contain reference to audio tracks, including edits, crossfades, and volume and pan automation. DP can import and export sessions in OMF and AAF formats. Any MIDI tracks can be separately imported and exported via Standard MIDI File format.

XML

Digital Performer supports XML import and export with Final Cut Pro 7. XML contains references to audio tracks, edits, sequence start times, and movie location.

Importing Video Into DP

Digital Performer can open a digital movie file and link that file to a sequence timeline. Go to the Project menu and choose Movie. A window will open that allows a MOV file on any connected drive to be selected and opened.

The selected movie will open in a Movie window for the currently play-enabled sequence chunk. Initially the movie will be locked to the sequence transport controls, and the first frame of the movie will be referenced to the current sequence start time.

The Movie Window

Each sequence chunk in a DP session has its own Movie window. The Movie window can be opened in a sidebar of the consolidated window, or it can be its own independent window. The default key command to open the Movie window is Shift-V.

If no movie file has been selected, the Movie window will open to show a black frame.

Movie Window Mini Menu

Right+Click or Control+Click on the Movie window to get the mini menu. The Movie window mini menu contains commands that are described throughout this section.

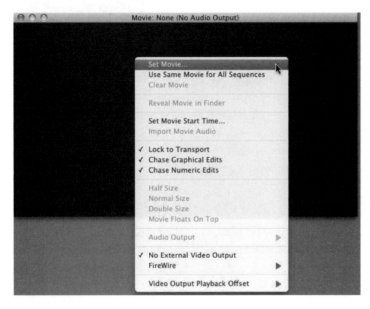

Figure 3.3

Movie Windows Controls

When the mouse is moved over the Movie window, the Movie window control bar becomes visible.

Figure 3.4

If there is audio embedded in the movie file, an audio volume control will be available. To the right of the audio volume control are the frame back, play, and frame forward buttons. At the far right is the button to lock movie playback to sequence playback. Below these controls is a timeline slider with elapsed time indicators.

If the movie window is displayed in a sidebar of the Consolidated window, Double+Clicking on the Movie window will cause it to pop out of the sidebar. When the Movie window is displayed as a stand-alone window, there is an additional control in the Movie window control bar. On the far right is a button that will cause the movie to go in or out of full screen mode.

When the movie playback is locked to sequence playback, the movie follows the DP transport controls like any other audio or MIDI track. If the Movie window is the front-most window, the left and right arrow keys on the computer keyboard will cause the movie to frame forward and backward. There is a setting in the Movie window mini menu to Always Float on Top. If this setting is checked, the arrow keys do not function to frame forward or backward.

Full Screen Mode

The Movie window can be dragged on to any video monitor connected to the computer. The Movie window can be displayed in full screen mode on any connected video monitor.

Figure 3.5

To display the Movie window in full screen mode, the Movie window must first be displayed as an independent window, outside of the Consolidated window. If the Movie window is displayed in the Consolidated window, Double+Click on the movie to pop it out, so it becomes a separate window. When the movie is displayed as a separate window, the movie control bar includes a full screen button.

Press the full screen button to enter or exit full screen mode for the movie. This function is especially useful in a multimonitor setup.

Video Playback

The movie will open with its first frame referenced to the beginning of the sequence timeline. By default, the movie will be locked to the DP transport. If the sequence plays, the movie plays with the sequence.

There is a lock button in the Movie window control bar. The lock function can also be toggled from the Movie window mini menu. If the movie is unlocked, playing or locating within the DP sequence will not play the movie. Playing or locating within the movie will not affect the DP transport.

External Video Output

The Movie window can be set to output through a general Firewire video converter, or MOTU video converter. This allows the movie to be displayed on an external video monitor or sent to an external video recording device.

Select the movie output destination from the Movie window mini menu. Movie output can also be selected from the drop-down menu of the movie track in the Sequence Editor window.

Digital Performer plays back the movie at its current frame rate. Not all consumer video monitors support all professional video frame rates. Make sure the frame rate of the movie is supported by the external video monitor.

Audio embedded in a movie file is not sent to the external converter as part of the video signal. Audio playback from a movie is routed to DP audio outputs via the Movie window menu.

External Playback Offset

If a Firewire converter is used, the video signal will be delayed on output. This will mean the movie on the external monitor plays late as compared to the DP sequence. Some external video monitors also delay video display. Digital Performer can compensate for this. Right+Click on the Movie window to open a menu. From the menu choose Video Output Playback Offset>Other... The Set Playback Offset window will open.

Set Playback Offset allows video played back from DP to be advanced relative to the sequence. This will advance the video in the DP Movie window as well as video signal sent to the external output. Therefore if a video playback offset is used, watch the movie on the external monitor but not on the computer desktop.

Figure 3.6

Playing Back Movie Audio

If there is audio embedded in the movie, that audio can be routed through DP like any other signal. Audio output from the movie is initially set from the Movie window mini menu, or from the Movie track in the Sequence Editor window.

Movie audio output can be mono, stereo, or multi-channel, depending on how the movie file was created. The audio output format is reflected in the output assignment in DP. For example, if the movie has a mono audio track, DP will only see a single channel of audio output from the movie.

The choices available in the movie audio output assignment are based on the available bus and output bundles in the Bundles window. If a desired output is not available in the movie audio output assignment, create that output in the Bundles window, and then it will be available to the movie audio output.

The movie audio can be routed directly to outputs on the audio interface. If a master fader is assigned to that output, the movie audio will pass through the master fader.

Figure 3.7

If the movie audio is assigned to a bus, it can then be further routed and processed in DP. For example, it is not uncommon for a movie audio track to contain dialog on one channel, and Foley sound effects on the second channel. If the audio is monitored in stereo, dialog is on the left and sound effects are on the right. Here is a better way to handle that situation:

- Create a new stereo bus in the Bundles window.
- Create two mono buses in the Bundles window. Move these bus assignments so they match the left and right assignments of the stereo bus.

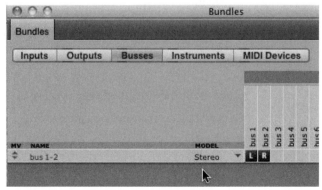

Figure 3.8

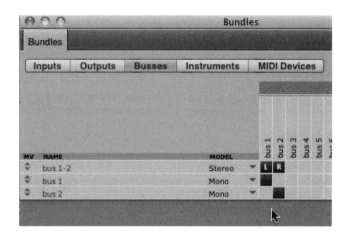

Figure 3.9

- Assign the movie audio output to the new stereo bus.

Figure 3.10

- Add two new aux tracks to the sequence.
- Assign the inputs of the aux tracks to the mono bundles. This splits the left and right output of the movie audio into the two mono aux tracks.
- Assign the outputs of the aux tracks to the main monitor outputs.
- The two aux tracks can now process the dialog and sound effects as separate audio signals within the mix.

Extracting Movie Audio

If there is audio embedded in a movie file, DP provides two ways to monitor that audio. Audio can be played back directly from the movie. Audio can be extracted from a movie and placed in a new audio track in the DP sequence.

To extract audio from the movie into a new track, go to the Movie window mini menu and choose Import Movie Audio. A new audio track will be created, and the extracted audio will be placed in the track, in sync with the movie file. If the movie has mono, stereo, or surround audio, the corresponding audio track type will be created. This allows the movie audio to be routed, edited, and processed like any other audio track.

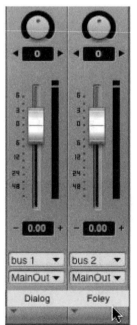

Figure 3.11

Timeline Offsets

When working with movies, it is common to offset the sequence start in relation to the movie. Therefore DP provides complete flexibility in terms of time format offsets.

Every point along a DP sequence timeline has a unique address. Address points on the sequence timeline can be described in different types of time formats. Multiple time formats can be displayed in DP simultaneously.

It is possible to offset the start times of different types of time formats in relation to the sequence. By default, DP initially displays time in bars and beats format. By default, a new DP sequence starts at bar 1, real time zero, and SMPTE frame time zero. By default, an imported movie starts at SMPTE time zero. By using time offsets, it is possible to assign any SMPTE start time to the movie. It is possible to assign the start of the DP sequence to any SMPTE location.

SMPTE Time Code

SMPTE time code is used to keep track of location within video. With SMPTE time code, a minute is always a minute and a second is always a second. However, within a second there are a specific number of frames, and that frame rate can vary depending on the source material.

When SMPTE time code is used for location within a sequence or movie, the frame rate of the time code must match the actual frame rate of the video. Therefore it is important to know the frame rate of the video. The DP sequence frame rate must be set to match the movie frame rate. The DP sequence frame rate can be set via the Project Settings when visible in the Control Panel.

Figure 3.12

Sequence frame rate can also be set via the Setup menu.

Figure 3.13

Time Formats

Sequence timeline location can be described in the following ways:

- Real Time: This is shown in seconds, minutes, and hours
- Bars and Beats:The spacing of bars and the beats within those bars is determined by a tempo map that is part of the sequence timeline. In DP, tempo is based on beats per minute in relation to meter.
- Samples: Digital Performer can display the sample number of any position of the sequence timeline. Numbering starts at the beginning of the sequence and is based on the current sample rate of the DP session.
- SMPTE Frame Time: This is a standard based on film frames. SMPTE time code is described as hours, minutes, seconds, and frames. There are different frame-per-second rates that can be used.

Timeline location is displayed in graphic editor windows, event lists, and selection boxes. In any place that a sequence location can be displayed, DP has the option to display that location in different formats.

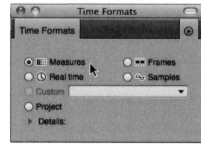

Time format display can be controlled and customized from the Time Formats window under the Setup menu. Initially, the Time Formats window

Figure 3.14

displays simple choices for universal time display throughout DP.

It is possible to customize the time format display in DP, and to create presets of different custom display setups. Click on the Details menu to show the time format customization options.

Set Movie Start Time

When a movie is opened in DP, its first frame is set to SMPTE location 0:00:00:00. In some cases that may actually be the correct SMPTE address of the first frame of the movie. It is also possible that the movie will not have a SMPTE start time of zero. For example, it is a common convention to assign a start time of 1:00:00:00 to movies. It's also possible that a composer may receive a movie file that contains a portion of the final movie. In that circumstance, it becomes important to have the correct SMPTE start time of the movie file.

When a composer receives a movie file for scoring, the composer is usually also informed of the frame rate and SMPTE start time of the movie file. In some situations, a movie file may have a SMPTE "burn-in window," which displays the current SMPTE location as the movie is played.

It is possible to set the SMPTE start time of a movie file in DP. If the SMPTE start time for the movie is set correctly, and if the DP sequence is set to the same frame rate as the movie, the SMPTE display in the DP counter will accurately match the current SMPTE location in the movie.

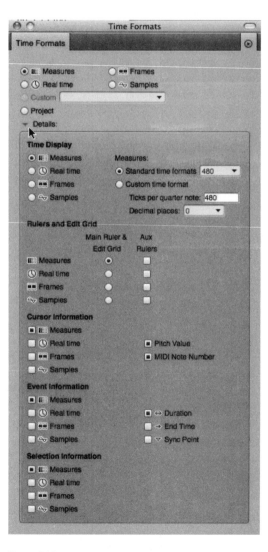

Figure 3.15

To set the movie start time, Right+Click or Control+Click on the Movie window to get the mini menu. Choose Set Movie Start Time... The Set Movie Start window will open.

Set Sequence Start Time

By default, a new file created in DP is set so that the start of sequence is bar 1, with a SMPTE location of 0:00:00:00. It is entirely possible that the composer will want music to start at some other SMPTE location than "time zero." Therefore it is possible to offset the bar and beat location in relation to the SMPTE location.

Once the movie start time is set correctly, the SMPTE display in the DP counter will accurately show the current SMPTE frame location in the movie. Locate to the position in the movie where the music is to start.

Figure 3.16

The next step is to offset the sequence start time to the current SMPTE location. To change the sequence start time, go to the mini menu in the Control Panel and choose Set Chunk Start Time...

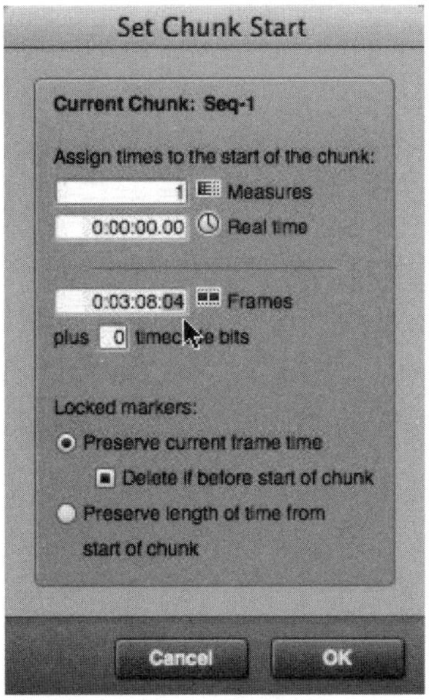

Figure 3.17

Set Chunk Start Time... is also available from the Chunks window mini menu.

Leave the Measure display set to 1. Set the Frame location to the current SMPTE location displayed in the counter. Now bar 1 of the DP sequence is matched to the specified SMPTE location in the movie.

Figure 3.18

Markers

Markers are pointers created within a sequence timeline. Markers have many uses:

- Markers are used to locate within a sequence.
- Markers are used to keep track of specific events on the sequence timeline.
- Markers are used to keep track of video events within a movie.
- Markers can be used for tempo calculation.
- Markers can be used for rehearsal markings.
- Markers can be used to trigger video streamers.

The Markers Window

The Markers window can be displayed in a sidebar of the Consolidate window, or it can be opened as a separate window. The default key command to open the Markers window is Shift+K. The Markers window can also be opened from the Studio menu.

In a new sequence, the Markers window is initially empty. As markers are added to the sequence, they appear in the Markers window in chronological order.

The Markers window displays a series of vertical columns. Clicking on the far left, next to a marker, will locate the DP sequence to that marker position.

![Markers window showing measure 9|1|000, time 0:03:2, with Marker-1 listed]

Figure 3.19

The next set of columns show the location for each marker. By default, the display is set to show bars and beats. It is possible to change time display to other formats, and to show multiple time formats simultaneously. To change the time format display in the Markers window, go to the Setup menu>Time Formats. Select a basic time format, or click on the Details button to customize the time format display. The time formats in the Markers window are set via the Event Information checkboxes.

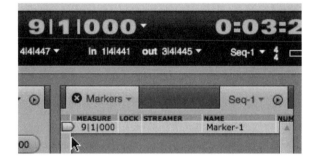

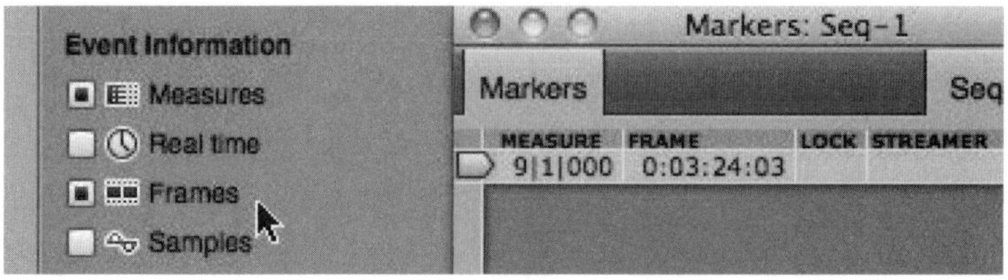

Figure 3.20

The next column is the Lock column. Click in the Lock column to set a Marker so that it is anchored to SMPTE time, rather than beat and bar location.

By default, the next visible column is the Name column. Option/Alt+Click to rename a marker.

It is also possible to display another column to the left of the Name column. If Show Streamers is selected in the Markers window mini menu, the Streamer column will be visible.

The NUM column is used for locating between markers with remote commands.

Find, Weight, and Hit Range columns are used for finding tempos that reference audio beats to marker locations.

The far right column is the Comments column. Click in the Comments column to open a text editor for the selected marker.

In the upper right-hand corner of the Markers window is a tab that allows selection between the Markers windows of different sequence chunks.

Adding and Deleting Markers

Markers can be created with a key command or by selecting Add Marker in the Markers window mini menu. The default key command to add a new marker is Control+M. When a marker is added, it is created at the current sequence location.

There is a separate key command and mini menu selection to add a New Marker with Options.

Figure 3.21

New Marker with Options will open a window that allows editing of the new marker as it is being created.

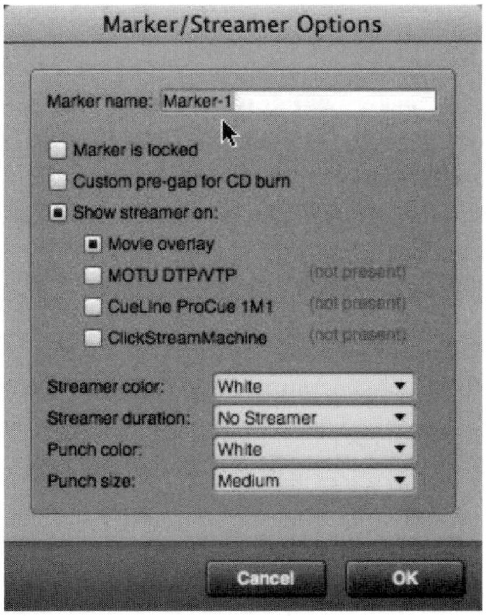

Figure 3.22

Markers can be deleted by selecting and choosing Delete Marker from the Markers window mini menu. Markers can also be selected and deleted from the conductor track in the Sequence Editor window or Event Edit List window.

Locking Markers

Like other sequence events, markers can be locked or unlocked in relation to sequence location. If a marker is locked, it will retain its SMPTE location, regardless of sequence tempo. If a marker is not locked, its location is based on bars and beats. That means that if the sequence tempo is changed, the marker will stay in the same position relative to bars and beats, but that means it is moving relative to SMPTE frame time.

An example of using an unlocked marker is that the marker describes a music location such as verse or chorus. If the tempo if the sequence is changed, the marker needs to be able to change with the sequence so that it continues to accurately describe the location of the verse or chorus.

An example of using a locked marker is that the marker refers to an event in the movie. If the tempo of the sequence is changed, the event in the movie does not change. Therefore a locked marker will stay in the same position relative to the movie, regardless of any sequence tempo changes.

Markers can be locked by clicking in the Lock column in the Markers window. Markers can also be locked by Option/Alt+Clicking on the marker in the Sequence Editor window.

Edit Decision List

An Edit Decision List is also known as an EDL. An EDL is a list of specific events within a video. EDL events have a basic description, and a SMPTE time code location. EDLs are used by a composer or post-production engineer as a reference for composition, editing, and mixing.

For example, an EDL may contain the start times of all musical cues within the video. The EDL may also contain references to video events that occur during musical passages. The EDL events can then be used to calculate musical "hit points" that reinforce the action in the video.

In some cases, an EDL is provided to the composer by a music editor or someone similar. The EDL would then be copied into the Markers window manually. In other situations, the composer may have free reign to make those musical decisions. In either situation, the Markers window is used to contain the EDL within the DP session.

The Markers window can be printed, and the print output can be sent to a PDF file. This allows the export of an EDL from the Markers window.

Clicks

A click is a metronomic pulse that is used to provide a tempo reference within a sequence. A click can be a sound, MIDI event, or visual event overlaid onto a movie.

Clicks can be played back as patterns. Click tracks can be programmed to change click patterns and to turn the click on and off.

Types of Clicks

Digital Performer can generate audio, MIDI, and visual clicks. A MIDI click can be sent to any internal or external MIDI sound module. An audio click can be generated from one of the included DP click sounds, or from any WAV or AIFF audio file. The click type is set up in the Click Preferences window.

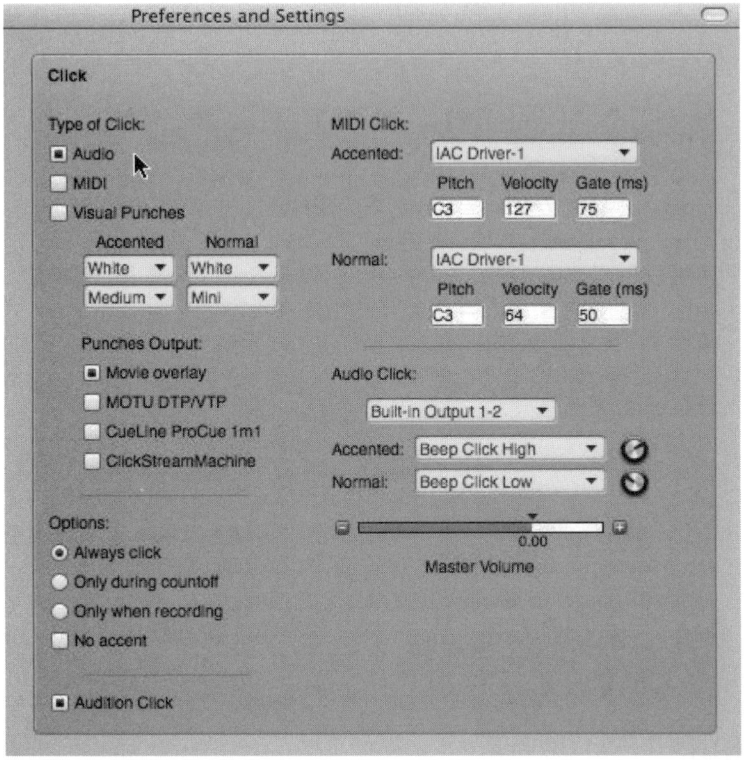

Figure 3.23

Programming Click Tracks

Digital Performer can play a simple click based on the beat value defined in the BPM indictor in the Control Panel.

The behavior of the click is based on settings in the click preferences, and whether or not the Click button is engaged.

Figure 3.24

Digital Performer can also play back a sophisticated click track that includes changing beat values, click patterns, and tacet sections (no click playback). Click programming is done in the conductor track.

Figure 3.25

Open the Event List window for the conductor track. At the top of the window are Insert Event and Delete Event buttons, and a pop-up menu to choose the type of event to insert. Choose Click Change from the pop-up menu and press the Insert Event button. A click change event will be inserted at the current sequence location.

The location of the click change event can be edited. The type of click event can be edited. Click on the click event type to get a menu.

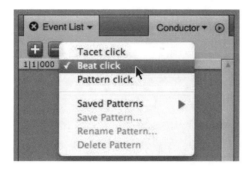

Figure 3.26

Beat click values and pattern clicks can be further edited in the Event List window. The following graphic shows a conductor track Event List with a programmed click track. The click starts off as a quarter note click. At bar 5, the click is silenced with a click tacet event. At bar 7, a click pattern is engaged. At bar 9, the click pattern changes to an eighth-note click.

Figure 3.27

Click Patterns

The most typical pattern for a metronomic click is a click on each quarter note beat. By default, DP is set to generate a click on the quarter note.

To change the default metronomic value of the click, click on the Current Beat Value icon in the Control Panel window. Choose the desired click value, including dotted note value beats.

Figure 3.28

Digital Performer also provides the ability to use sophisticated, programmable click patterns. Click patterns are inserted as events in the conductor track. In the Event List window for the Conductor track, select Click Change from the insert menu and press the add button. A click event will be inserted at the current counter location.

Click on the click event to get a menu that allows the event type to be changed. This menu provides the choice of a new click pattern or a saved click pattern. If a new click pattern is created, it can be saved, renamed, or deleted.

A click pattern is described as a series of numbers. The last number, after the forward-slash, is the beat division for the pattern. The valid values are 1 for a whole note, 2 for a half note, 4 for a quarter note, 8 for an eighth note, 16 for a sixteenth note, and 32 for a thirty-second note.

The numbers before the forward slash represent the clicks within the pattern. Each number represents a multiple of the beat division value. If the beat division is 4 (quarter note), a number 1 to the left of the forward slash represents a quarter note. If the beat division with 8 (eighth note), a 1 to the left of the forward slash would represent an eighth note. 2 doubles the value of the beat division. If the beat division is 8, a 2 to the left of the forward slash represents a quarter note (double the value of the eighth note beat division). Here are some examples of click patterns:

- 1111/4: Four quarter notes
- 111/4: Three quarter notes
- 11111111/8: Eight eighth notes
- 111111/8: Six eighth notes
- 221111/8: Two quarter notes, followed by four eighth notes
- 42211111111/16: One quarter note, followed by two eighth notes, followed by eight sixteenth notes
- 33111111/16: Two quarter notes, followed by six eighth notes. This would typically be used for a 3/4 meter

Click patterns are not affected by meter changes in the sequence. For example, a click pattern of three quarter notes will play that pattern regardless of the meter. If the meter is 4/4, the downbeat of the three quarter note pattern will change with each bar. Typically, the pattern is matched to the meter. In other words, a pattern with three quarter notes would usually be used within a 3/4 meter sequence. Another example is a pattern of six eighth notes, which would typically be used with a 6/8 meter.

The DP click provides for an accented click and a normal click. The sounds or MIDI assignments for accented and normal clicks are assignable in the Click Preferences window. When a simple beat value is used for a click, the first click of the bar is accented. When using click patterns, any clicks within the pattern can be designated as accent clicks. To accent a click, select it and choose Command+B on the keyboard. The selected click will highlight to show that it is accented.

Figure 3.29

Tempo Maps

In order to compose music that is synchronized to picture, a tempo map is created that references hit points in the movie. Tempo and meter changes can be used to create downbeats or beat referenced hit points.

Conductor Track

Every sequence in DP has a single conductor track. The conductor track can not be deleted from the sequence.

The conductor track is used for the following event types:

- Tempo change events: Tempo change events can be embedded in the conductor track to create a tempo map. Tempo events will change the playback tempo of the sequence. In order for the sequence to follow tempo events in the conductor track, the sequence must be set to Conductor track mode in the Tempo Control menu in the Control Panel window.

Figure 3.30

- Meter changes: Meter change events change the position of barlines in relationship to beats within the bar
- Key changes: Key change events change the key signature markings in the notation windows. Key change events can influence transpose functions.
- Markers
- Click changes
- Video Streamers, Punches, and Flutters

All types of events can be entered into and edited in the Event List window for the conductor track. Key changes, meter changes, and tempo change events can be added and edited in the Sequence Editor window. Markers and streamers can also be added and edited in the Markers window.

Tap Tempo

Tap tempo is a way to create a tempo map in real time by tapping on a MIDI key. Tap tempo will not change the tempo of audio files in real time. Therefore tap tempo works best with MIDI tracks or a simple click.

- Go to the Setup menu>Receive Sync. The Preferences window will open.

Figure 3.31

- Select Tap Tempo as the Type of sync.
- Choose the MIDI input beat data: Source. Any configured MIDI input device can be selected as the tap source. It is also possible to use MIDI Keys as the tap source. This allows the tap to be controlled from the computer keyboard. Open MIDI Keys from the Studio menu.
- Choose the MIDI Event type for the tap source. Highlight the Event field and trigger a MIDI key. The Event field will "learn" the MIDI event.
- Sync countoff beats: allows the tap to start with a specified number of countoff taps. The default setting of 4 means that there must be four taps before the sequence starts and follows the next tap. If the tempo of the sequence was 3/4, it would make sense to set the Sync countoff beats to 3.
- Click the Done button to close the Preferences window.
- Set DP to Slave to External Sync: Slave to External Sync can be engaged from the Setup menu. The default key command is Command+7. Slave to External Sync can also be engaged from the Control Panel.

Figure 3.32

- Record-enable the conductor track.

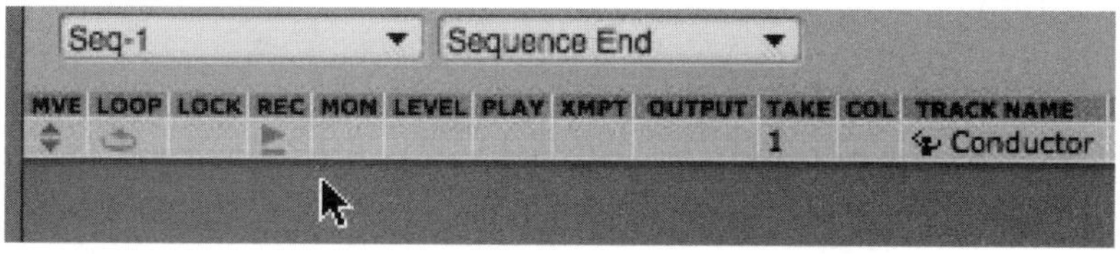

MVE	LOOP	LOCK	REC	MON	LEVEL	PLAY	XMPT	OUTPUT	TAKE	COL	TRACK NAME
									1		Conductor

Seq-1 ▼   Sequence End ▼

Figure 3.33

- Put DP into Record mode.
- DP will now wait for the tap signal. As DP receives the tap, the sequence will play. If a Sync countoff beats value has been set, the sequence will play after the countoff. MIDI tracks and the click will follow the tap. The tap signal will generate tempo events, which will be recorded into the conductor track.
- Press stop at any time to exit the tap record mode.
- Disengage Slave to External Sync.
- DP will now play back and follow the tempo created by the tap.

Change Tempo

Digital Performer provides many tools for tempo control. One way to set tempos and create a tempo map is to define bar number locations based on real-time locations. DP can calculate the correct tempo required to hit specific bar and beat locations based on real time. DP can create gradual tempo changes based on real-time locations of start and end tempos. This can be a quick way to create a tempo map change based on two hit points in a movie.

Go to the Project menu>Conductor Track>Change Tempo. The Change Tempo window will open. The Change Tempo window is a calculator that can create tempo changes in the conductor track. The Options button will toggle the Change Tempo window between two modes of operation.

Initially, the Change Tempo window will display the tempo start and end times, and a tempo. There are five selectable tempo curve types. If the first button is selected, that indicates no desired tempo change between the selected start and end times. The desired tempo can be set between those two points. Pressing the OK button will place the appropriate tempo event in the conductor track.

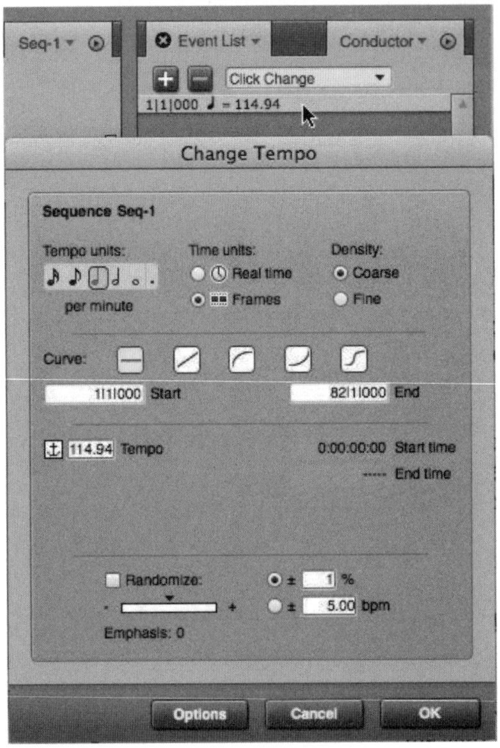

Figure 3.34

To enter a tempo change over time, choose a tempo curve type. The window now displays adjustable start and end tempos for the start and end times. When the OK button is pressed, DP will create tempo data that causes the sequence to follow the assigned tempo at the assigned bar locations.

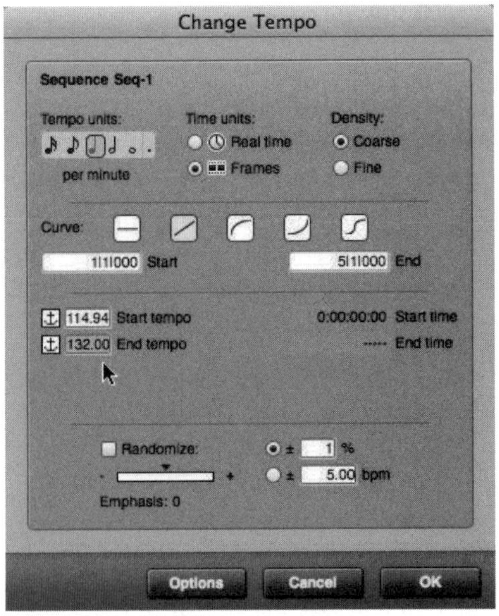

Figure 3.35

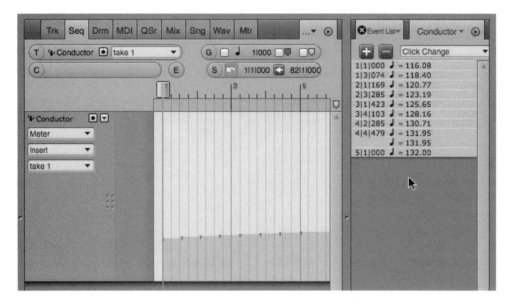

Figure 3.36

Press the Option button to change the mode of the Change Time window. The SMPTE End time of the the tempo change can be programmed. This allows tempo changes to be based on hit points in a movie. By selecting a SMPTE location for a bar location, the Change Tempo window will calculate the correct tempo events.

In the following example, the Change Tempo window is set to generate tempo information so that there is a linear tempo change between bar 3 and bar 8. The lock button is pressed for the start tempo, so that the tempo at bar 3 does not change with the calculation. Bar 8 has been designated and a specific SMPTE location has been entered. When the OK button is pressed, DP will insert the correct tempo change events so that bar 8 is now aligned to the specified SMPTE location. In this example, the SMPTE location being aligned with bar 8 has caused DP to create a tempo accelerando. If a different SMPTE time had been specified, DP may have needed to create a tempo retard in order to line bar 8 up correctly.

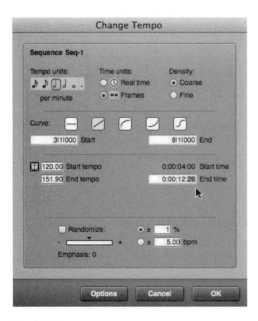

Figure 3.37

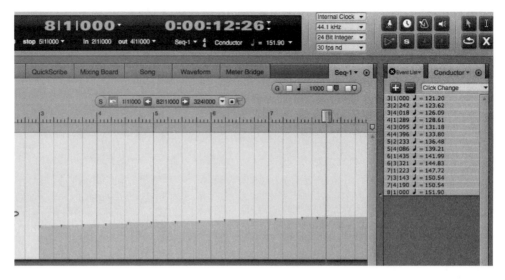

Figure 3.38

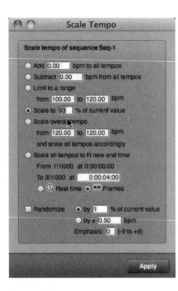

Figure 3.39

Scale Tempo

Scale Tempo is a region-based command that changes tempo event data in the conductor track. Select a time range in any graphic edit window and choose Scale Tempos... from the Region menu. The Scale Tempo window will open.

There are many options to change the tempo of the selected region. Select the desired options and press the Apply button. Appropriate tempo events will be added or changed in the conductor track.

Scale Time

Digital Performer has the ability to change the tempo of recorded MIDI and audio data without changing the sequence tempo in the conductor track. Audio and MIDI data can be selected and speeded up or slowed down, and the tempo of the sequence can remain the same.

Scale Time is a function found under the Region menu. Select a region (any combination of tracks and time), and choose Scale Time... from the Region menu. The Scale Time window will open.

A new time length for the region selection can be made based on bars and beats or percentage. There is an option to time scale any audio in the region selection. Click OK and the tempo of the selected data will be changed within the current sequence tempo.

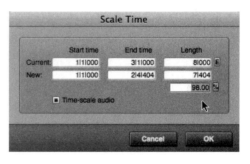

Figure 3.40

Calculate Tempo based on SMPTE Hit Points

There are many ways to create and edit tempo maps in DP. When composing music for video, a common task is to create a tempo map that references audio beats to specific events within that video. It is possible to calculate a tempo that lands beats on two specific SMPTE locations. It is also possible to calculate a common tempo that lands beats on, or close to, multiple SMPTE locations. The Change Tempo window is useful for creating tempo changes based on two hit points. To find common tempos for multiple hit points, the Find Tempo for Locked Markers window in the Markers window mini menu is the appropriate tool.

Find Tempo for Locked Markers

Finding a tempo that is common for multiple SMPTE hit points is much more complicated than finding a tempo common to only two hit points. Digital Performer features a sophisticated calculator to find common tempos for multiple SMPTE hit points.

- In the Markers window, click in the Lock column to lock markers to their SMPTE time locations. If the tempo of the sequence is changed, the markers will stay in the same location relative to SMPTE time code and the movie.
- Click in the Find column to include locked markers in the tempo calculation.
- Click in the Weight column to set the importance of the marker in the tempo calculation. The tempo calculator will look for a common tempo for all checked markers. If markers do not fall on exact beats at specific tempos, the tempo calculator will consider which markers are more or less important in terms of finding common tempos.
- Click in the Hit Range Before and Hit Range After columns to expand the range of the marker in terms of representing a hit point. If the hit point must be exactly at the marker location, do not edit the hit ranges.

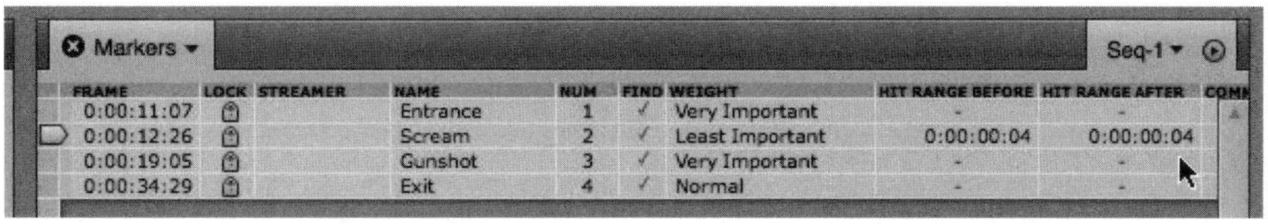

Figure 3.41

- Go to the Markers window mini menu and select Find Tempo for Locked Markers... The Find Tempo window will open.

The Find Tempo window will display a list of tempos, based on the selected markers and the current parameters in the window. The tempos are displayed in order of the most likely tempos to land beats on the selected markers. These choices are influenced by the marker weights and hit range offsets. Click on a displayed tempo and the selected markers will appear at the bottom of the window. Sequence locations based on bars and beats will be displayed for each marker in the find selection. Clicking on different tempos will display the bar and beat locations of the markers at the selected tempo.

Clicking the Apply window will enter the selected tempo information into the conductor track, starting at the sequence location specified in the upper left-hand corner of Find Tempo window.

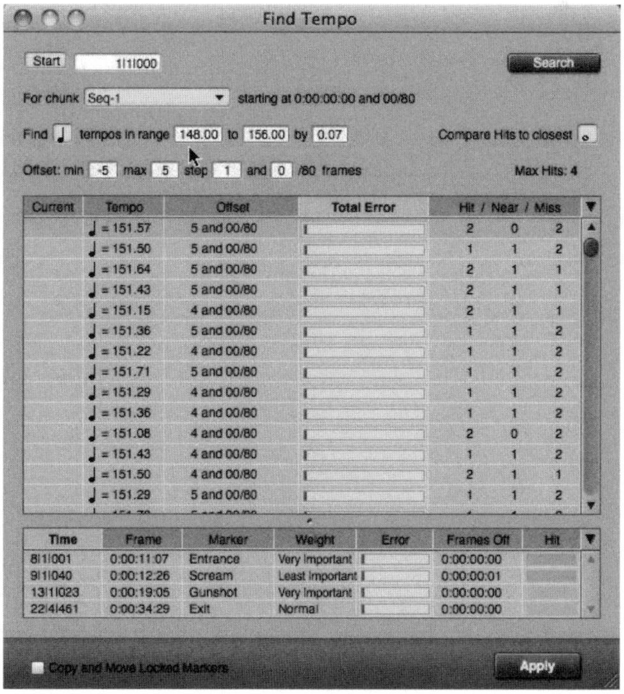

Figure 3.42

Figure 3.43

There are many options available in the Find Tempo window. Check the Digital Performer User Guide for a description of each parameter.

Sequence Chunks and the Song Window

When composing music for picture, it is common that there will be multiple cues throughout the video. The Chunks feature in DP is specifically designed for handling multiple musical cues that belong to the same movie.

Individual sequence chunks can reference different SMPTE locations in the movie. This allows each cue to be worked on independently.

Chunks as Cues

The Chunks window provides the ability to have multiple sequences within a single session file. This feature has many uses, but its original design and intention was to be used to provide a way to work with multiple musical cues within a movie timeline.

In a movie, there may be many separate pieces of music, known as cues. Each of these musical cues start at a different location within the movie. Each cue starts at its own bar 1. If a single sequence timeline was used for all the musical cues within the movie, only the first cue would start at bar 1 on that timeline. Also, if any tempo changes or edits were made in that single sequence, that would affect every cue after the edit or tempo change. Therefore it is desirable that each cue be contained in a separate sequence. If each cue is its own sequence, that means that each cue starts at bar 1, and any edits or tempo changes made in one sequence will not have any effect on any other sequences.

Movies and Sequence Chunks

By default, an imported movie will be assigned to all sequence chunks in the Chunks window. If a new sequence chunk is added to the Chunks window, the movie will automatically be assigned to the new sequence. Initially, an imported movie is assigned to the start of the sequence. Each sequence chunk can have different movie start times. If the movie start time is edited in one sequence chunk, that will have no effect on the start times in other sequences. This allows a single movie to be used for multiple musical cues. Each sequence represents a separate musical cue that is assigned to a unique location within the movie.

It is also possible to assign different movies to different sequence chunks within the DP session file. To do this, go to the Movie window mini menu and deselect Use Same Movie For All Sequences. If this is deselected, an imported movie will only be assigned to the currently play-enabled sequence chunk. If different movies are then assigned to different sequence chunks, changing the currently play-enabled sequence will change the currently visible movie.

The Song Window

It is possible to assemble a larger sequence based on the individual cues. This is done with the Song window. A song is a container. Sequence chunks can be dragged into a Song window and assigned to specific SMPTE locations. A final sequence can then be created that is the sum total of all the included cues.

- In the Chunks window, select New Song from the mini menu. A new item will appear in the Chunks window. Option/Alt+Click to name the new song.

Figure 3.44

- Double+Click on the name of the song to open the Song window.
- Go to the Song window mini menu and check Frames. This will display SMPTE times in the Song window.

Figure 3.45

- Go to the mini menu and choose Insert Column... The Insert Column window will open.

Figure 3.46

- Set the SMPTE start time of the first cue. This will be the same SMPTE start time as the the sequence chunk that is used for the first cue. Click OK. If the SMPTE time was set to anything other than zero, a new column appears in the Song window with the programmed SMPTE start time.

Figure 3.47

- Drag the first cue sequence chunk icon from the Chunks window into the Song window. Drag the sequence chunk to the correct SMPTE start time. The sequence chunk will appear as an icon on the song timeline.

Figure 3.48

- Go to the Song window mini menu and choose Insert Column... again. This time, enter the SMPTE start time for the second cue. Press OK. A new column will appear in the Song window with the SMPTE start time for the second cue. Drag the sequence chunk icon for the second cue from the Chunks window to the column in the Song window.

Figure 3.49

- Once all the cues are assigned to their correct SMPTE locations, select all the sequence chunks in the Song window, go to the mini menu, and choose Copy Conductor Tracks. This will copy the tempo change information from each sequence chunk into the conductor track for the song.

- With the sequence chunks selected in the Song window, go to the mini menu and choose Merge Markers. This will copy the markers from each sequence into the Song window conductor track.
- With all sequences selected, go to the mini menu and select Merge Chunks to Sequence... A window will open asking if tracks with identical names should be merged. If the different sequence chunks have tracks in common, it is probably desirable to merge tracks with similar names so that the final sequence does not have duplicate tracks for common instruments.
- In the Merge Chunks window, press the OK button. A new sequence chunk will be created in the Chunks window. This new sequence chunk will be an assembly of the separate cues on a single timeline. The appropriate tempo changes and SMPTE start times are all preserved for each cue. The movie can now be viewed from start to finish with this final sequence, and each cue will play at the correct time in the movie.
- At any time, the composer can go back to an original cue sequence chunk and make edits. The final sequence can then be re-merged in the Song window to include the updated cue.

Notation

Digital Performer can display MIDI as notes as standard part and score notation. DP has two separate windows for working with notation. The Notation Editor window is used for single staff note entry and MIDI controller editing. The Quickscribe window is used to create part and score page views that are appropriate for print output.

Notation Editor window

The Notation Editor window displays one MIDI track at a time. The default key command to open the Notation Editor window is Shift+N. The windows can also be opened from the mini menus of the Sequence Editor, MIDI Editor, and Quickscribe windows.

The Notation Editor window is not set up for print display or page formatting. The Notation Editor window is similar to the MIDI Editor windows in that it scrolls from left to right. MIDI information in the track is displayed on a Grand Staff. The bottom portion of the window displays additional MIDI information such as velocities and continuous controllers.

The purpose of the Notation Editor window is to provide a way to create and edit MIDI data, while viewing the MIDI notes as traditional notation on a staff. Notes and other types of MIDI data can be entered with the pencil tool. To add a MIDI note, click on the staff. Drag right to extend the note duration. The menu in the bottom left corner of the window allows selection of other types of data to be entered.

Quickscribe Window

The Quickscribe window is designed to create printed sheet music output. The Quickscribe window is set up to

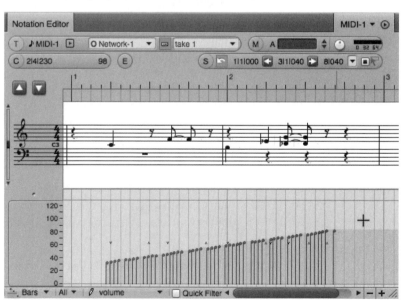

Figure 3.50

display a page. The size of the page is determined by the settings in the print driver. Any combination of MIDI tracks can be displayed as staves. This provides a way to create part and score views for printout.

Open the Quickscribe window from the button in the Consolidated window or from the Project menu. The default key command to open the window is Shift+Q.

The track selector is used to hide or show MIDI tracks. By default, DP will choose bass or treble clef for each displayed track based on the general range of the notes. It is possible to designate different staves, including Grand staff for each MIDI track. Go to the Quickscribe window mini menu>Options>Track Options... The Track Options window provides options for default display, as well as individual track display. These options include transposition, which will transpose the notation view without changing the playback pitches.

The Quickscribe window mini menu provides many additional choices and options for creating, editing, and displaying sheet music. Staves can be "hidden" inside other staves to create repeat sections for lead sheets.

Dynamic markings and arrangement markings can be added via palettes. There are different types of text tools, including a chord tool that will follow any transposition changes. Notes can be added from the note palette. There are extensive key commands available for note entry and editing.

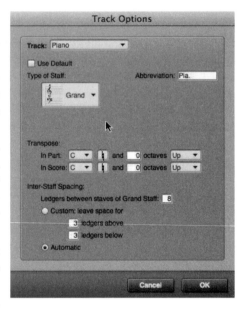

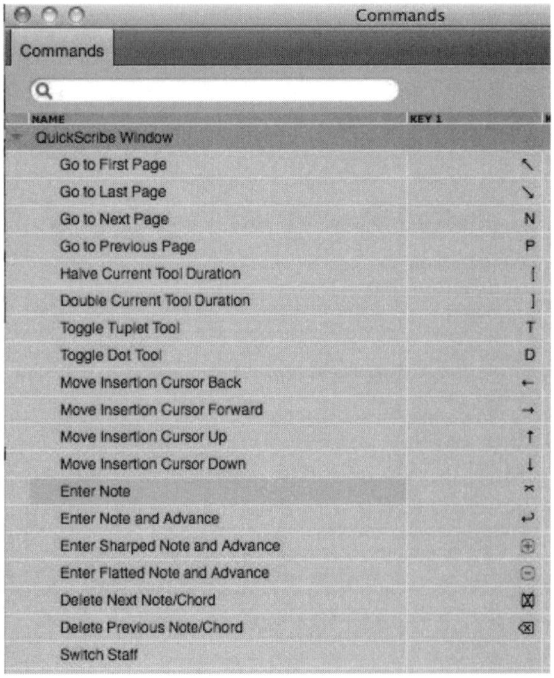

Figure 3.51

Figure 3.52

Film Scoring Events as Video Overlays

Digital Performer has the ability to superimpose visual cues onto the movie window. DP can also send control information to external video cue overlay devices. Configure Film Scoring Events in the Preferences window.

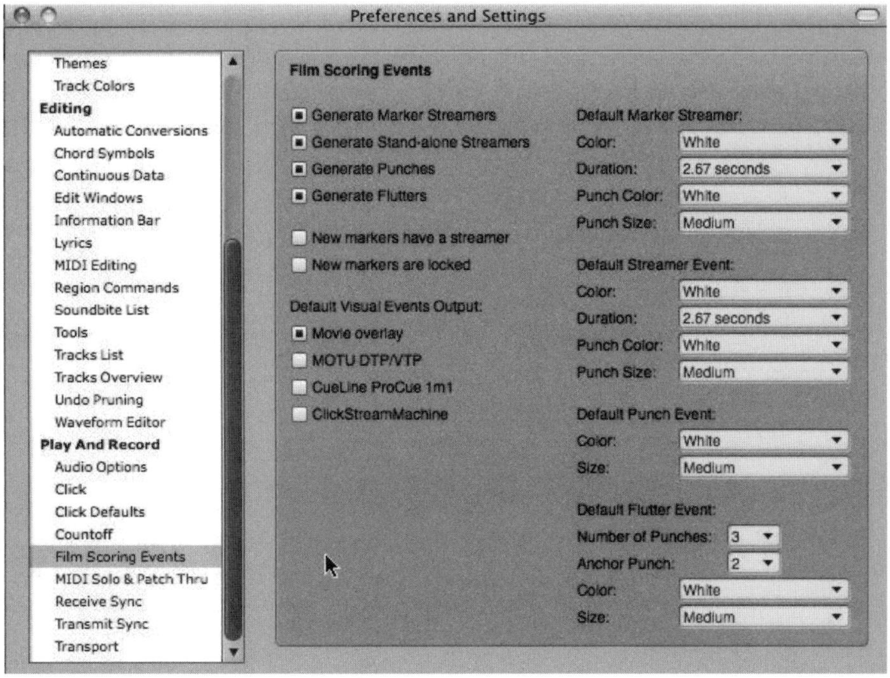

Figure 3.53

Digital Performer can generate the following types of visual cues:

- Video click: The video click follows the DP Click settings. This includes click patterns and tacet click. Video click settings are configured in the Click preferences.

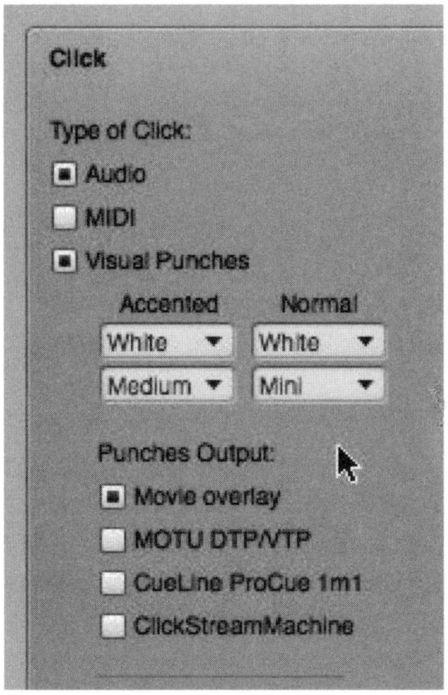

Figure 3.54

- Streamer: A streamer is a horizontal bar that moves from left to right across the movie window. The streamer is timed so that when the bar reaches the right-hand edge of the window, that is a hit point. A streamer is typically followed by a punch or flutter. Streamer default settings are configured in the Film Scoring Events preferences, and Streamers can be created in the Markers window and the conductor track Event List window. In the Markers window mini menu, select Show Streamers. The Markers window will display a Streamer column. Streamers can be assigned to markers. The streamer will be timed to start before the marker so that it hits the right side of the screen at the specific marker location. If the marker location is changed, the streamer will update to the new marker position.

Figure 3.55

Streamers can be added as events to conductor tracks. This allows creation of streamers that are not associated with markers. The streamer start will be timed so that the streamer hits the right edge of the movie window at the streamer event insert time.

- Punch: A punch is a single video flash. Punches are added as events in the conductor track. Punch defaults are set in the Film Scoring Events preferences. Individual punches can be edited in the conductor track Event List window.

Figure 3.56

- Flutter: A flutter is a series of punches, typically used to denote a video event where there must be some sort of musical or sound effect reference. Flutters are created and edited in the conductor track.

Figure 3.57

When DP bounces to a movie file, the movie can include the film scoring event overlays.

Synchronization

Digital Performer has the ability to lock to incoming MIDI Time Code (MTC), or MIDI beat clock information. DP can generate MIDI Time Code and MIDI beat clock based on tempo and SMPTE location.

Receiving Sync

Digital Performer can slave to external sync, as well as slave to MIDI clock or MTC.
- Go to the Setup menu>Receive Sync... Choose the type of sync and the incoming sync port.
- Go to the Setup menu and choose Engage Slave To External Sync. This can be done from the Setup menu, key command, or Slave To External Sync button in the Control Panel.
- Instantiate Play or Record. The Play or Record button in the Control Panel will flash, indicating that DP is waiting for sync. When DP receives sync, the Play or Record button will go solid and the DP transport will roll.

If DP is recording while slaved to external sync, and the incoming time code is interrupted, DP will go out of record mode.

If DP records or plays audio while slaved to MTC or MIDI clock, the audio file is seen as a single record event. That means audio will be recorded or triggered to play on time, but after that point, if the incoming time code varies in speed, the audio in DP will no longer be in sync with the time code. For proper audio sync, the DP audio interface needs to also be in sync with the time code. A MOTU audio interface can slave to LTC SMPTE, and it will lock its audio speed to the incoming code. If DP is using a non-MOTU audio interface, ideally the device that is generating the external time code will also be able to generate a resolved word clock signal to the audio interface. If that is the case, make sure to set the clock source in the DP Audio Hardware Driver window to that external source.

Generating Sync

Digital Performer can generate MIDI beat clock and MTC (MIDI Time Code). Go to the Setup menu>Transmit Sync. The Transmit Sync preferences will open.

There are separate pop-up menus for assigning MTC and MIDI clock outputs. The available choices in these menus are based on the MIDI Devices that are configured in the Bundles window. If MIDI Devices in the Bundles have the checked properties of MIDI Beat Clock and/or MIDI Time Code, they will show up as available destinations for transmit sync.

Digital Performer can also work with a MOTU audio interface to generate LTC SMPTE time code. The MOTU audio interface drivers include a utility application called MOTU SMPTE Setup.

Post-Production

Post-production is the editing of audio for picture. Post-production may or may not include musical editing. Post-production can include dialog and Foley sound effects. Digital Performer is a powerful tool for post-production editing.

Organizing Stock Audio Clips

By default, DP stores all recorded, processed, and imported audio into the Audio Files folder in the Project folder. When working with stock audio libraries, it may be desirable not to copy imported audio into the project folder. In the Audio Files preferences, DP can be set to never copy imported audio files. DP can also be set to store any converted or processed files either with the original files, or in the project folder.

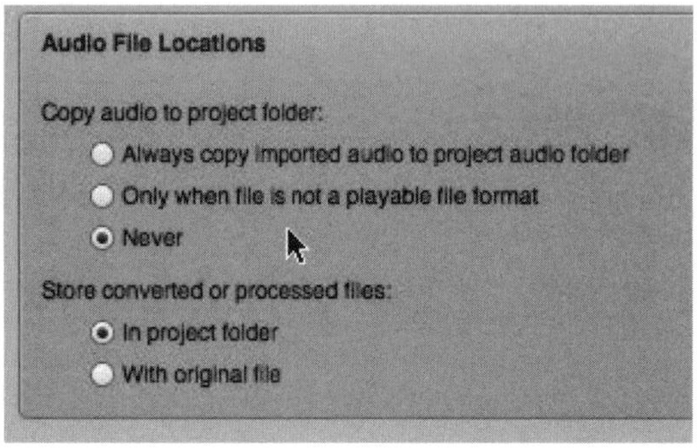

Audio File Locations

Copy audio to project folder:
- Always copy imported audio to project audio folder
- Only when file is not a playable file format
- ⦿ Never

Store converted or processed files:
- ⦿ In project folder
- With original file

Figure 3.58

Digital Performer will attempt to play audio files that are referenced over network connections. If the network can not deliver the files fast enough, they may need to be copied to a locally connected hard drive.

An excellent tool for organizing stock audio (and MIDI) clips are Clippings windows. Clippings windows can contain aliases to Soundbites. Soundbites can be dragged directly from the desktop into clippings windows. Multiple clippings windows can be created and named for sophisticated organization. Audio and MIDI clippings can be dragged from clippings windows into tracks as needed.

Soundbite Gain

There are two ways to non-destructively change the volume of audio playback in DP. Audio tracks in DP have volume control via the track fader in the Mixing Board window, or via track automation. It is also possible to embed volume automation directly into a soundbite. This is called soundbite gain.

Soundbite gain is associated with the soundbite, as opposed to being separate data in a track. This means that if a soundbite has edited gain, that automated gain will stay with the soundbite wherever it is used in the sequence.

Soundbite gain can be changed with menu or key commands, or graphically in an edit window. Select one or more soundbites and go to the Audio menu>Bite Volume and Gain.

Figure 3.59

To edit soundbite gain in the Sequence Editor window, set the track view to Bite Volume. Click on the soundbite gain line to edit the same way track automation is edited.

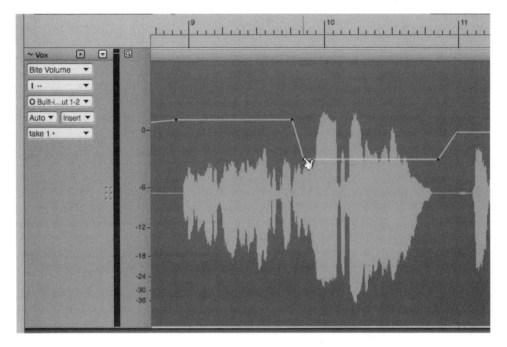

Figure 3.60

Soundbite gain can be edited in the Waveform Editor window.

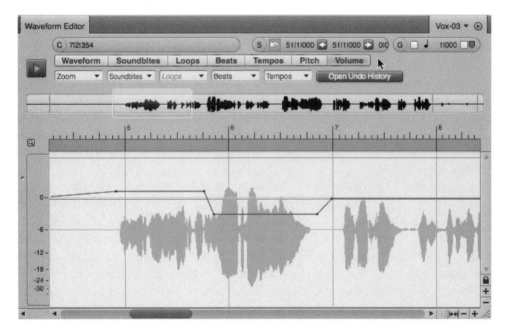

Figure 3.61

Soundbite gain can be edited in the Sound File Information window.

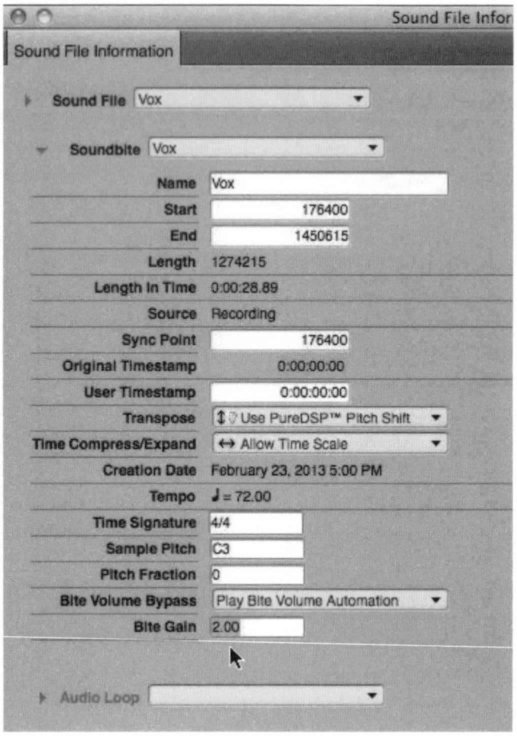

Figure 3.62

Spotting to Time Code

Soundbites can be dropped onto the sequence timeline and spotted to SMPTE or bar/beat locations. Any MIDI or audio event can be moved to a specific location via any window where that event can be selected.

A Soundbite can be dragged from the computer desktop or from the Soundbites window directly into an audio track. Soundbites can also be referenced as clippings and dragged from a clippings window. If audio is dragged into an existing track, it must be dragged into a track with the corresponding number of channels. Stereo audio can only be dragged into a stereo track. Mono audio can only be dragged into a mono track.

Soundbites can also be dragged into the left side of the Tracks window. The window will highlight. When the mouse cursor is released, a new track will be created and the Soundbite will be placed in the new track. If there is time stamp information in the Soundbite, the Soundbite will be placed at that location. Therefore if the sequence starts at SMPTE time zero, but the Soundbite has a time stamp of one hour, don't be surprised when the Soundbite is placed one hour into the sequence timeline.

Once an event is selected in a track, it is simple to move that event to any time line location. The Event Information window will update to show information about any selected event. Time location can be displayed in multiple formats, based on what is selected in the Setup menu>Time Formats window.

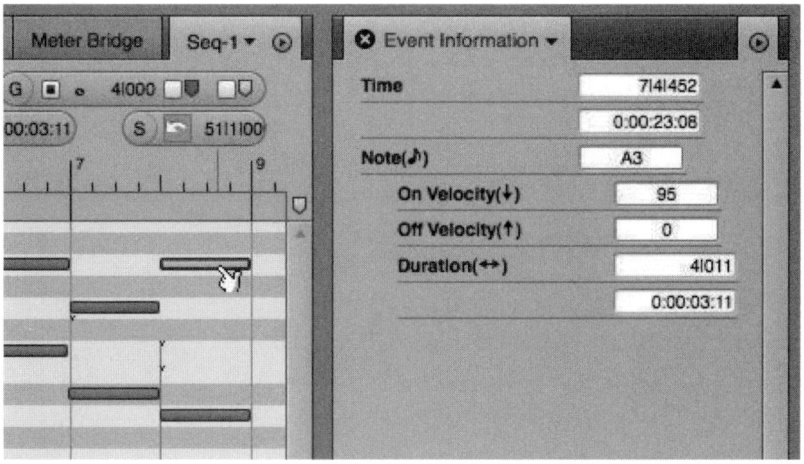

Figure 3.63

Event location information can also be displayed and edited in graphic editing windows and Event List windows. The Information Bar preferences provide a way to to select which windows will display event information.

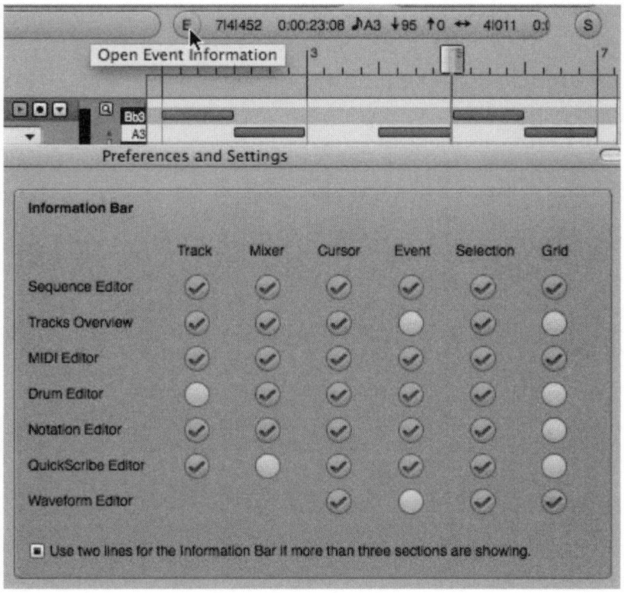

Figure 3.64

When event information is displayed in a graphic editor window, it can be selected and edited. This makes spotting any event a simple process.

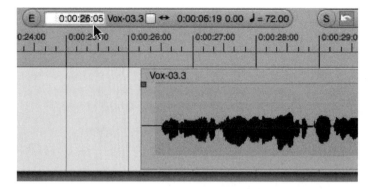

Figure 3.65

Locking Tracks to Time Code

In the Tracks window, there is a lock column. The lock column is available for all tracks except the conductor track. When the track is locked, events in that track will not change position relative to SMPTE time if the sequence tempo is changed. This allows tracks to contain data that is not specific to musical locations, but must stay in a fixed position relative to picture.

Locking Markers to Time Code

Markers can be locked to time code. There is a lock column in the Markers window. Markers can also be locked and unlocked in the Sequence Editor window. Option/Alt+Click on the marker in the ruler to lock or unlock.

Figure 3.66

Insert Measures

Digital Performer can insert time at any point in the sequence. Go to the Project menu>Conductor Track>Insert Measures... A window will open.

The number of bars to be inserted and the insert location can be selected. The inserted bar length will be based on the current meter at the insert location. If the option to Maintain all

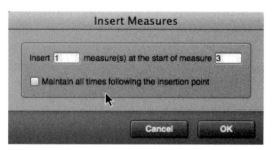

Figure 3.67

times following the insertion point is selected, events before the insertion point will be moved earlier in time. If the option is not checked, all events after the insertion point will be moved later in time.

It is important to understand that Soundbites are handled as individual events. Inserting measures will not split the Soundbite at the insertion point. If the goal is to insert space into any Soundbites at the insertion point, locate the cursor to the insertion point. Select all Soundbites. Choose Split At Counter from the Edit menu. The Soundbites will all be cut at that location. If measures are now inserted, there will be space between the Soundbites at the new edit points.

Snip

Snip is an edit command that deletes the selected data from the region, and moves all data on the right side of the edit point to the beginning of the left side edit point. Snip works within tracks, or across the entire sequence. Make a selection in any graphic editing window. Choose Snip from the Edit menu. The default key command for Snip is Command+J

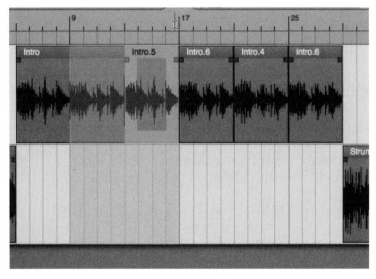

Figure 3.68

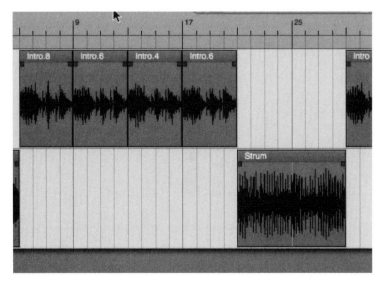

Figure 3.69

Bounce and Export

There are many ways to export final product from DP. The Bounce to Disk function will create rendered mixes based on region selections. Bounce to Disk can bounce to a variety of audio formats and can also bounce to a movie file. Individual soundbites can also be exported in a number of formats.

Bounce to Stems

It is not uncommon that a composer is asked to deliver their mixes as stems. Stems are submixes of the overall composition. For example, a mix may be separated into percussion stems, orchestra stems, and special effects stems. To create submix stems, select only the tracks to be included in the submix and choose Bounce to Disk from the File menu. A separate bounce will need to be done for each separate submix of tracks.

Bounce to Quicktime Movie

Digital Performer can bounce selected tracks into a movie file. Since bounce is based on a region selection, DP will cut off the beginning or end of the movie, or insert video black at the beginning or end of the movie as may be required.

Exporting Audio

Selected soundbites can be exported via the File menu or from the Soundbites window. Export provides a range of audio format options.

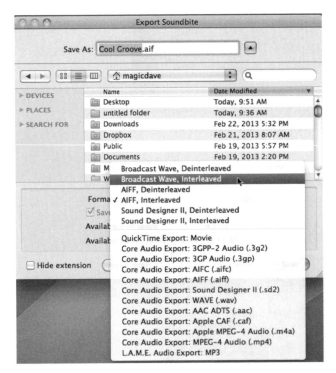

Figure 3.70

Exporting Other File Formats

The Export command under the File menu allows selected regions in a DP sequence to be exported as a Standard MIDI File, DP clipping, OMF, AAF, or XML format file.

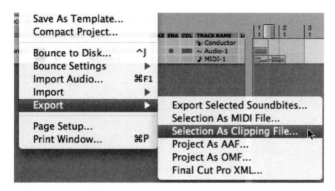

Figure 3.71

Chapter 4
MUSIC PRODUCTION

Digital Performer can provide a complete production environment for writing and recording music. DP can be used as a simple songwriting template, for cutting-edge production and mixing, and for final mastering and assembly of musical projects.

The following section will describe some of the more unique and powerful music production techniques available within DP. This includes audio routing and effects, advanced editing, creating and working with tempo maps, quantization, mastering, and much more.

Hardware Setup

A current generation laptop and a pair of headphones may be all that is required to do serious production work with DP. At the other end of the scale, every piece of hardware found in a recording studio can have some sort of involvement with a DP-based system.

As always, system requirements are based on the task at hand. Computers have become powerful enough that all aspects of recording, production, and mixing can be handled "in the box." In many cases, the choice to use external hardware as part of the production process is strictly a preference of the musicians and engineers. The following section will describe basic requirements for a DP-based music production system.

Computer Requirements

DP8 requires an Intel or AMD processor running Mac OS 10.6.8 or later, or Windows 7 or later. Minimum RAM to run the software is 4 GB. Any current generation Mac or Windows computer that can run a compatible version of OS will work with DP.

Some tasks use a relatively small amount of computer resources. For example, DP could be used to edit and assemble stereo tracks for a radio or internet broadcast. This task would require a few audio tracks, no virtual instruments, and very little in the way of effects processing. Therefore an absolute minimum computer setup would be entirely adequate.

When building up a DAW system, it's useful to know how different tasks use different computer resources:

- Audio track recording and playback uses significant amounts of hard drive space. Also, a faster drive will provide higher track counts for both recording and playback.
- Sample-based virtual instruments often use disk streaming technology to play back sounds. Disk streaming uses hard drive resources.
- Video playback requires significant hard drive space, and a faster drive will improve playback performance.
- Using separate drives for audio and video playback, as well as sample libraries, may increase overall system efficiency.
- Audio interfaces can use significant bandwidth to pass signals in and out of the computer. Higher sample rates multiply the amounts of data that need to pass through these connections. If hard drives are connected on the same buses as audio interfaces, that also increases how much data is passing over the connection. Therefore it may be helpful to use multiple connection types on the computer to spread the bandwidth load for external drives and interfaces. These connections could include USB, Firewire, PCI, or Thunderbolt.
- For large DP sessions, more RAM is required. For example, if the task is to record 24 tracks of audio for 2 continuous hours, DP will need enough memory to draw the waveforms for all that audio. For work with high track counts and long audio files, at least 8 GB of RAM is a good idea.
- Effects processing typically relies on CPU power and to a lesser extent, RAM. DP takes full advantage of multi-core CPUs, so more and faster CPUs will result in the ability to run more effect plug-ins.
- Virtual instruments are one of the most demanding functions within any DAW. Virtual instruments use hard drive resources, RAM, and CPU power. If the goal is to run the most possible simultaneous virtual instruments, the solution is to get the most powerful computer that is available. Since DP8 can take advantage of all available RAM in the computer, 16 or 32 GB of RAM could be used in large virtual instrument setups.

Audio and MIDI Interfaces

The purpose of an interface is to provide input and output to the computer. The requirements of a MIDI or audio interface are based on the type and number of signals that need to passed in and out of the computer.

Here are some typical uses of audio and MIDI interfaces in the studio:

- Connection of multiple external MIDI modules to the computer requires a MIDI interface with the corresponding number of inputs and outputs.
- Stereo audio mixing in the computer requires an audio interface with two channels of audio output. This can be as simple as the built-in audio output on the computer.
- Surround-sound monitoring requires enough channels of audio output for each portion of the surround signal. For example, 5.1 surround monitoring requires six channels of audio output through the audio interface.
- In order to patch external audio processing gear into a computer-based mix, audio inputs and outputs are required on the audio interface for each channel of external processing.
- Some mix engineers prefer to mix outside of the computer. In order to mix on an external mixer, there needs to be enough channels of audio output on the audio interface for each external mix stem.
- Some audio and MIDI interfaces also include time code functions. SMPTE time code may be transmitted or received as MTC (MIDI Time Code), or LTC (Longitudinal Time Code, which is an audio signal).

Monitor System

The choice of audio monitor speakers can be very much a personal preference on the part of the listener. The basic goal with audio monitoring in the studio is to get an accurate playback so that the final result works outside of the studio. In other words, studio monitor speakers don't have to sound good. They have to be effective.

Most engineers have worked with enough different monitor systems that they know what they prefer in order to get a useful playback sound. The bottom line with mixing and mastering is that the final product sounds acceptable on a wide range of speakers and headphones outside the recording studio.

Many studios use multiple monitor speaker setups, so the mix can be compared on different playback systems. It's not uncommon for an engineer to burn a mix to a CD, and take that CD out to listen with a car stereo or boombox.

One effective way of evaluating a monitor system is to play back a well-known commercial mix through that system. Many engineers have a favorite CD or mix that they use as a reference to test any new speaker or listening environment.

Control Surfaces

There are two fundamental ways to externally control DP. It is possible to send commands in the form of keystrokes or MIDI messages, and it is possible to use an interactive hardware or software control surface. The difference is that with keystrokes or MIDI commands, the communication is in one direction – into DP. With a dedicated software or hardware control surface, the communication is in two directions – in and out of DP.

There are several standardized control surface protocols that allow DP to work with any device that supports one of these protocols. There are also protocols that are custom designed for DP.

Two of the most common control surface protocols are HUI and Mackie Universal Control. These protocols are originally described by Mackie, a brand of LOUD Technologies Inc., and made available to other manufacturers. There are control surfaces made by a number of different companies that use one or both of these protocols. HUI is the older of the two standards and was originally designed for 8 mixer faders. Mackie Universal Control is a new standard and can support multiple banks of faders. If a control surface offers both protocols, the Universal Control protocol is generally the better choice.

Some control surfaces also have specific modes designed to custom support DP. For example, the Mackie Universal Controller can work with DP in HUI mode, Universal Controller mode, and Digital Performer mode.

Another example of a control surface that has both general support and custom-designed support for DP are the Avid MC Mix and MC Control devices.

Digital Performer can also be controlled via remote software applications. MOTU has released the free DP Control app for iPhones, iPads, and iPods. DP Control provides transport, mix, and take management functions. It uses multiple pages to display the mixer, transport controls, and track parameters. Because DP Control works on a wireless device, that makes it convenient for remote control in the studio. The engineer or artist can control DP from any location that accesses the same wireless network as the DP computer.

Digital Performer also supports remote control protocol called OSC (Open Sound Control). OSC commands can be generated by local or remote software applications.

A control surface typically has control over all the basic transport and mix functions of DP. Depending on the model of control surface, there may be sophisticated support for many parameters within DP, and even remote parameter control of effect plug-ins. What the control surface can do, and how to access those controls is up to the device itself. Each control surface comes with documentation that describes its available functions and options.

Instructions for configuring remote control of DP are located under the Help menu>Control Surfaces Help/DP Control App User Guide.

External Processing

When recording and mixing, it is possible to use a combination of internal and external signal processing. Usually, external processing is done because there is a piece of hardware available that has capabilities that are not duplicated by available software plug-ins. Using external hardware for processing can also be a matter of personal preference. An audio engineer should never be limited to working one specific way. There are many ways to record and mix, and it should be up to the engineer and artist how they want to work. If there is a desirable piece of external processing gear available, it is not difficult to bring that gear into the DP mix. This includes sending recorded guitar signals through real guitar amplifiers for "re-amping" the sound.

External effects processing can be used when recording, mixing, or mastering.

Typical hardware processing during the recording stage can include microphone preamps, EQs, compressors, or any other special effect added into the signal chain. For example, a guitarist may want to record their guitar as it is being processed by an amplifier and their "stompboxes" or other guitar effects. Another example could be recording a singer whose vocal signal is processed by a mic preamp, compressor, and EQ.

In many situations, a singer may ask for additional effects in their monitor mix as they perform. Typically, the engineer would not want to record a vocal track with added reverb or echo. Therefore it is not uncommon to set up a monitor mix that includes effects, but only the direct signal of the microphone is what is actually recorded. If an external mixer is in use, it's easy enough to set up an effect send and return that provides echo or reverb to the singer's monitor mix, while not routing that effect into the computer for recording. If no external mixer is in use, it may be possible to set up monitor effects by some sort of routing through the audio interface.

Some audio interfaces have built-in effects processing. For example, the MOTU 896mk3 Hybrid interface provides available microphone limiting, compression, and EQ. If any of these effects are applied to an input signal, that signal is routed into the computer. The 896mk3 Hybrid also provides internal reverb processing. However, the reverb signal is separate from the input signal, and therefore can be used for monitoring, without being recorded.

It is possible to do an entire multitrack mixdown within the computer. It is possible to route audio playback from the computer to an external mixer or through external effects devices or signal processing chains. This includes such techniques such as sending a recorded guitar track out of the computer to a guitar amplifier, which is then mic'd and re-recorded back into DP.

In order to mix outside the computer, there must be enough available outputs on the audio interface to provide the separate channels. It is not a requirement that every individual track in DP is sent to a separate output on the audio interface. Some tracks in DP can be submixed to common outputs. For example, if there are four background vocal tracks, they could be submixed to a stereo output pair in DP, and mixed externally as a combined stereo mix. In the following graphic, the kick and snare tracks are routed directly to mono outputs on the audio interface. Because the track outputs are mono, there are no panners for those tracks. The graphic also shows four additional drum tracks that are routed to a stereo output pair. A master fader has been created to control the summed level of the stereo submix. Bass and guitar tracks are also sent to separate mono outputs for external summing.

Figure 4.1

Mixing on an external mixer is usually done because the mixer (or summing device) imparts a sound that is difficult or impossible to get inside the computer. In this case, the external mixer or summing bus is usually adding some sort of harmonic distortion to the sound that is pleasing to the ear. There are many software plug-ins available that emulate external mixers and summing buses, but some engineers prefer to use actual hardware.

When mixing with external hardware, it is not uncommon for the mixed signal to be routed back into the computer to be recorded as a final stereo or surround mix. When recording the mix back into the computer, make sure the mix record track is not passing signal back out to the mixer as it records. This will cause a feedback loop! The mix record track in DP can be play-disabled, or the audio monitoring mode in DP can be set to not patch the input signal through to output. To disable input monitoring in DP, go to the Studio menu>Audio Patch Thru, and set the parameter to Off. The following graphic shows audio tracks that are routed from the computer to external outputs, and a mix track that is set up to record the returning mixed signal.

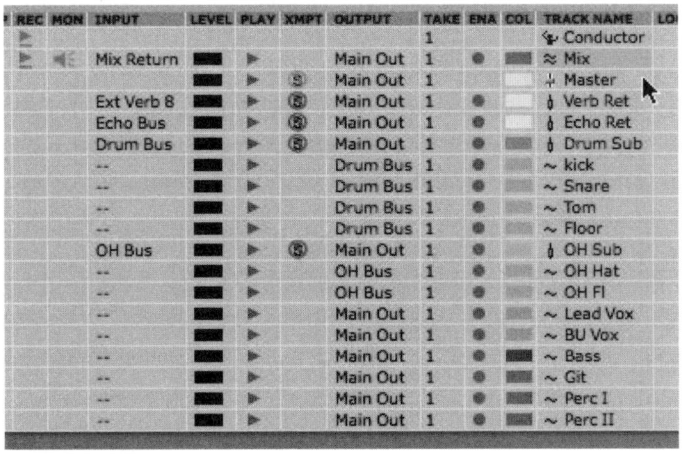

Figure 4.2

It is possible to mix inside the computer, but use external processing as part of the mix. For example, there may be a hardware compressor or reverb that is desirable to use on a track in the mix. There are several ways to set up routing to use external effects devices. Tracks in DP can use sends that are routed to outputs on the audio interface. This is similar to using effects sends on a hardware mixer. Varying amounts of multiple signals can be sent out of the computer and into an effects processor. It may be desirable to set up a master fader on the send output to control overall level of the signal going out of the computer. In the following graphic, three audio tracks are set up with sends that are routed to analog output number 8 on the audio interface. A master fader has been created to control the summed level of the send signals.

The output of the external processor is then routed back into the audio interface. The returning effect signal can be monitored either through the audio interface (assuming the audio interface has some sort of direct monitoring capability), or through DP. There are two ways to monitor an external audio signal through DP. External audio can be monitored through an aux track, or through an audio track. In order to monitor through an audio track, the following settings must be made in DP. Go to the Setup menu>Configure Audio System>Input Monitoring Mode... In this window, check the option to Monitor record-enabled tracks through effects. If the audio interface does not have direct hardware monitoring capabilities, this parameter will already be set to monitor through the record-enabled tracks. Next, go to the Studio menu>Audio Patch Thru. Set Audio Patch Thru to either Auto, Blend, or Input Only. Any of these settings will allow signal going in to an audio track to be passed through for live monitoring.

Figure 4.3

The most common setting for this application would be Auto. Auto input monitoring means that if the track is recording or if the input monitor button is selected for the track, signal will patch through. If audio is recorded into the track, that audio will then be heard on playback. Once the Audio Patch Thru mode has been set, record–enable the audio track, or engage the input monitoring button. The purpose of the input monitoring button is to allow patch through without having to put the track into record mode. This allows monitoring through the audio track while other audio and MIDI tracks are recording. In the following graphic, a reverb return track has been created and set up to monitor the live input signal. Other audio tracks are armed for recording separate signals.

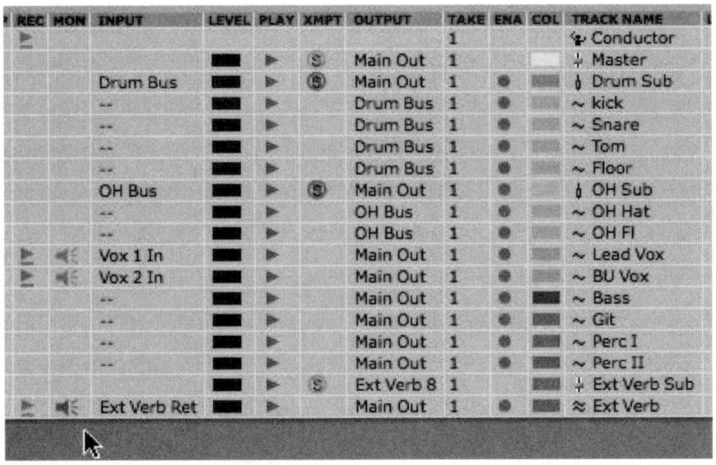

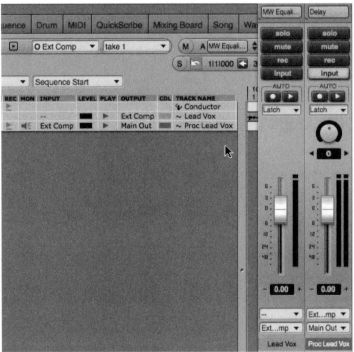

REC	MON	INPUT	LEVEL	PLAY	XMPT	OUTPUT	TAKE	ENA	COL	TRACK NAME
							1			❧ Conductor
			■	►	⑤	Main Out	1			↓ Master
		Drum Bus	■	►	⑤	Main Out	1	●		◊ Drum Sub
		--	■	►		Drum Bus	1	●		~ kick
		--	■	►		Drum Bus	1	●		~ Snare
		--	■	►		Drum Bus	1	●		~ Tom
		--	■	►		Drum Bus	1	●		~ Floor
		OH Bus	■	►	⑤	Main Out	1	●		◊ OH Sub
		--	■	►		OH Bus	1	●		~ OH Hat
		--	■	►		OH Bus	1	●		~ OH Fl
►	◄€	Vox 1 In	■	►		Main Out	1	●		~ Lead Vox
►	◄€	Vox 2 In	■	►		Main Out	1	●		~ BU Vox
		--	■	►		Main Out	1	●	▬	~ Bass
		--	■	►		Main Out	1	●	▬	~ Git
		--	■	►		Main Out	1	●	▬	~ Perc I
		--	■	►		Main Out	1	●	▬	~ Perc II
			■	►	⑤	Ext Verb 8	1		▬	↓ Ext Verb Sub
►	◄€	Ext Verb Ret	■	►		Main Out	1	●	▬	≈ Ext Verb

Figure 4.4

Returning the external effect signal into an audio track allows the return signal to be recorded. Once the return signal is recorded, the external hardware is no longer required.

Using sends for external effects means that the direct signal from the track is still "inside the box." The dry signal is mixed within DP, and the external effect signal is then added back in to the DP mix.

In some cases it may be desirable to insert an external effect directly into the DP audio track. In DP8, the effects inserts do not provide external input and output routing. In order to insert an external effect into a DP audio track, the output of the track must be routed to the external effects processor. The returning signal can then be monitored and recorded. If it is desirable to place additional plug-in effects on the returning signal, that can be done with an aux track or or second audio track. In the following graphic, a vocal track has an EQ plug-in applied, and then the signal is routed out of the computer to an external compressor. The returning signal is routed through a second audio track, which has a delay plug-in on its insert. This means the vocal signal is processed by the EQ plug-in, then the external compressor, and then finally the delay plug-in on the return track.

Figure 4.5

External effects processing can be used on sub-groups or even the entire mix. In the following graphic, six drum tracks are routed to an aux track for subgrouping, and the aux track is then routed out of the computer to an external compressor. That signal is returned into a stereo audio track. The entire mix is then routed back out a different set of outputs on the audio interface, and through an external analog EQ. That return signal is routed into a stereo track for final mixdown.

REC	MON	INPUT	LEVEL	PLAY	OUTPUT	COL	TRACK NAME	L
▶	◀	Ext Comp Ret	■■■	▶	Main Out	■■	≈ Drum Mix	
		Drum Bus	■■	▶	Ext Comp		♪ Drum Sub	
		--	■■	▶	Drum Bus		~ kick	
		--	■■	▶	Drum Bus		~ Snare	
		--	■■	▶	Drum Bus		~ Tom	
		--	■■	▶	Drum Bus		~ Floor	
		OH Bus	■■■	▶	Drum Bus		♪ OH Sub	
		--	■■	▶	OH Bus		~ OH Hat	
		--	■■	▶	OH Bus		~ OH Fl	

Figure 4.6

When an external audio signal is monitored through DP, it is delayed by the computer CPU. This is called latency delay. It is possible to shorten the monitoring latency delay by lowering the Buffer Size in the audio hardware driver window (Setup menu>Configure Audio System>Configure Audio Hardware). However, no matter how low the buffer is set, there will still be some delay. In some situations, latency delay is not a problem in a mixdown. For example, if the final mix is sent out of the computer and through an effects processor and then back in to the computer for re-recording, latency delay does not cause any problems. If external effects are used within the mix as effects send/returns or inserts, any latency delay will cause timing offsets to those signals relative to other audio tracks. DP8 does not have any type of latency compensation for external effects processing. Therefore latency delay must be dealt with manually.

If an external audio signal is recorded to a track in DP, there is no latency delay when that track is then played back. Therefore, recording external effects returns is one one way to eliminate latency in the mixdown.

It is also possible to apply delay compensation manually within the mix. Delay

Figure 4.7

compensation delays all audio signals within the mix to match a specific signal that has been delayed either by an internal plug-in, or an external audio patch through. Digital Performer automatically applies delay compensation in the mix for any plug-ins. To apply delay compensation for an externally patched signal, there are plug-ins available that cause DP to compensate the mix to match the returning audio signal. One example of a manual delay compensation plug-in is the Voxengo Latency Delay plug-in. The plug-in is available for no charge for Mac and Windows systems. It can be downloaded at http://www.voxengo.com/product/latencydelay/.

The latency delay plug-in is applied to the insert of an audio track which is then sent out through an external processor. If an effect send is used, the latency delay plug-in can be applied to an insert on a master fader which assigned to the send output. The latency delay plug-in does not delay the signal of the track to which it is applied. The latency delay plug-in delays all other tracks so that they match the returning external audio signal. The amount of latency compensation can be set by listening to the return signal and comparing it with other signals. A more precise way to the set the delay compensation is to record the returning signal and compare it to the original signal. Adjust the latency delay and re-record the return signal until it lines up exactly with the original track.

External Mixing and Summing

It is possible to route individual tracks or mixed combinations of tracks to separate outputs on an audio interface. These separate audio signals can them be mixed together with an analog or digital mixer that is external from the computer and DP.

There are a number of reasons an engineer may want to mix "outside the box." Some analog gear is designed specifically for mix summing. Analog summing hardware may provide distortion or coloration that is desirable in the final mix. In some situations, a mix engineer may prefer to use an external analog or digital mixing board for the sake of familiarity, features, or sonic characteristics. External mixing may also include using hardware processing gear such as vintage analog EQs and compressors. If an external mixer has automation functions, DP can be synchronized to the externally automated mix.

In order to mix outside of the computer, the audio interface must have enough analog or digital channels to pass each track or sub-group of tracks. In order to get the best sonic results from the audio interface, DP audio track output signals should use the full range of the interface outputs. Check the VU levels of individual tracks assigned to outputs. Make sure the level is hot, without clipping. If multiple tracks are assigned to the same output, it is a good idea to use a master fader, or buses and an aux track, so there is a way to control the summed levels on the way out through the audio interface.

It is also possible to route an external mix back into inputs on the audio interface, to be recorded onto new tracks within DP. Set up a record track and assign the appropriate inputs. Make sure the mix record track is not set to output back into the live mix, otherwise there will be a feedback loop. This can be done by play-disabling the mix audio track, or setting Audio Patch Thru to None.

Interface Tips

Digital Performer has the most customizable interface of any available DAW software. The interface can be as simple as a single window. Multiple windows can be spread out over multiple computer monitors. DP allows for saved window sets, and provides many ways to change the interface and window setup on the fly.

In addition to window layout, DP provides for customization of the "skin" of the software. DP ships with a list of preset "themes," and also allows the user to further alter and customize the graphic elements of the program.

Each DP user ends up molding the workspace to their personal preference. There are many ways to do similar things in DP, and often the choice of how to work comes down what is more comfortable or familiar to the engineer or artist.

It is worth taking some time to explore the possibilities of the DP interface. The more familiar the software is to the user, the more productive the overall experience.

Preferences

Like most software applications, DP has configurable preferences. Some preference settings are specific to individual files. Other preference settings are global, and affect any file created or opened in DP.

The Preferences window is available under the Digital Performer menu on Mac OS, and under the Edit menu in DP running on Windows. The Preferences window can be opened via key command, or from many other locations within DP. For example, Double+Clicking on the Click button will open the Preferences window to the Click preferences.

For any user of DP, it is worth reading through the available preference options in the Preferences window. This is an excellent way to get to know DP, and to customize the interface and workflow.

One popular troubleshooting technique for software in general is to "trash the preferences." This is usually done in the hope that a problem is being caused by an incorrect preferences setting. It is not necessary to trash any preferences in DP. At the bottom of the Preferences window there is a button to reset to factory default preferences. If DP is not functioning in an expected way, resetting the preferences to factory defaults can often solve interface or unexpected behavior problems within DP.

Consolidated Window

There are many windows available within DP and it is possible to place individual windows at any location on the computer desktop. If multiple video monitors are connected to the computer, a common technique is to set DP up with primary windows displayed on different monitors. For example, the Mixing Board window can be placed on one monitor and the Sequence Editor window could be placed on a second monitor.

It is also possible to work with DP using a single window that works as a "container window" to display other windows. The Consolidated window is that container window.

By default a new file in DP will open to display the Consolidated window. The factory default preferences are set to display the Control Panel and Tracks window within the Consolidated window. The Consolidated window is highly customizable, depending on user preference.

The first thing to notice about the Consolidated window are the tabs.

Tracks	Sequence	Drum	MIDI	QuickScribe	Mixing Board	Song	Waveform	Meter Bridge

Seq-1

Figure 4.8

These tabs change the currently displayed window within the Consolidated window. This makes it easy to switch between windows without having to close one window before opening the next.

It is possible to configure the Consolidated window to display multiple windows. This can be done by horizontally dividing the main window. To add a second or third horizontal window, Double+Click on the bottom edge of the Consolidated window, or click and drag up on the bottom edge.

Each horizontal window in the Consolidated window has its own set of tabs. This makes it easy to switch between primary windows.

Figure 4.9

It is possible to create left or right sidebar windows. This can be done by Double+Clicking, or clicking and dragging from the left or right edge of the Consolidated window.

Figure 4.10

Once a sidebar window has been created, the tab at the top of the window can be used to switch between which window is currently displayed.

It is possible to add multiple windows into a sidebar. This can be done by adding tabs. To add tabs to a sidebar, choose Add Tab from the tab menu.

It is possible to add sidebar windows by Double+Clicking or clicking and dragging from the bottom of the sidebar.

Figure 4.11

Figure 4.12

By default, if a window is selected from one of the main menus, it will open inside the Consolidated window. This preference can be customized. Go to the Digital Performer Preferences>Display>Consolidated Window.

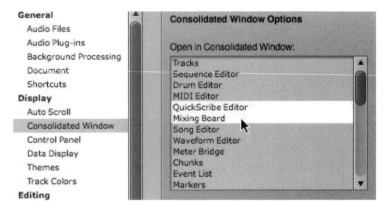

Figure 4.13

These preferences determine which windows are displayed within the Consolidated window. If a window is deselected in the preferences, it will open as a separate window when called up via key command or menu selection.

To customize the Control Panel within the Consolidated window, go to Digital Performer Preferences>Display>Control Panel. These preferences determine whether the Control Panel will be displayed within the Consolidated window, and if so, which specific components will be displayed within the Control Panel.

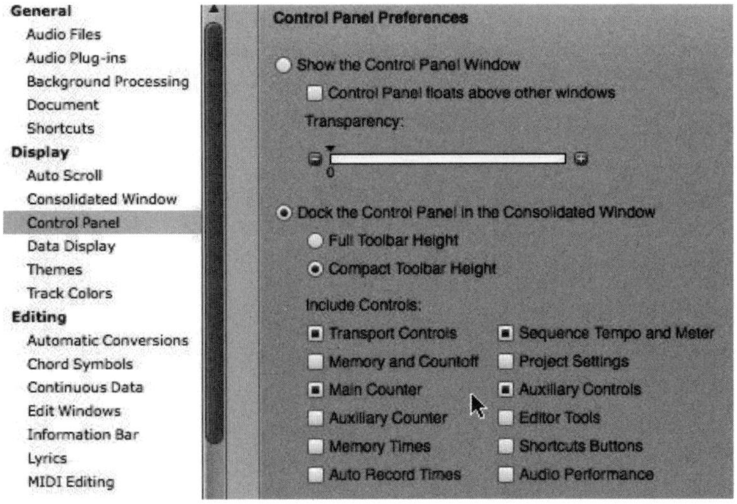

Figure 4.14

The Editor Tools and Shortcut buttons can be displayed in their own windows or within the Control Panel. If either of these windows are displayed within the Control Panel, they will not be available from the main menus.

Track and Waveform Colors

It can be useful to use different colors to identify tracks. For example, similar colors can be used to identify groups of tracks or types of tracks. For example, perhaps drum tracks are always displayed in green, and master faders are always displayed in red. It is up to the preference of the DP user how track colors are used.

Track colors appear in the Tracks window, Sequence Editor window, Track Inspector window, and Mixing Board window. In the MIDI Editor window, track colors are used to display the actual MIDI notes within the tracks.

Track colors can be assigned to individual tracks or to groups of tracks. Track colors can be assigned in the Tracks window.

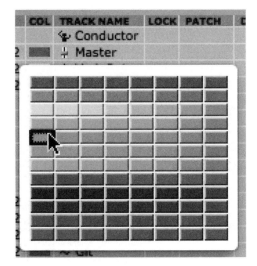

Figure 4.15

Track colors can be assigned in the Sequence Editor window.

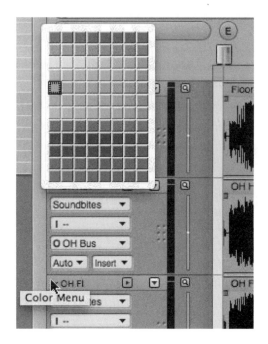

Figure 4.16

Track colors can be assigned in the Track Inspector window.

Figure 4.17

To assign colors to multiple tracks, make a selection that includes multiple tracks, go to the Setup menu>Colors>and choose Assign Track Colors... The Assign Colors window will open to provide options.

There are also additional customizations that can be made as to how colors are used in DP. Go to the Preferences window>Display>Track Colors.

Figure 4.18

Figure 4.19

Waveform colors can also be adjusted from the Preferences window. For example, the Waveform Lightness control can be used to display an audio waveform as completely black or completely white.

Track Grouping

It is possible to group tracks together so that an action performed to a single track will be repeated for all tracks within the group. There are two ways to group tracks in DP. Tracks can be grouped temporarily, or they can be part of a track group.

Temporary track grouping is done by holding down a hot key and making a change in an Edit window or the Mixer window. The default key command for temporarily grouping visible tracks is the W key. While the W key is held down, any track edit will be duplicated on all visible tracks. By using the Track Selector, it is possible to display only the tracks that need to be temporarily grouped. For example, just the faders for the drum tracks in a multitrack project are displayed in the Mixer window.

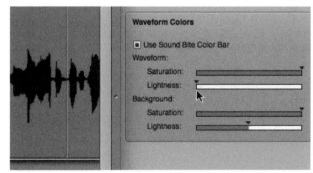

Figure 4.20

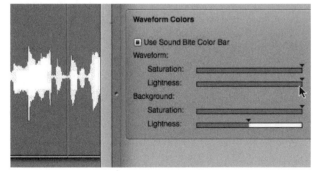

Figure 4.21

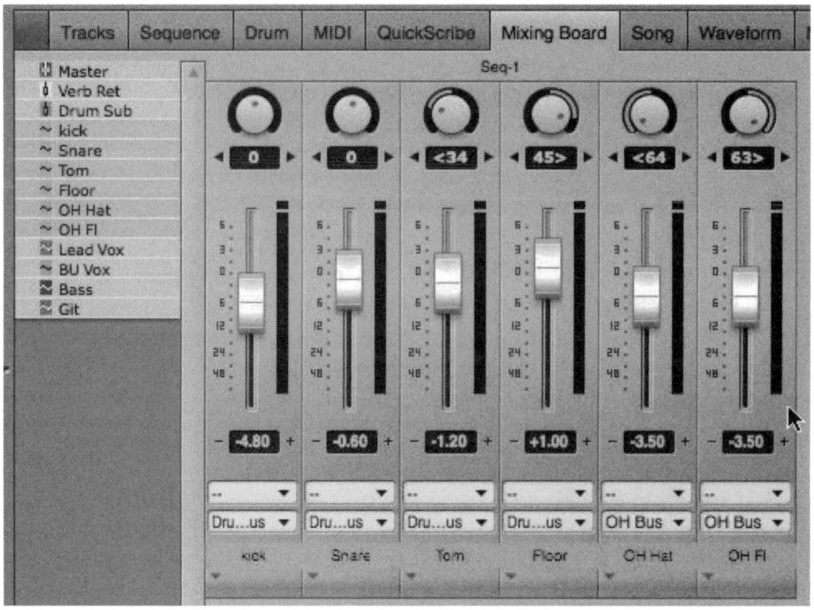

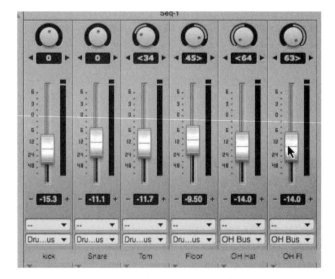

Figure 4.22

By holding down the W key and moving a single fader, all faders are moved together. A useful feature of this function is that faders are scaled within the relative mix.

Figure 4.23

In this example, Automation is added to a single track while holding the W key, and therefore simultaneously duplicated to all other visible tracks.

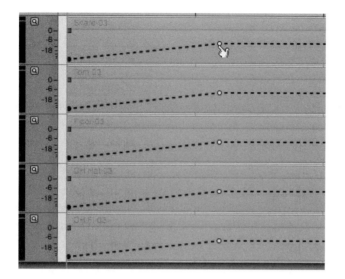

Figure 4.24

Tracks can also be assigned to track groups. There is a Track Groups window that lists all current track groups. Open the Track Groups window from the Project menu, or as a sidebar window. The default key command to open the Track Groups window is Option/Alt+Shift+G.

There is always at least one Track Group called All Tracks. By default, this track group is disabled.

The Track Groups window mini menu has an option to customize which functions are controlled within a temporary group. From the mini menu choose Set Temporary Group Type...

Track groups can be created two ways. A track group is based on a selection of tracks. To create a new track group, at least two tracks of any type must be selected. This can be done from any edit window that allows selection of multiple tracks. Once at least two tracks are selected, a track group is created via the Project menu.

Figure 4.25

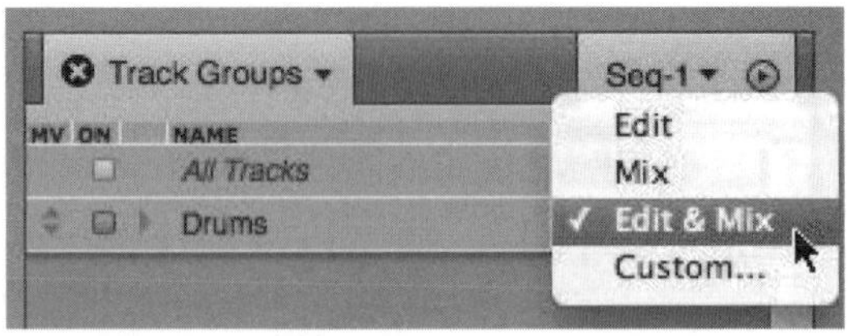

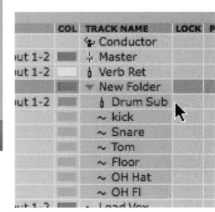

Figure 4.26

When a track group is created, a window appears that allows the track group to be named. There is a button to enable or disable the track group. There is a pop-up menu that allows assignment of what specifically will be grouped within the selected tracks.

Option/Alt+Click to rename a track group in the Track Groups window. Click on the down arrow to expand the track group to show all included tracks.

The Custom selection for a track group allows for a customized selection of functions to be part of the track group.

Once a track group is created, tracks can be added or deleted from the group. To add or delete tracks from a track group, make a selection within one or more tracks, select the track group in the Track Groups window, and choose Add Selection to Group or Remove Tracks from Group from the Track Groups window mini-menu. It is possible for a track to be included in multiple track groups.

Track groups can be enabled or disabled at any time. Track group functions can be modified at any time.

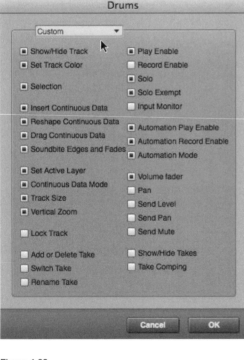

Figure 4.27

Track Folders

Track folders are a way to show or hide multiple tracks within an edit window or the Mixing Board window. This is a powerful organizational tool, especially for large projects. Any combination of tracks can be placed into a folder. Folders can be nested inside other folders.

Select one or more tracks, go the the Project menu>Track Folders>New Track Folder From Selected Tracks. The default key command for this function is Command+Shift+R. A new track folder will be created and the selected tracks will appear inside the folder.

Option/Alt+Click to rename the track folder.

Figure 4.28

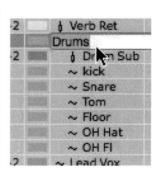

Figure 4.29

Figure 4.30

The track folder can be opened or closed with the arrow icon.

Figure 4.31

Tracks can be dragged out of a folder in the Tracks window. Do this by dragging the track move icon up or down out of the folder.

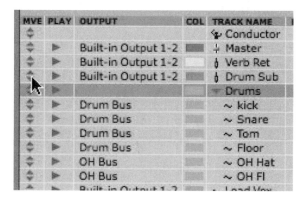

Figure 4.32

Tracks can be dragged into folders, and folders can be dragged into other folders. To do this the folder must be open. Drag the move icon of a track or folder to the open folder.

Track folders are visible in the Track Selector window, allowing multiple tracks to be shown or hidden with a single click.

Figure 4.33

Track folders can be named. Track folders have the same color assignments functions as tracks. All tracks within a folder can be play-enabled or disabled with a single click. It is also possible to disable all tracks within a folder so they use no memory or CPU resources. This is useful for retaining tracks in a project that have plug-ins or virtual instruments instantiated, but are not currently in use.

If a selection is made in the Tracks window that includes a closed folder, the selection will include all tracks contained within the folder. This means that for example, if a region is selected in the Tracks window ruler and deleted or snipped, all data, including data hidden in closed track folders, is affected by the edit.

Window Sets

Any configuration of windows can be saved as a window set. Window sets can be assigned to key commands. Go to the Window menu>Window Sets. This will display the options to create, edit, and recall window sets.

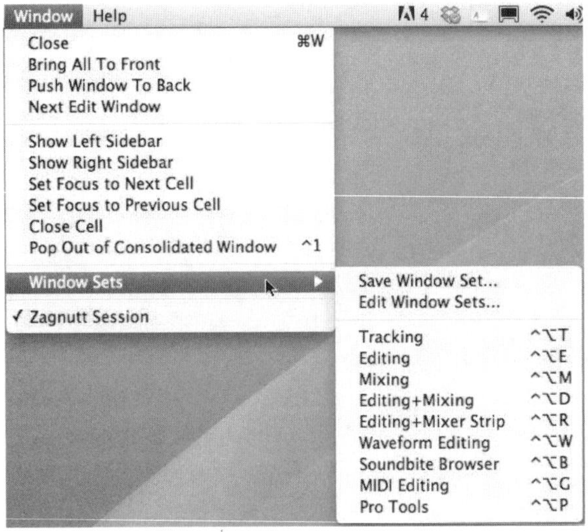

Figure 4.34

In the Edit Window Sets window, click on the key assignment column to assign a key command to the window set.

Figure 4.35

File Management

A significant part of working with any DAW involves file management. There are potentially many different types of files associated with a DAW project. The files may be large and spread out over multiple locations.

It is always a good idea to back up or archive critical files. It is also important to keep files and hard drives organized. This will ensure that files don't get lost and hard drives don't fill up with unused data.

Project Folder

When a new file is created in DP, a folder is created at the save location. The folder is named based on the file name, with "Project" added to that name. A DP session file is then created within that Project folder. For example, if a new file is created in DP called "Opus 7," and the save destination is the computer desktop, a new folder will be created on the desktop called Opus 7 Project. Inside that folder will be the Opus 7 DP session file. DP also creates other folders within the Project folder. Here is a list of what DP creates and sets up within a Project folder:

- DP session file: The DP session file is a proprietary format and can only be opened with DP. DP can always open session files created in older versions of the application. An older version of DP cannot open a session file created in a newer version. It is possible to save a DP file to an older version format. That will be described later in this section. The DP session file contains any MIDI data and all setup information relating to the project. This includes track setup, automation, and plug-in information. The DP session file does not contain any audio files or movie files. Those files are referenced by the session file. The DP session file does not contain any audio samples used by virtual instruments. Those files are also referenced by the session file.
- Auto Save version of the session file, depending on the autosave preferences.
- Audio Files folder: This is the default location for any audio recorded by or imported into the DP session. It is also possible to direct DP to record or access audio on any drive location accessible to the computer.
- Analysis Files folder: When DP imports or records audio, it analyzes that audio for waveform calculation, as well as pitch and tempo control. Analysis files are created and stored in the folder. These files can be trashed. If the analysis files are deleted from the hard drive, DP will create new analysis files as it needs them.
- Bounces folder: This folder is created when a bounce to disk operation is done within DP. DP can write bounce files to any hard drive location. The default location is the Bounces folder in the Project folder.
- Undo folder: This is where DP stores audio files that have been deleted or discarded during work within the DP session. Depending on the workflow, it is possible to generate a great deal of unused audio. Therefore DP features built-in undo history management tools. If the contents of the Undo folder are manually deleted from the hard drive, the DP session will still open and play, but it will not be possible to undo edits that involve the deleted audio.
- Plug-In Data folder: This folder is created if samples are saved in the MOTU Nanosampler virtual instrument, the Model 12 virtual instrument, or if impulse responses are saved from the ProVerb plug-in. This provides a way to store samples and impulse responses associated specifically with the project.

File Locations

DP Project folders can be created on any drive location accessible to the computer. In general, network connections are not fast enough to play back multi-channel real-time audio, therefore it's not a good idea to try to create or open DP files over a network. The best protocol is to work with files that are on locally connected drives. Projects can be copied onto USB thumb drives. However, a USB thumb drive will also be too slow to play a multitrack audio session directly.

Digital Performer will not open a session file that is on a DVD or CD-ROM. The session file should be copied to a local hard drive before opening.

The project folder is designed to keep files organized, and to keep related files in the same place. It is possible to move files from the project folder to different hard drive locations, but that can cause problems if done carelessly. When a DP session file is opened, the first place it looks for any related audio files is the Audio Files folder in the project folder. If the DP session file was previously saved while referencing audio files in other locations, the session file will know to check those locations. If the audio files are moved, DP will attempt to find them when the session is opened. If DP can't find the associated audio files, it will present a dialog box on launch that allows the missing files to be relocated.

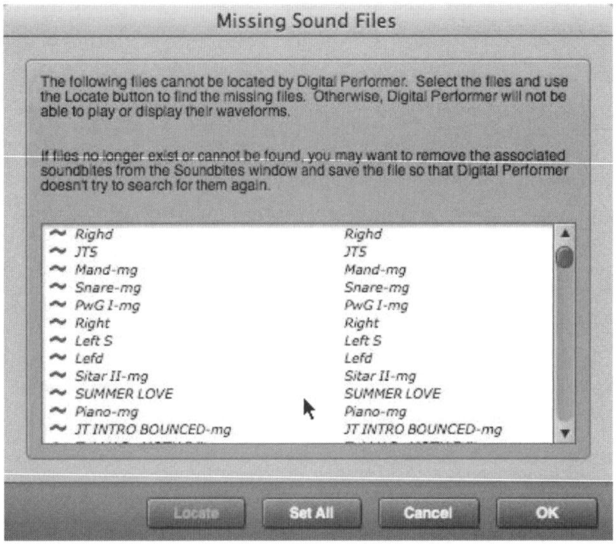

Figure 4.36

Typically, the best protocol is to keep all referenced files within the project folder. There may be exceptions to this. For example, if audio take file locations are spread over multiple hard drives, that may allow for a higher number of tracks to be simultaneously recorded. Another common example is that video files may be played back from a different drive than audio files. This may also increase system efficiency. If there are files associated with the session that are not stored in the project folder, care must be taken to keep track of these additional files.

Undo History
DP keeps track of every edit made in a session. The Undo History window displays a list of past edits. Open the Undo History window from the Edit menu.

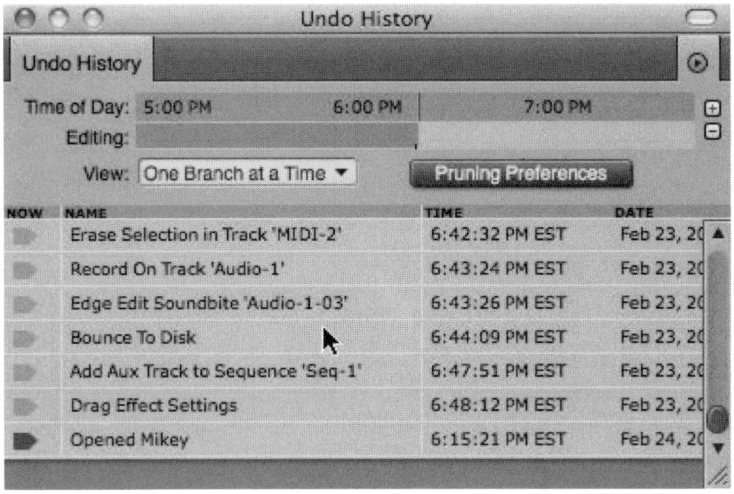

Figure 4.37

It is possible to jump to any point in the undo history by clicking on the left edge of the Undo History window. The undo history is linear. That means that if the undo history is moved back five steps for example, all five edit steps will be undone.

If edits involve deleting or creating audio, audio files are moved to the Undo folder in the project folder. Over time, this can create a large amount of unused audio data on the hard drive. Therefore the undo function has specific preferences for pruning the undo history. Basic pruning functions can be accessed from the Undo History window mini menu. Additional pruning customizations can be done in the Undo Pruning preferences.

Save As/Save A Copy As

When a DP session file is open, there is always the choice to create and save a new version of the file. This can be useful for creating incremental backups or modified versions of the file. Go to the File menu and choose Save As or Save a Copy As.

The difference between the two choices is that if Save As is chosen, a new session file is created and that file is now the currently open file. The file that was previously open is closed without saving. If Save a Copy As is chosen, a new file is created on the hard drive, but the current file continues to stay open.

Both Save As and Save a Copy As have the option to duplicate audio data and copy shared samples. This will cause all the audio files currently referenced in the Soundbites window, any custom samples for Nanosampler and Model 16 instruments, and any custom impulse responses for ProVerb to be duplicated with the newly created session file. This is an effective technique for creating a backup or archive of the project, and ensuring that all referenced audio is included with that backup.

Both options also include the ability to save the session file to an earlier DP file format or a different file format, including Audiodesk, Standard MIDI File, OMF, and AAF.

Auto Save

Digital Performer has an automatic save function that will save the session file or save to a backup file. Go to Digital Performer Preferences>Document>Auto Save.

Figure 4.38

Auto Save can be disabled. There is an option for how often auto save engages. There is a choice for automatically saving the current session file, or automatically saving to a backup session file, which is created in the same directory as the original session file.

If Auto Save saves changes that the engineer or artist does not want to keep, the undo history can be used to go back to an earlier edit point.

Import/Export Between DP Session Files

Data within DP session files can be imported or exported to other DP session files. To import data from one DP session file to another, the Load function is used. There are two ways to load data from one session to another.

Go to the File menu>Load... A window will open to select the session file that is to be imported into the currently open session. Locate and select the session to be loaded and click Open. The Load window will open.

Select the data to be imported and click the OK button. Any selected sequences from the Load window will now appear in the Chunks window of the open session.

It is also possible to drag a DP session file from any window open on the computer desktop into the Chunks window or Tracks window of a currently open DP session. If a DP session file is dragged into the Chunks Window or the left-hand side of the Tracks window, the Load window will open to allow selection of what will be imported.

If a chunk is loaded into the left-hand side of a currently open sequence, it will be added to that currently open sequence. This is a way of importing track layouts and mixes from one session or sequence to another. For example, if a sequence chunk is loaded, but the option to not import soundbites

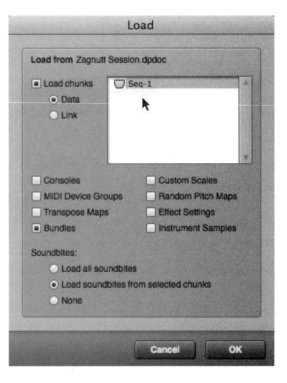

Figure 4.39

is also checked, only the track layout and any plug-ins will be loaded. Audio from the original sequence tracks can be copied into the newly loaded tracks to update the mix.

Virtual Instruments

Virtual instruments can run as plug-ins in DP, as stand-alone applications, or as ReWire applications. VIs create audio output, which can be monitored and recorded in DP. Some VIs have the ability to export audio and MIDI files, which can also be used in DP sequences.

Virtual instruments can be automated via automation data in the instrument track, as well as data in the MIDI tracks that trigger the VI.

Digital Performer can assign one or more MIDI tracks to the input of a virtual instrument. MIDI tracks can be assigned to different MIDI channels within multitimbral VIs.

Some virtual instruments have the ability to send audio signals to multiple outputs. Those outputs can be assigned to audio or aux tracks in DP for further processing and recording.

Virtual instruments, instrument tracks, and V-Racks are discussed in further detail in the section on live performance.

Audio Effect Plug-Ins

An audio effect plug-in is a piece of software that is called up within DP and placed somewhere in the audio signal chain. Effect plug-ins can be instantiated into the signal path of audio tracks, aux tracks, master fader tracks, and instrument tracks. This allows for complex processing of signals for both live input and track playback.

DP8 ships with over 70 different audio effects. Digital Performer can also host third-party plug-ins that support MAS, Audio Unit, or VST2 formats. The following section will describe some of the stock plug-ins that ship with DP8, and how to use them effectively in a session.

Plug-In Management

In addition to the stock DP plug-ins, it is possible to add many more third-party plug-ins into the DP system. Some plug-ins are available in different plug-in formats. When DP launches, each plug-in must check in with its copy protection and then load. This can take some time. Therefore DP provides a way to choose which plug-ins are loaded and which versions of plug-ins are used within DP. It is possible to create plug-in "sets" in DP and to choose which plug-ins will load when DP is launched.

The first time DP8 is launched after installation on a Mac, a window will open that asks the user to choose between VST or Audio Unit as the preferred plug-in format. If there are plug-ins installed in the computer that have both VST and Audio Unit versions, this preference will determine which version of the plug-in to load.

DP8 on Windows supports VST plug-ins. Audio Unit is a Mac standard, therefore there is no choice between VST and Audio Units when DP8 runs on a Windows computer.

Once DP is launched, go to the Preferences window>General>Audio Plug-Ins. The Preferences window will display all currently loaded plug-ins. The Preferences window allows the creation and selection of plug-in sets. Individual plug-ins can be enabled or disabled within a plug-in set. If a new plug-in set is selected, or any changes are made to the current plug-in list, closing the Preferences window will open a window. The window allows the user to restart the audio engine to initiate the new plug-in set.

It is also possible to select a plug-in set as DP is launching. Hold down the Option key on a Mac or Alt key under Windows as DP launches. A window will open allowing the user to select a plug-in set.

Figure 4.40

Effect Inserts

Effect inserts are found in the Mixer window. Effect inserts can be displayed or hidden in the Mixer via the mini menu.

It is possible to configure the number of available inserts for each sequence chunk. Up to 20 inserts can be configured via the mini menu.

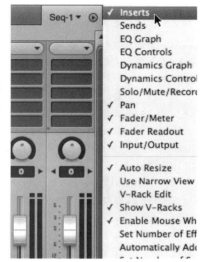

Figure 4.41

The signal flow through the effect inserts can be pre- or post-fader. Signal flow is from top to bottom through the inserts. By default, all inserts are pre-fader. This means that if the fader is turned down, that controls the volume of the signal after any effect. To make an effect insert post-fader, there is a handle at the bottom of the insert list that can be dragged up. Inserts below the handle are now post-fader.

Here are two examples of pre- or post-fader use of inserts.

Figure 4.42

- A reverb plug-in is placed on a snare drum or vocal track. The track is automated to fade out at some point. If the reverb is pre-fader, the automated fader will fade the output of the reverb signal. The original signal going into the reverb will not change, therefore the reverb will sound the same as it is faded. If the reverb is post-fader, that means the output of the reverb is not attenuated as the track fader is lowered. Instead, the signal from the audio track is attenuated as it passes into the reverb processor. The sound of the reverb changes naturally as the original signal fades away.

- A mastering limiter is placed on a master fader. The purpose of the mastering limiter is to make sure the final output of the mix does not clip. The mastering limiter may also be used to quantize the mix to 16 bits and to add dither for audio CD preparation. If the mastering limiter is pre-fader, that means the master fader does not affect signal going in to the limiter. Turning the master fader up or down will not affect how much limiting is applied to the input signal. In DP, audio faders in the mixer have 6 dB of available gain. This means a master fader can be used to add up to 6 dB of gain to the signal. If the mastering limiter is used to attenuate the signal to prevent clipping, that signal can still be boosted by raising the master fader. This would then cause clipping on final output. If the mastering limiter is placed after the master fader in the signal chain, it doesn't matter if the master fader adds gain to the signal. The limiter will still control that level to prevent clipping. As the master fader is attenuated, the limiter will have to do less limiting to the input signal.

The Effects Chooser window

When the mouse cursor is placed over an audio effect insert, the cursor changes to the effects chooser icon. Click to open the Effects Chooser window.

Figure 4.43

The Effects Chooser window is a powerful tool for managing audio plug-ins and effects presets. The Effects Chooser window provides multiple ways of organizing and displaying both plug-ins and plug-in presets, which may include chains of multiple plug-ins.

At the top of the window are two buttons to change the display between Effects or Presets. When the display button is set to Effects, the Effects Chooser window displays the plug-ins that are currently available within DP. Which plug-ins are displayed is based on the folder or category selected on the left. When the display button is set to Presets, the window shows effect presets, which may refer to one or more plug-ins.

Below the display buttons is a search field. The search field searches based on what is selected in the top display buttons, and which folder or category is selected on the left.

On the left side of the window are folders, categories, and buttons to create new categories and folders. A folder is a way to organize categories. Categories are ways to organize the actual plug-ins or presets. By default, DP displays a basic set of folders and categories. Selecting a folder or category will display a specific set of plug-ins or presets. For example, plug-ins or presets can be viewed by manufacturer or format.

It is also possible to create and customize folders and categories. For example, a folder could be created that is the named "Ambience Effects." In that folder, categories could be created and named "Reverbs," "Echoes," and "Special Effects." Plug-ins can then be dragged from the right side of the Effects Chooser windows into the appropriate categories.

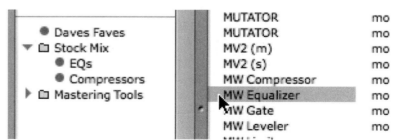

Figure 4.44

To save a preset into the Effects Chooser window, go to the menu above the effects inserts in the mixer. From the menu choose Save Insert Settings... A window will open that allows the preset to be named and saved into a sub-folder. The preset will include all plug-ins in the channel strip.

If the mouse is Right+Clicked on an effect insert, that will open an Effect Insert menu. It is possible to customize what is displayed in the menu. In the following graphic, the stock MOTU dynamics plug-ins have been chosen as the default effects menu category. The Insert Effect menu is also displaying recently selected plug-ins.

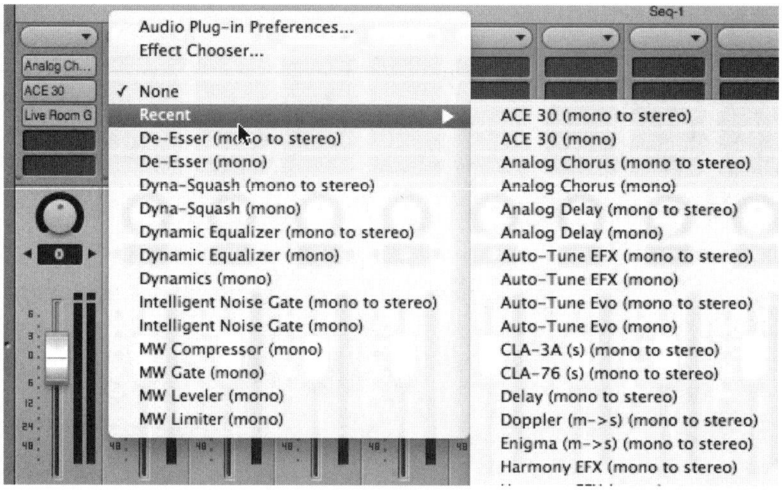

Figure 4.45

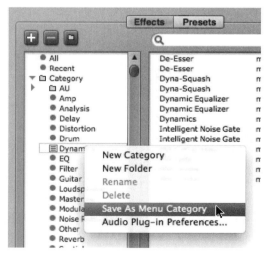

Figure 4.46

In the Effect Chooser window Right+Click on a folder or category to get a menu. Choose Save As Menu Category.

Hardware and Convolution Modeling

Many of the stock plug-ins in DP8 are based on existing hardware devices. This allows the DP user to process sound the same way as if the original hardware was available and in the signal chain. Digital Performer includes hardware modeled plug-in effects based on classic analog devices such as optical compressors, tube guitar amps, bass and guitar speaker cabinets (with variable microphone placement), "stompboxes," and much more.

Figure 4.47

Hardware modeling is a process of writing software that emulates a physical piece of audio processing equipment. For example, it is possible to develop a software model of a guitar amplifier. This allows a clean guitar signal to be processed inside the computer, and end up sounding as if it had been played through an actual amp and speaker cabinet.

Convolution modeling is a process of making an audio sample, and using that sample as the foundation for signal processing. For example, it is possible to make an audio sample of the ambient response of any acoustic space. This sample is called an impulse response. The impulse response can then be used to provide ambience for a signal that passes through a convolution-based plug-in such as ProVerb. The result is the original sound combined with the actual ambience of the sampled acoustic space.

A convolution reverb does not simulate ambience or reverb. A convolution reverb puts the processed signal in the actual sampled space. Therefore a convolution reverb can provide any ambient effect, as long as the impulse response sample is available. Impulse responses can be made from natural acoustic spaces. Impulse responses can also be made from hardware processing devices. It is therefore possible to model the sound of a hardware reverb processor, and use that impulse response in a software-based convolution reverb.

Some plug-ins can use a hybrid of technologies. For example, the Live Room B, Live Room G, and Live Stage plug-ins all emulate speaker cabinets, microphones, and acoustic spaces. Hardware modeling is used to re-create the sound of the speakers and microphones. Convolution modeling is used to provide the ambient space for the cabinets and mics.

EQs

An EQ (equalizer) provides controls to boost or attenuate specific frequencies within an audio signal. Frequency equalizers are often referred to as "tone controls." An EQ works by using frequency-dependent filters that add or subtract gain within a specific frequency range. A parametric EQ provides precise control over what frequencies will be boost or cut, and by how much. An EQ plug-in may have one or more bands of parametric frequency control.

Stock DP EQ plug-ins include the ParaEQ 2-band, ParaEQ 4-band, ParaEQ 8-band, and MW EQ. The Dynamic Equalizer plug-in is a multifunction plug-in that combines frequency control with frequency-specific compression or expansion. The Dynamic Equalizer is described in the mastering section.

Other plug-ins also affect frequency response and can be used as dramatic special effects. Stock DP plug-ins that use forms of EQ for special effects include the Multimode Filter, Hi-Top Booster, Sonic Modulator, and Wah Pedal. Many other plug-ins use EQ features as part of their functions. For example, the PreAmp-1 plug-in includes an EQ section. These specialized plug-ins will be described in following sections.

The ParaEQs are basic parametric equalizers with different numbers of frequency bands. The MW EQ provides addition control over the slope of the frequencies that are boost or cut. The MW EQ also provides an FFT display. The FFT display provides a graphic representation of the frequency response of the audio signal. Both types of EQs provide a graphic representation of the boost or cut applied by the plug-in.

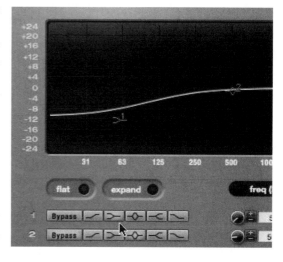

Figure 4.48

Individual bands within a stock DP EQ can be configured as high- or low-pass filters, shelving filters, or fully parametric filters. The type of filter is selectable per band in the ParaEQs.

In the MW EQ, there are dedicated high- and low-pass filters and five configurable parametric filters. Two of the parametric filters can also be configured as shelf filters.

Figure 4.49

Dynamics Processors

A dynamics processor controls the volume of an audio signal. Compressors and limiters are dynamics processors. DP includes a variety of dynamics processors including compressors, limiters, expanders, gates, de-esser, and multiband compressors.

Typical controls for a dynamics processor include attack and release times, ratio, and threshold controls. The MW Leveler is an exception in that is has a gain reduction control, makeup gain control, and response control. The response control introduces a high frequency notch filter into the detector circuit path. This makes the leveler less sensitive to high frequency input triggering. The attack and release times of the MW Leveler are constantly variable, based on input signal. There are four models of the MW Leveler,

Figure 4.50

based on original analog optical compressor components. The MW Leveler can be a smooth way to control overall gain of a track.

The MW Leveler models a photo emitter and sensor circuit. In the original hardware, this was called a "T4 Cell." The way that circuit works is that input volume over time will saturate the T4 Cell. The amount of saturation is based on a number of variables, including how much gain reduction is being applied, the transient nature of the input signal, average signal strength, and time.

The MW Leveler is always adjusting to input, so it is always in "warm-up" mode when signal is going through. When signal stops going to input on the plug-in, the T4 Cell model starts to cool down. This cool-down can last as long as a minute or more. Again, how long depends on the characteristics of the signal before signal stropped coming in.

Control+Click or Right+Click on the MW Leveler meter to get a sub menu. The sub menu

Figure 4.51

includes the option to save the T4 Cell state. When the save option is selected, the state of the T4 Cell at that moment is saved.

Once a T4 Cell state has been saved, that state will be reset in the Leveler under specific conditions. For a bounce to disk operation, that causes the Leveler to reset at the start of the bounce. That way, if bouncing from a cold start, the MW Leveler will already be "warmed up" for the bounce.

Closing the MW Leveler window will reset the T4 Cell state.

If bypass is automated for the MW Leveler, the T4 Cell state is reset when the plug-in is un-bypassed. So for example, there is a vocal track that comes in half-way through the song. Play back a section of the vocal track to get the MW Leveler "warmed up." Save the T4 Cell state at that point. Now automate a bypass for the Leveler that un-bypasses just before the vocal comes in. The MW Leveler will be warmed up when the vocal track comes in.

Utility Plug-Ins

A utility plug-in is used to do a specific job in the audio signal chain. Utility plug-ins in DP include:

- Buffy: This plug-in reports latency delay to the audio system, based on a Buffer Size multiplier. Buffy is used for audio or aux tracks that have a plug-in or live audio signal that is not being properly delay-compensated.
- DC Notch: Used to correct any DC offset in the audio waveform.
- Invert Phase: Used to invert the phase of the audio signal.
- MS Decoder: The MS Decoder is used to decode two channel signals that have been recorded with mid-side microphone configurations.
- Precision Delay: This plug-in can be used to correct timing offsets for phase-related audio signals.
- Gates: A gate is a form of dynamics processor that attenuates the audio signal based on some sort of trigger. Gate functions are included in the Intelligent Noise Gate, De-Esser,

Dynamics, Pattern Gate, and MW Gate plug-ins.

- Calibration: This plug-in is used to correct levels and phase relationships of studio monitor speakers. The plug-in works by generating a noise signal, which is then picked up by a microphone placed in the listening position. The microphone signal is routed back to the Calibration plug-in. Noise signals are sent to each speaker output and analyzed for amplitude and phase offset. The plug-in can then be used on a master fader as a speaker calibration processor.
- Trim: Trim is a powerful plug-in for controlling level, phase, and pan position within multichannel signals. The Trim plug-in also provides precise, zoomable level metering.

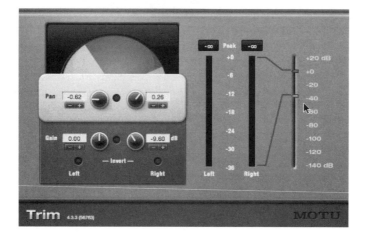

Figure 4.52

Modulation Effects

A modulation effect is usually made by oscillating a parameter such as a filter, delay, or amplitude. Modulation effects include phasers, flangers, choruses, and filter effects.

DP has many modulation-based plug-ins. Depending on the plug-in, it may be able to synchronize its modulation effect with the sequence tempo. For example, this is the Sonic Modulator, a mono to stereo effect. The Sonic Modulator has four tempo-synchable LFOs and an amplitude envelope, which can be used to control filters, upper and lower frequency pitch, delay, and amplitude.

Figure 4.53

Reverb and Delay Effects

The difference between reverb and delay or echo is whether or not individual repeats can be heard. If there are enough delayed repeats of the audio signal, this is called reverberation.

DP has four different delay plug-ins, and eight different reverb plug-ins. Each plug-in has its own characteristic controls and sounds.

The ProVerb is a convolution reverb that includes a collection of ambience samples (Impulse Responses). Any WAV or AIFF file can be dropped onto ProVerb to be used as an IR. There are many free and paid ambience samples available for download. Do an Internet search for "Impulse Response Samples." To set up an ambience in ProVerb, load an IR from the stock library or any imported IRs. The IR can then be further shaped with predelay, damping, a ducking compressor, room size, and a four band EQ.

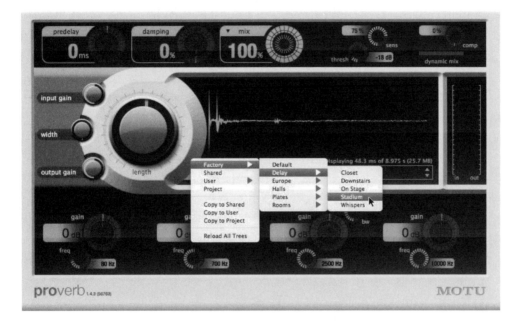

Figure 4.54

Amps and Speaker Cabinets

DP8 ships with plug-ins that model well-known guitar amplifiers. Digital Performer also has plug-ins that model speaker cabinets, including microphone placement. This allows the DP engineer to create the true sound of a guitar amplifier set up in a studio (or stage) with sophisticated microphone placement. In addition to guitar speaker cabinet models, there are also models for bass guitar speaker cabinets. The included amps and cabinets provide a wide range of effects from clean tones to the sounds of highly overdriven vacuum tubes.

Because the amp models and cabinet models are in separate plug-ins, that means different amps can be mixed and matched with different speaker cabinets. Up to three microphones can be used to record each speaker cabinet. Different microphone types and positions are available. Room size can be changed. All this allows the artist or engineer absolutely precise control over guitar and bass amplifier and cabinet recording. Of course, these plug-ins are not limited to use with just bass and six-string guitars. Want to find out how a mandolin track sounds through a high gain guitar amp? Digital Performer makes it easy to get exactly the right tone.

- Custom '59: This plug-in is a combination of models of the Marshall JTM amp and the Fender Bassman amp. The input tube, preamp type, tone controls, and power amp sections can all be customized to create hybrid versions of these two classic guitar amps. Neither the JTM nor the Bassman amps have an overdrive section. The way to overdrive these amps is to either use a distortion pedal before the amp, or to just increase the gain going to the input. Even a simple Trim plug-in before the amp will provide gain that will bring out smooth overdrive tones. The Custom '59 has two input channels, and each of those channels has a hi and lo Z input. Each of these inputs has a slightly different tone, just like the original hardware. The Custom '59 can be a good choice for bass guitar processing. The amp model will provide just a touch of tube warmth for a great bass sound.
- ACE 30: The ACE 30 is a model of the Vox AC30 guitar amp. The AC30 has been the secret weapon of many well-known guitar players. The ACE 30 provides two channels, including a switch in the Top Boost channel for modern or vintage tone controls. Vox Amplification changed the design of the original AC30 amp, and the ACE 30 plug-in has models of both versions of the tone stacks.
- Soloist: The Soloist is a model of the Mesa Boogie Dual Rectifier amp. This amp is designed for high gain and heavy tube saturation. The Dual Rectifier amp is an excellent choice for maximum distortion and "shredding" type sounds. The Soloist has three channels and provides a way to blend two of those channels. The Orange channel can be switched between Normal and Clean. The Red channel is a Vintage distortion channel. There is also a switch to combine the red and orange channels.
- Live Room G/Live Room B: Live Room G and Live Room B provide modeling of guitar and bass speaker cabinets, multiple microphone types, and room ambience. There are controls for cabinet drive and output gain of the cabinet in the room. Live Room G has speaker cabinets and microphones that are optimized for recording electric guitars. Live Room B includes classic bass guitar speaker cabinets and appropriate microphones to record those cabinets.

Choose the cabinet model from the drop-down menu.

Choose the microphone type and position from the drop-down menus.

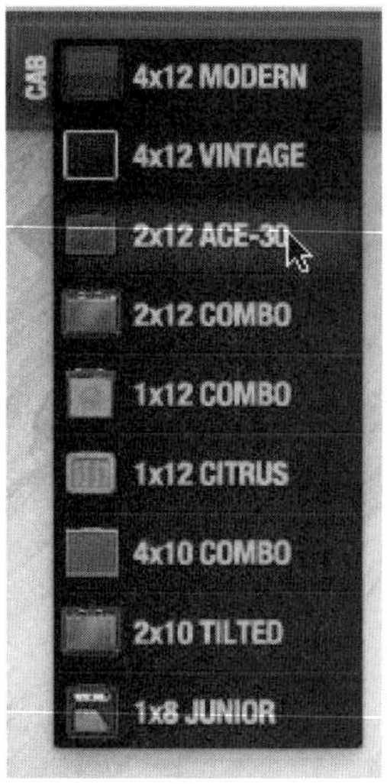

Figure 4.55

Figure 4.56

Up to three microphones can be used to capture the sound of the cabinet. Mics can be placed in different positions relative to the speaker. Mics can be moved closer or further from the cabinet. There is an internal mixer for the microphones, including tone and pan controls. The output of the audio track includes a mono or stereo mix of up to three microphones.

The channel 2 and 3-4 microphones can also be split to separate audio outputs for additional processing. Create aux or audio tracks. The additional mic outputs will be available as audio input assignments. They are listed as CLOSE MIC and ROOM MIC. Turn down the chan 2 and chan 3-4 mics in the Live Room mixer so that only the chan 1 mic appears at the original track output.

Figure 4.57

The room size can be changed with the Decay control. The Damping control attenuates high frequency in the ambience signal.

- Live Stage: Live Stage is a simplified version of Live Room G and Live Room B. Live Stage includes all the cabinet models from those two plug-ins. Live Stage provides for a single variable position microphone. Because Live Stage uses one microphone model instead of three, it uses one-third the processing power of the larger plug-ins. Live Stage also includes gain, room decay, and damping controls.

Figure 4.58

Stompboxes

Stompbox is a term used to describe effects processors typically used by guitarists. The term refers to an effects device housed in a small box that is placed on the floor and has a footswitch. To turn the effect on or off, the guitarist "stomps" on the footswitch. From the 1960s through the present, many companies have developed signal processing hardware that includes a footswitch. Many of these older effects devices have unique sounds that are still useful onstage and in the studio. Some of these classic effects devices are no longer manufactured and are difficult to find on the used market. Older "stompboxes" used batteries, had high impedance inputs, and could be extremely noisy.

Digital Performer includes a compliment of plug-ins that are convolution and physics models of classic stompbox effect pedals. As with the amp and speaker cabinet plug-ins included with DP, these stompbox plug-ins are faithful recreations of the original hardware. The only difference is that the plug-ins don't require batteries and do not have the noise problems of the originals.

The DP user should not feel that these plug-ins are only for guitar signals. Each of these plug-ins provides unique processing, and can be used on any audio signal for interesting effect.

The stompbox plug-ins included with DP 8 are:

- Distortion pedals: These includes D Plus, Delta Fuzz, Diamond Drive, Hi-Top Booster, RXT, Tube Wailer, and the Uber Tube. Each of these distortion plug-ins offers unique tone and control over the distortion effect.

- Analog Delay: This plug-in is a model of a specific analog delay technology called "bucket brigade delay." Part of the sound of a bucket brigade delay effect is that each echo repeat has diminished high frequency content. Another interesting aspect of this effect is that if the Repeat control is turned all the way up, the delay will self-oscillate, and generate its own tone. If the delay parameter is then changed, the tone will change pitch.

- Dyna-Squash: This device was originally sold as a sustain pedal for guitarists. It is a brick wall limiter. It will work as a sustain effect for guitar or bass, but it can also be a powerful dynamic effect for snare drum, vocals, or any other audio signal.

- Intelligent Noise Gate: This is a gate that is optimized to clean up noise introduced in a typical guitar effects chain. In addition to gate controls, there is also a filter removal of 60 cycle AC noise. Typically a noise gate will be the last effect in an effects chain.

- Wah Pedal: A wah pedal works by using a variable filter with high gain and a sharp Q curve. The DP Wah Pedal can be automated via MIDI or audio track automation. The Wah Pedal can also be controlled in real time via external control. A MIDI footpedal or any device that can be set up to generate continuous controller data can be used. Set the Sweep Control to MIDI. Choose the continuous controller number for the filter control. The Wah Pedal can also be bypassed with a continuous controller message. To pass the MIDI data from the external controller to the Wah Pedal, use a record-enabled MIDI track, or set up a slider in a custom console.

- Springamabob: Springamabob is a convolution model of three different types of spring reverbs. Spring reverbs are found in some guitar amps or self-contained boxes.

- Analog Chorus, Analog Flanger, Analog Phaser, Clear Pebble: There are modulation effects based on classic guitar effect pedals from the 1970s. Each of these effects works by delaying the input signal, and combining the delayed signal with the original. The delayed signal is then modulated, which causes slight amounts of pitch shifting. The general difference between a phase shifter and a chorus is that a phase shifter uses a shorter delay time as compared to a chorus effect. A flanger routes the delayed signal back to input to create a variable feedback loop. Each of these effects produces its own unique modulated filter effect

Mixing

The mixer in DP is based on a traditional analog metaphor. There is a standardized flow to all signal paths. Effects can be inserted at any point in a mix. Subgroups, inserts, sidechains, effects send and returns, and master faders can be used to create simple or complex mix paths. Buses are used for internal patching. Audio interface inputs and outputs can be patched in for monitor mixes, external summing, external effects processing, live input signals, and re-recording back into the computer.

Digital Performer offers complete automation of all mix parameters. Multiple mix takes can be created and recalled. The DP mixer, including plug-in effect parameters, can be controlled via remote hardware or software devices. Onscreen mixing can be done in the Mixing Board window, or via automation in graphic editing windows.

Digital Performer provides comprehensive ways to manage plug-ins and plug-in presets. This includes the ability to store multiple plug-ins as effect preset chains. DP supports standard third-party plug-in formats. The mix functions and stock plug-ins included with DP provide the tools required for complete mix down, as well as final output mastering.

Because DP is an integrated audio/MIDI sequencer, MIDI is treated very much like audio in terms of mixing. MIDI tracks have inserts for real-time MIDI effect plug-ins. MIDI can be routed to internal and external destinations. MIDI automation works the same way as audio automation.

Mixing Board Window Basics

The Mixing Board window can display any combination of audio, MIDI, and instrument tracks. Tracks can be shown or hidden via the Track Selector window or list. To make the track selector part of the mixer, select the preference to Always open the edit window's Track Selector.

The button in the bottom left-hand corner of the Mixing Board window will open and close the track selector. Tracks nested in folders can be displayed or hidden with a single click on the folder.

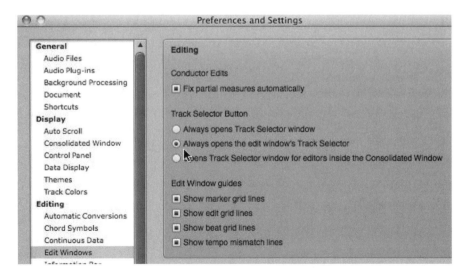

Figure 4.59

The Mixing Board window mini menu provides many options for configuring the mixer.

Figure 4.60

Currently displayed faders and panners can be temporarily grouped and scaled by holding the W key and moving a single fader or panner.

A single sequence can have multiple mix takes. The initial mix is described in the bottom left-hand corner of the mixer as Mix Mode Off. Click on this menu to duplicate the mix take or create a new mix take. Mix takes can be renamed, recalled, and deleted. A mix take contains all assigned effect plug-ins and all track automation. Switching to a new mix take is a quick way to disable all effect plug-ins.

To the left of the mix mode menu is the Automation Snapshot button. Press this button to get the Automation Snapshot window.

The mixer automation snapshot button will capture volume, pan, and track mute information. If a send is assigned to a working output, the mixer snapshot can also capture send level, pan, and mute information. The mixer automation snapshot does not capture plug-in parameter automation.

The numerical calibration to the left of audio faders describes the position of the fader. The numerical calibration does not describe the vertical VU meter to the right of the fader. Audio faders in DP have six dB of additional available headroom. If the audio fader is set to 0 in the mixer, it is at unity gain. Double+Click on any audio fader to set it to unity gain. The fader now has six additional dB of available gain.

Figure 4.61

The VU meter to the right of the fader shows a relative level of signal with a clip indicator at the top. If the clip indicator turns red, that indicates the digital audio sample has exceeded the 24-bit range. If the clipped signal goes directly to an audio output or is printed to a file, it will contain square wave clipping distortion. However, it is important to understand that if a signal exceeds the range of a 24-bit sample inside DP, it still has available dynamic range. The mix path of DP uses 32-bit floating point resolution. As long as the final output of DP is within the 24-bit range, it will not be clipped on playback or printing to file. This means that a track in DP can cause its VU meter clip indicator to light, without actually clipping the audio signal. If the track is routed through another gain stage such as a master fader, and the gain is reduced there, the original signal maintains its dynamic range, and does not clip on final output. This is important to understand in a mixdown. Clip indicators on audio tracks are not a problem as long as the sum of the mix does not clip the final output. A master fader with a mastering limiter inserted is a typical way to control summed mix output.

The Trim plug-in does provide precise numerical VU metering of the actual audio signal. Place the Trim plug-in post-fader in the insert list to view the final output from the track.

Tracks Types

Figure 4.62

The following types of tracks can be added to a DP sequence. Different icons are used to denote each track type.

- MIDI track
- Mono audio track

Figure 4.63

- Stereo audio track

TRACK NAME
≈ Audio-2

Figure 4.64

- Surround audio track (choices include Quad, LCRS, 5.1, 6.1, 7.1, and 10.2)

TRACK NAME
s.1 Audio-3

Figure 4.65

- Instrument track

TRACK NAME
⊟ Instrument-1

Figure 4.66

- Aux track

TRACK NAME
⌀ Aux-1

Figure 4.67

- Master fader track

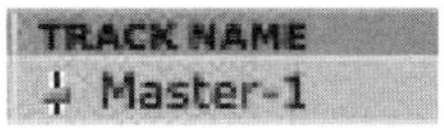

TRACK NAME
⌀ Master-1

Figure 4.68

Every sequence in DP has a conductor track and a movie track. These tracks cannot be deleted from the sequence. It is not possible to have more than one conductor and movie track per sequence. This is the icon for the conductor track:

TRACK NAME
⌀ Conductor

Figure 4.69

MIDI Signal Flow

MIDI data goes in and out of MIDI tracks. In order for MIDI data to be recorded or passed through a MIDI track, the MIDI track must be record enabled. If DP is in multirecord mode, the input assignment for the MIDI track must match the actual source and channel of the incoming signal.

The output of a MIDI track can be assigned to any external MIDI device that is configured in the Bundles window. The output of a MIDI track can be assigned to any currently active virtual instrument. The output of a MIDI track can also be assigned to multiple destinations. This is done by clicking in the MIDI track output column and choosing New Device Group...

Some effect plug-ins can accept MIDI input. For example, the MasterWorks Gate plug-in can use a MIDI signal to control an audio gate. Set the Key Source to MIDI Notes.

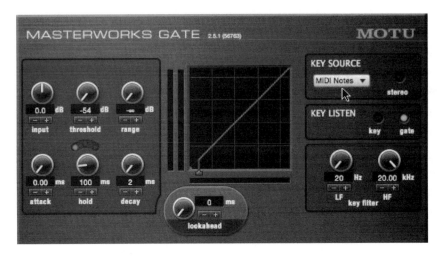

Figure 4.70

Now the MW Gate will be an available output destination for MIDI tracks. This allows the MIDI track to pass real-time or recorded MIDI notes to trigger the audio gate.

PLAY	XMPT	OUTPUT	COL	TRACK NAME
▶		MW Gate : Audio-1 : Insert D-in		♪ MIDI-1

Figure 4.71

MIDI data can be translated in real time in DP. There are two ways to translate different types of MIDI data in real time. In the mixer, there are inserts for MIDI tracks that provide for real-time MIDI plug-ins. It is also possible to generate, translate, and convert MIDI data with a Custom Console.

Bundles Window

The Bundles window is used to configure audio and MIDI inputs and outputs within DP. Audio bundles can be mono, stereo, or multichannel. External MIDI devices can be configured. Virtual instruments with auxiliary outputs can also be configured.

Open the Bundles window from the Studio menu. The default key command is Shift+U. The Bundles window has tabs to switch between the different types of bundles. What is displayed with each of the bundles tabs depends on what audio and MIDI hardware is connected to the computer, and what virtual instruments are currently running. In this graphic, the Bundles window is set to display input bundles. The available inputs of the currently connected audio interface are listed on the right. Input bundles have been created and named for each of the available interface inputs. These input bundles will now be available as track input selections in other windows.

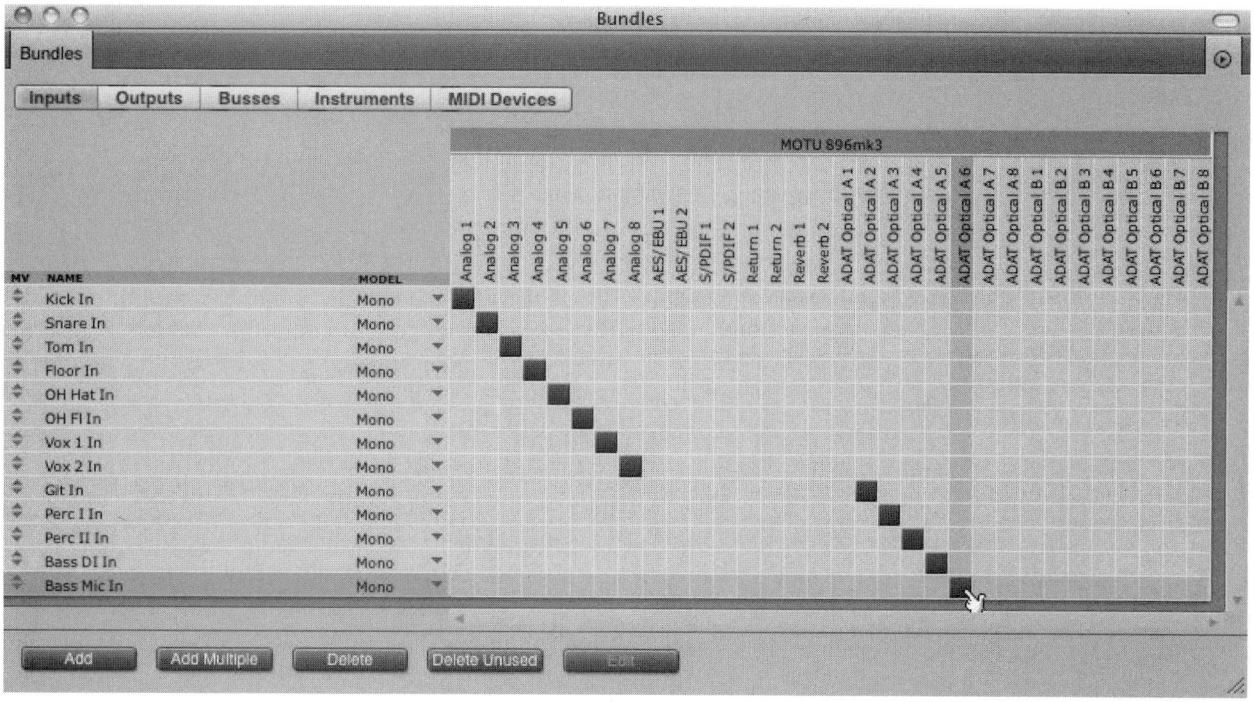

Figure 4.72

Buses

A bus is a "virtual patch cord" inside DP. Buses can be mono, stereo, or multichannel for surround sound. Buses can be configured in the New Mono Bundle and New Stereo Bundle selections for audio and aux track inputs and outputs. Buses can also be configured, named, and deleted in the Bundles window.

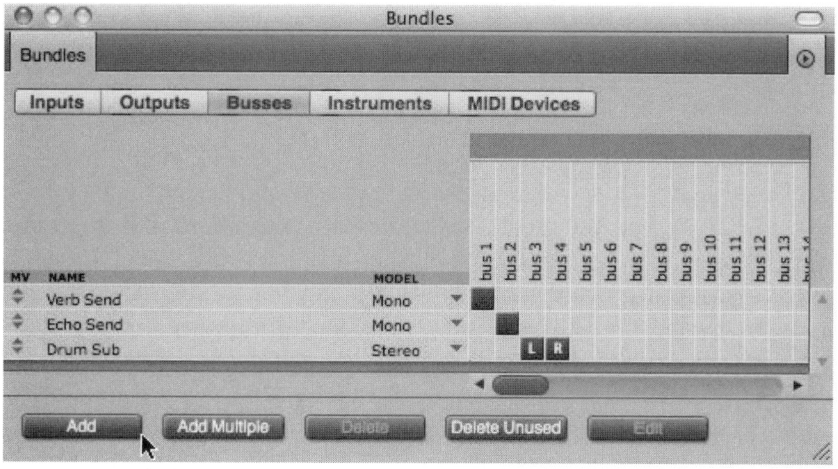

Figure 4.73

Buses are typically used for connecting the outputs of audio tracks to inputs of other audio tracks (for re-recording) or aux tracks (for subgroups routing). Buses are used for effect sends (typically routed to aux tracks, which are used for the effect return). Buses are used for side-chain connections.

Analog Signal Levels

As any audio engineer knows, proper signal level is critical to good sonic quality. A great deal of effort goes into the making of hardware and software for audio recording and processing. In order for any component of the audio signal chain to work its best, care must be taken to properly match signal levels. Improper audio signal level matching can result in distortion or noise.

With a DP system, signal level is a concern for both analog and digital audio. With analog gear, signal level is a function of electrical voltage. Correct impedance matching is also important with analog audio connections. Analog gear can produce distortion or other sonic artifacts depending on how levels are set. In some cases this may be desirable. For example, an overloaded vacuum tube can add harmonically based distortion to an audio signal. Harmonic distortion may be pleasing to the ear, depending on how it is used. When an audio signal is referred to as "warm," that usually means that the signal has been distorted in some way. Distortion may be added to analog signals as a desirable sonic effect.

Not all analog audio gear creates pleasing harmonic distortion. Harmonic distortion is not always a desirable effect. In some cases, audio distortion in analog gear may be simple square wave clipping, which generally is not a pleasing effect. Therefore it is useful to know if analog hardware is adding audible distortion to the signal, and what nature of distortion is added, if at all.

In general, computer audio interfaces are not designed to be signal processors. Some models of audio interfaces do have signal processing capabilities built in, but this is a secondary function to the basic job of providing audio input and output to the computer. Unless the interface has some sort of analog input limiter, an overloaded input to an audio interface will usually result in clipping of the waveform, and undesirable audio distortion. If the input signal is too low, amplification of that signal will also increase the level of any noise present in the signal. Dynamic range specifications of an audio interface are irrelevant if proper level matching is not used on input and output.

In DP, the Audio Monitor window shows the input level to a record-enabled audio track. Digital Performer has no control over the level of the audio signal being recorded. If the audio interface does not do any additional processing of the incoming audio, the Audio Monitor window in DP provides an accurate measurement of the signal coming in to the interface.

If the interface has additional internal processing, the Audio Monitor window in DP will reflect the level of the incoming signal as it is being processed. Therefore, if the audio interface does feature internal signal-processing capabilities, it is important to make sure that the signal coming into the interface is at a proper level. It is also important to make sure the signal is still at a proper level after being affected by any internal interface processing.

Digital Signal Levels

Digital audio works by taking samples of an analog waveform. An individual digital audio sample measures the amplitude of the waveform at the point at which the sample is taken. In simple terms, a single digital audio sample is a measurement of audio volume.

A digital audio sample is described by a specific number of bits. For example, a 16-bit sample is using 16 binary bits to describe the amplitude of the waveform at any given point. 16 bits has enough resolution to describe a dynamic range of 0 to 96 dB. 24 bits has enough resolution to theoretically describe a dynamic range of 144 dB. 16- and 24-bit samples are "fixed integer" numbers, which mean they only describe whole numbers. A 16- or 24-bit sample does not have the ability to describe a fractional number that uses a decimal place. It is possible to add extra bits to an audio sample to extend the dynamic range of the sample. A 32-bit floating point sample is a 24-bit sample with 8 extra bits added on. The 8 extra bits are used to describe a floating decimal point. The dynamic range of a 32-bit floating point sample is around 1500 dB.

It is generally accepted that the maximum dynamic range of a healthy human ear is around 120. Most adults have considerably less dynamic range than that. Music that is produced and mastered for radio typically is compressed to make it sound apparently louder. A pop song on the radio may have as little as 12 dB of actual dynamic range. By comparison, a soundtrack for a movie may have a wide dynamic range.

With a fixed integer 16- or 24-bit sample, there is no headroom above the top of the sample. If a signal is overloaded when recording or playing back a fixed integer sample, the result will be simple clipping of the waveform. This will result in unpleasant distortion. It is important to understand that audio interfaces do not record or play back floating point samples. Any analog signal sent into an audio interface for recording must not clip the input of the interface. Any digital audio signal being sent from the computer to the audio interface for playback must not exceed the dynamic range of the fixed integer sample, otherwise it will clip on output.

It is possible to record to a 32-bit floating point sample in DP, but initially, the dynamic range of the sample will be limited by the analog-to-digital conversion of the audio interface. 32-bit files are more useful for audio that is processed inside DP.

The internal audio path of DP is 32-bit floating point resolution. Plug-ins can use 64-bit floating point processing, depending on how they are designed. When DP works with 16- or 24-bit samples, it adds additional bits to each sample for internal processing. When audio is played back from DP, or is printed to a 16- or 24-bit file, DP rounds off the extra bits and turns the floating point sample into a fixed integer sample.

Because of the internal 32-bit floating point mix path, it is almost impossible to clip a digital audio signal inside DP by adding gain. That also means that when audio is played back or printed to a 16- or 24-bit file, care must be taken to ensure that the level of the signal does not exceed the dynamic range of that 16- or 24-bit fixed integer number.

Digital Performer includes precise tools to monitor internal signal level, and to control that level. From simple volume faders to sophisticated multiband compressors and limiters, DP provides many ways to control volume and dynamic range of digital audio, both within the software, and when playing back or printing to a file.

Automation

One of the distinct advantages of computer-based music production is the ability to recall and automate complex mixes. Digital Performer provides the capability to automate every parameter of a mix. Automation can be created and edited in real time via a variety of control methods. Automation data can be created and and edited in various DP edit windows.

Automation can be enabled or disabled for any data type. Automation preferences are configured in the Setup menu>Automation Setup... window.

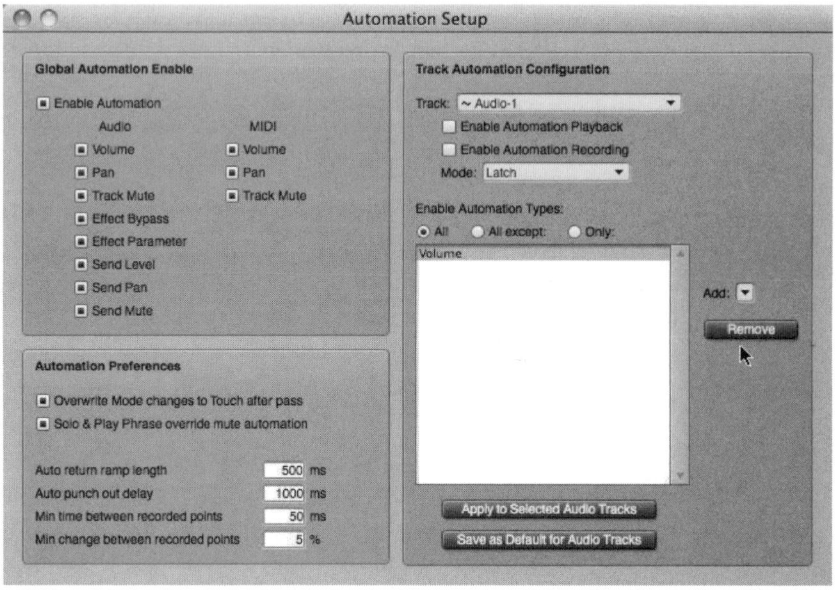

Figure 4.74

Automation Record

Parameters in the mixing board and within plug-ins can be automated in real time. Each fader strip in the mixer has an automate record button. Automation record mode for plug-ins can be enabled from the menu in the upper right-hand corner of the plug-in window.

There are nine different automation record modes. The default mode is Latch.

To record automation, press Play (not Record) in the DP Control Panel. If automation record is enabled for any track, moving a parameter in that track or any plug-in assigned to the track will create automation data.

Figure 4.75

Automation Play Mode

In order for automation data in a track to play back, automation play mode must be enabled for that track. The automation play button is next to the automation record button in the Mixing Board window. Automation play can also be disabled or enabled via menus in the plug-in windows and in the Sequence Editor window. Specific types of automation data can be enabled or disabled in the Automation Setup window.

Snapshots

A snapshot is an instant insertion of automation data based on the visible types of automation and the current location of the playback wiper. Snapshots can be taken from the Mixing Board window or from any plug-in window.

The Snapshot button in the Mixing Board window can take snapshots of faders, panners, track mutes, and send parameters. The Snapshot button in the Mixing Board window does not capture any plug-in parameters.

Editing

Automation data can be edited like any other sequence data. Automation can be edited in graphic editor windows or Event List windows. The pencil and reshape tools in the Tools window can be used to enter and edit automation data. When drawing or reshaping automation data, the edit grid can be used for precise edit points of data. Hold down the Option/Alt key while dragging the Pencil tool or Reshape tool to snap to grid.

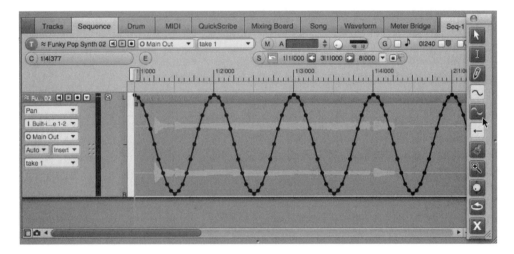

Figure 4.76

Click on any point of an automation line to add an automation point.

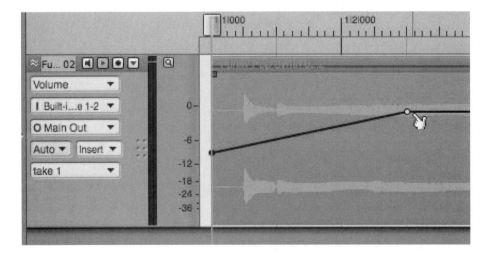

Figure 4.77

For audio tracks, if automation is play-disabled, automation data will show up as a dotted line in the Sequence Editor window.

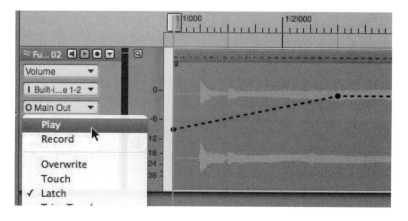

Figure 4.78

Figure 4.79

Editing Tips

Digital Performer contains a complete set of tools for editing audio and MIDI data. Editing can be done with mouse clicks, keyboard commands, and external control devices.

Edit Tools

The Tools window contains edit tools that work in different graphic editing windows. Some tools are for audio only or MIDI only. Some tools are common to both types of data.

When a graphic edit window is open, the mouse cursor has multiple functions depending its position in the edit window and which tool is selected in the Tools window. Tools can be selected by clicking in the Tools window. Tools can also be selected with key commands. Double+click the key command to invoke the tool. To temporarily invoke a tool, hold down its key command while editing with the mouse.

When the mouse cursor is set to the default arrow tool, it becomes context sensitive and will change its function depending on its position in each edit window. Here are some of the functions of the mouse cursor when set to arrow tool and used in the Sequence Editor window:

- Time Stretch tool

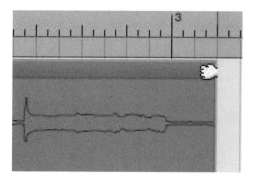

Figure 4.80

- Edge Edit tool

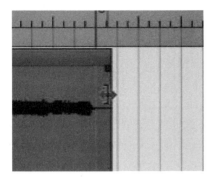

Figure 4.81

- Fade tool

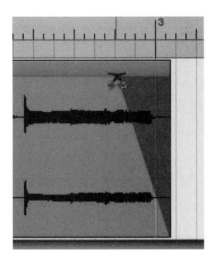

Figure 4.82

- Move tool (with soundbite selected)

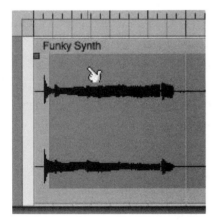

Figure 4.83

- Selection tool (cursor over bottom third of soundbite)

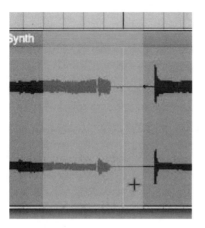

Figure 4.84

- Copy tool (with Option/Alt key held down)

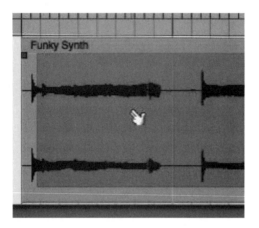

Figure 4.85

- Throw tool (with Control key held down)

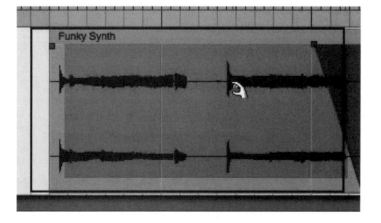

Figure 4.86

- Lasso tool (with Control+Option/Alt keys held down)

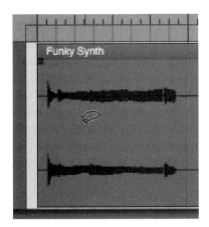

Figure 4.87

Sequence Editor Window

The Sequence Editor window can display any combination of tracks. Tracks are displayed above and below each other. Tracks can be displayed zoomed down to sample level resolution. Audio and MIDI data can be simultaneously edited.

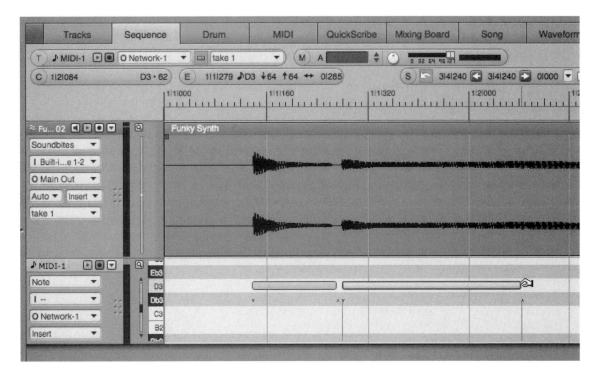

Figure 4.88

MIDI Graphic Editor Window

The MIDI Graphic Editor window displays only MIDI tracks. Controller data is displayed below the note data. Any combination of MIDI tracks can be displayed in the window. When multiple MIDI tracks are displayed, they are super-imposed over each other. It is useful to use track colors to be able to tell different tracks apart from each other. In the track selector list, the pencil icon denotes the master edit track.

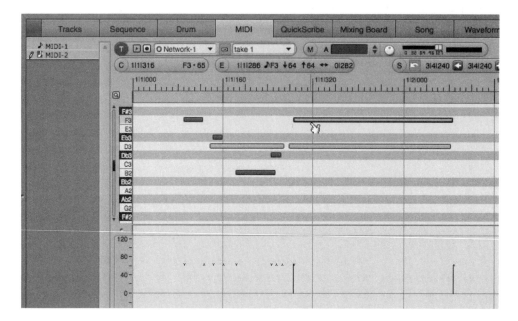

Figure 4.89

Drum Editor Window

The Drum Editor window displays MIDI data in a grid. Any combination of MIDI tracks can be displayed. Within each MIDI track, individual MIDI note values can be named and shown or hidden. This allows for creation and display of drumsets where different MIDI notes represent different drum sounds.

Individual note values can be muted, allowing for muting or soloing of drums within kits. Individual note values can be quantized. For example, a kick drum part could be quantized, while no quantization is applied to the snare drum.

The Rhythm Brush tool can be used to "paint" custom-made or stock MIDI patterns.

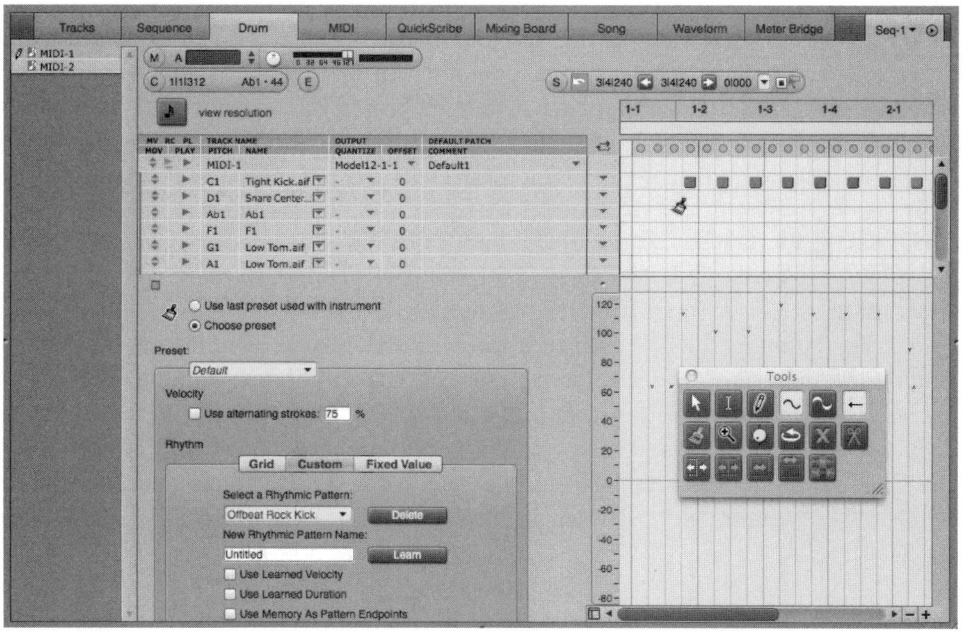

Figure 4.90

Printing Audio Effects

Effects for audio can be added as a non-destructive playback process. This can be done by using plug-ins in the mixer, or by adding pitch or soundbite volume automation from within audio tracks. Effects can also be printed to soundbites. When DP prints an effect to a soundbite, it actually makes a new audio file and soundbite with the printed effect. This allows for the edit to be undone if the original audio needs to be restored.

Plug-ins can be used to print an effect to audio:

- Select a soundbite or soundbites in the Soundbites window, or make a selection in any audio editing window.
- Go to the Audio menu and choose Audio Plug-Ins. A list will display all currently available plug-ins.
- Select any plug-in from the list. The plug-in window will open.
- At the bottom of the plug-in window, press the Preview button to play the selected soundbite. This allows the soundbite to be auditioned while changing the plug-in parameters.
- The pre roll and post roll settings allow additional audio to be created before and after the original selection. This can be useful for an effect such as reverb, where the effect generates sound that lasts after the initial audio selection.
- The Apply button will cause new audio to be created that represents the original selection. Each originally selected soundbite will be replaced by a new soundbite with the printed effect.

If pitch automation or soundbite volume changes have been added to a soundbite, those changes can be printed. Select the soundbite (or multiple soundbites) and choose Merge Soundbites from the Audio menu.

It is also possible to print plug-ins, edits, and automation by using the freeze or bounce functions.

Sequence Tempo

A sequence timeline in DP has an implied tempo map. By default, the tempo map starts with bar one at 120 BPM. The sequence timeline tempo can be controlled remotely in real time. It can be set to a fixed tempo with the Tempo Slider. It is also possible to create a complex tempo map within the conductor track..

Working Without a Tempo Reference

The concept of musical tempo can be ignored in DP. There is no requirement that the tempo map of the sequence timeline has to have any relationship to audio or MIDI tracks. For example, if DP is used to work with dialog and sound effects for a video soundtrack, there may be no use for any musical tempo information in the session.

It is possible to work with music in DP and not use any reference to tempo in the sequence timeline. This is similar to recording to magnetic tape. Digital Performer can be set to show real-time location represented as hours, minutes, seconds, and hundredths of seconds. Set DP to display real time in the Time Formats window under the Setup menu.

Figure 4.91

It is possible to create a tempo map after a musical performance is recorded or after audio tracks have been imported into a DP sequence. Therefore it is possible to begin a project with no reference to tempo, and then create a tempo map later in the workflow. This can be a useful technique if an artist prefers not to work with a click track, or if prerecorded audio with no tempo information is imported into DP.

Advantages of an Accurate Tempo Map

There are significant advantages to having a sequence tempo map that accurately references the music in the timeline.

- A tempo map will provide numbered barlines that correspond to musical locations.
- A tempo map allows for accurate display of score and part notation.
- A tempo map allows for predictable quantization of audio and MIDI events.
- A tempo map provides the foundation for altering the tempo of an existing performance.
- A tempo map provides the foundation for matching audio and MIDI that originally have different tempos.

Embedded Tempo in Audio

WAV and AIFF digital audio files have the capability to contain tempo information. If there is tempo information embedded in the audio file, DP can use that information to manipulate the tempo of the audio, or to match the sequence tempo to the audio tempo.

Digital Performer can also embed tempo information into an audio file. To embed tempo information into an audio file:

- When DP records audio, the current sequence tempo is automatically embedded in the newly recorded audio files.
- It is possible to select Soundbites in an edit window, and choose Copy Sequence Tempo to Soundbites from the Audio menu.
- Select any soundbite, go to the Audio menu, and choose Soundbite Tempo>Set Soundbite Tempo... Set Soundbite Tempo will calculate tempo based on the length of the soundbite. If the soundbite tempo is already known, it can also be assigned in this window.

Figure 4.92

- Soundbite tempo can also be assigned in the Waveform Editor window.

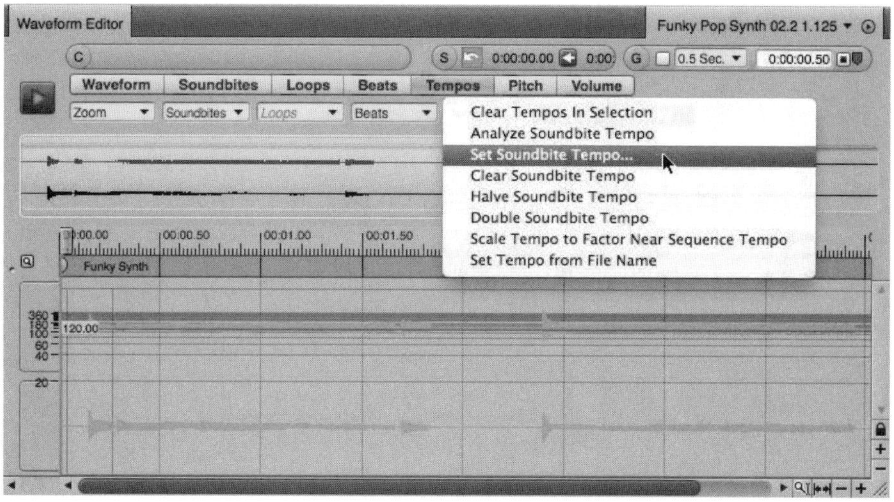

Figure 4.93

Creating a Sequence Tempo Map from Audio or MIDI

If audio or MIDI tracks were recorded while referenced to a click in DP, that means the tempo of the musical performance is roughly accurate and matches the tempo and bar lines in the DP sequence. One way to check that the sequence matches the tempo of the music is to engage the click in DP and play that back along with the music tracks. If the DP click matches the tempo of the recorded music, that means the sequence tempo map matches the actual tempo of the music in the tracks.

If the music doesn't match the DP sequence tempo, it is possible to build a tempo map based on the musical performance. If there is already tempo information embedded in audio soundbites, that tempo information can be copied to the conductor track. To do this, select the soundbite and choose Adjust Sequence Tempo to Soundbite tempo from the Audio menu. If there is no tempo information embedded in soundbites, it is possible to manually create a sequence tempo map based on the musical content of MIDI and audio tracks.

Automatic Tempo Detection

Digital Performer can attempt to find the tempo of a soundbite or a MIDI performance. This is based on DP analyzing the beats in the audio or MIDI performance. To find tempo based on MIDI, select a region of MIDI data, go to the Region menu and choose Set Sequence Tempo from MIDI. This command provides the option to set the tempo slider to an average of the detected MIDI tempo, or to set DP to use the conductor track for detected tempo changes.

To detect tempo from a soundbite, select the soundbite and go to the Audio menu>Soundbite Tempo>Analyze Soundbite Tempo. In order for this function to work, DP must have already found beats in the soundbites. Automatic beat detection is enabled in the DP preferences by default. If automatic beat detection has been disabled, open the soundbite in the Waveform Editor window. Select all, and choose Find Beats from Selection from the Beats menu.

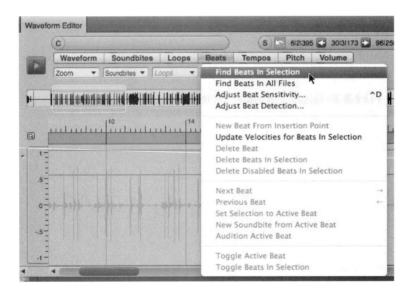

Figure 4.94

It is important to understand that tempo detection of MIDI or audio does not then move the downbeat of the MIDI or audio to a bar line. Digital Performer creates the tempo map based on the position of the detected downbeat of the audio or MIDI. Therefore it may be a good idea to shift the MIDI or audio performance left or right so that the downbeat lines up with a sequence bar line.

It's also important to understand that automatic tempo detection does not have any effect on the sequence meter. The default meter of a DP sequence is 4/4. Digital Performer may detect the tempo of an audio or MIDI performance based on beats, but it will not be able to detect meter. If the meter is other than 4/4, meter changes must be manually created in the conductor track.

Automatic tempo detection can have varying degrees of accuracy. Some audio or MIDI performances have obvious downbeats and tempos. Other performances do not. Also, there can be different interpretations of tempo. Depending on the content of the performance, a soundbite or MIDI performance could be detected as a multiple of the tempo. For example, is the accurate tempo or a performance 60 BPM or 120 BPM? Sometimes only the artist or engineer can make that decision. If DP does not accurately detect the tempo of audio or MIDI, it is possible to manually create a tempo map based on the performance.

Manual Tempo Map Creation

Manual tempo mapping is based on identifying downbeats audibly and visually, and dragging the sequence bar lines to match those downbeats. Dragging bar lines will create tempo data in the conductor track. Digital Performer includes powerful features for creating accurate tempo maps for complex audio and MIDI performances.

By default a DP sequence is set to be under the control of the tempo slider, with a tempo of 120 BPM. If DP is switched to conductor track tempo control, and there are no tempo events in the conductor track, the starting tempo of the conductor track is assumed to be 120 BPM.

- In the Tracks window, lock all tracks. This will cause the data in the tracks to stay in the same relative position while the tempo map is being created.

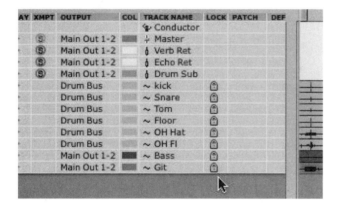

Figure 4.95

- Put DP under the control of the conductor track.

Figure 4.96

- Open the Sequence editor window and display all audio and MIDI tracks.
- Identify the first downbeat in the music. In many cases, the first downbeat won't be at the exact start of an audio file.
- It may be necessary to move audio and MIDI data in order to line up the first musical downbeat with a bar line in the DP sequence timeline. It may not be possible to slide audio or MIDI to the left past the beginning of the sequence, so it may be that the data

must slide to the right. In such a situation, the first musical downbeat won't line up with bar 1. It may line up with bar 2, 3, or whatever is the nearest available bar line. If audio or MIDI data is moved to line up with a bar line, it is important to move all the data in the sequence together so that it all stays relatively in sync. Make sure that all audio and MIDI in the sequence is selected before dragging any musical downbeat to a bar line. Once this is done, the first downbeat of the music is now accurately lined up with a bar line in the DP sequence. In the following graphic, the music starts with a pickup figure on the guitar. The downbeat of the first bar has been identified and the audio files have been moved to the right so the musical downbeat lines up with barline number 3 in the DP sequence timeline.

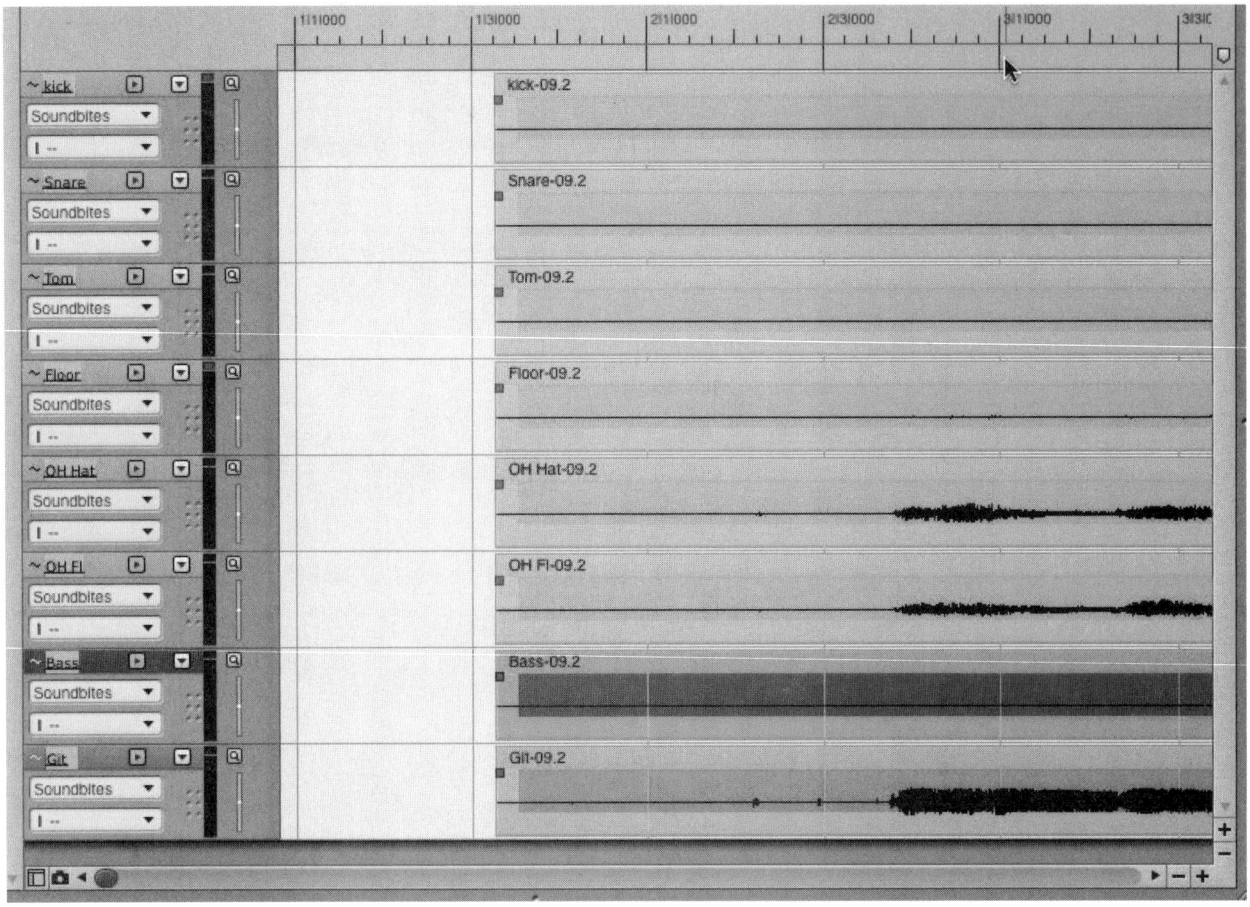

Figure 4.97

• Play the sequence to listen for and identify the downbeat of the next bar. Depending on the content of the audio and MIDI tracks, a downbeat may be visually obvious in the Sequence Editor window.

The downbeat of bar 2 of the music may be either before or after the next bar line in the DP sequence timeline. The goal is to line up the bar line with the actual downbeat of the music. This will be done for each bar line, all the way to the end of the sequence. When this is done, a tempo map will have been created in the conductor track that matches the tempo of the music.

• To move a bar line relative to the musical performance, go to the Project menu>Modify Conductor Track>Adjust Beats… The Adjust Beats window will open.

Figure 4.98

- In the Adjust Beats window, set the following options: Drag Beats in Edit window, Adjust: Measures, Apply adjusted beats tempo until end of sequence, Preserve Real Time Performance, Snapping: Notes or Audio Beats.
- It is now possible to drag a bar line to the left or right in the Sequence editor ruler. In the following graphic, the mouse cursor is over the timeline ruler and in adjust beats mode. The downbeat of the second bar of the music performance has been identified, and the adjust beats cursor has dragged the barline to that point.
- It is also possible to drag bar lines within audio or MIDI tracks. If there are audio beats detected in a soundbite, the bar line will snap to the audio beat. This can make the bar line dragging fast and accurate. In the following graphic, beats have been detected in the kick drum track, and the bar line is being snapped to the beat within the soundbite:

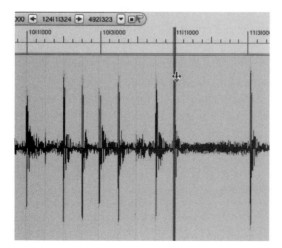

Figure 4.100

Figure 4.99

- Work from the beginning of the sequence. Check the work by listening to the music along with the DP click. If the DP click matches the musical performance, that indicates the tempo data in the conductor track is accurate.
- It is possible to go back earlier in the sequence and make adjustments without affecting later tempo events. To do this, select the option in the Adjust Beats window to Move one beat at a time. This will allow a bar line to be adjusted without disturbing tempo data before or after that point.
- In some cases there may be noticeable tempo changes within a bar. In the Adjust Beats window, set the Adjust pop-up menu to Beats. Now individual beats within a bar can be dragged.
- The final test of the accuracy of the tempo map is to play the music from start to finish while also listening to the DP click. If the DP click matches the music in the tracks, that means the tempo map in the conductor track is accurate.

For some musical performances, tempo may not be obvious from the individual audio or MIDI tracks. One trick is to create a manual click track by recording a MIDI or audio track by listening and tapping along with the music. The manually created click track can be edited for accuracy (relative to the music), and then used as a reference to create a tempo map.

Once the bar lines have been aligned and the DP click matches the music, select all soundbites. Go to the Audio menu and choose Copy Sequence Tempo to Soundbites. This will embed the tempo information into the audio. Now it will be possible to do tempo correction and accurate audio and MIDI quantization.

Adjusting Tempo

Once audio has an accurate tempo map, it can be time-stretched to fit any new tempo, including tempo variations. For example, if a tempo map has been created in the conductor track to match the varying tempo of a live performance, the tempo data from the conductor track can be copied back to the soundbites in the audio tracks. If the sequence tempo is now changed, including switching to the tempo slider mode, it will no longer match the tempo map embedded in the soundbites. Select the soundbites and choose Adjust Soundbites to Sequence Tempo from the Audio menu. DP will create new soundbites and will conform their tempo to the new sequence tempo.

Quantization

Quantization is the process of changing the timing of events in a track based on a grid or some sort of template. Any type of MIDI event, soundbite, or automation data can be quantized. Digital Performer also has the ability to quantize audio beats within soundbites.

Quantization is a region-based operation. Selected data can then be quantized by choosing Quantize... or Groove Quantize... from the Region menu.

There is also a Region menu called Smart Quantize... Smart Quantize is used to prepare MIDI data if it is to be exported to an external notation program. Smart quantize will "clean up" the MIDI notes so that an external notation program has an easier job of accurate rhythmic transcription.

In addition to region-based quantization, it is also possible to quantize MIDI data on playback only, by using a MIDI quantize plug-in.

Grid-Based Quantization

Grid-based quantization moves events based on the bar and beat locations of the sequence timeline. The Quantize window offers many options for grid-based quantization.

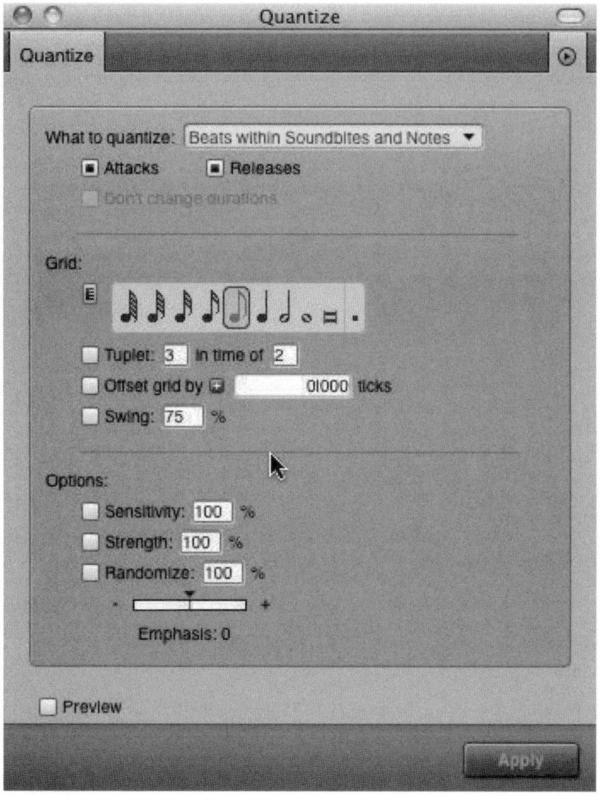

Figure 4.101

Quantize Audio Beats

When DP has detected audio beats within a soundbite, those beats can be quantized. This is done by creating a new soundfile and soundbite, applying time compression and time stretching to move the beats. In the Quantize menu, there are menu choices to quantize beats within soundbites, as well as beats within soundbites and MIDI notes. This allows simultaneous quantization of audio and MIDI data.

In some cases, it may be necessary to edit the beat map of the audio so that DP only quantizes specific beats. Display the soundbite in the Waveform Editor window. Click the Beats button. Select any region of the soundbite. Go to the Audio menu>Audio Beats, and choose either Adjust Beat Sensitivity... or Adjust Beat Detection... Either selection will open a window with a slider that will adjust the currently enabled audio beats. It is also possible to manually enable or disable individual audio beats with the Mute tool.

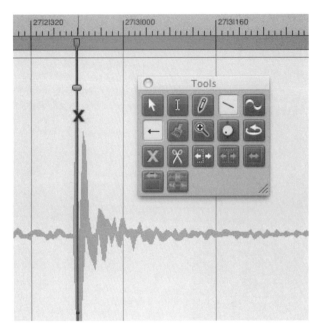

Figure 4.102

Quantizing Phase-Related Audio Tracks

When multiple tracks of audio are recorded that include common signals, those tracks are phase related. For example, it is a common technique to record a drumset with multiple microphones. The audio within the multiple drum tracks is phase related.

Digital Performer examines soundbites and looks for beat transients. From this information DP creates a beat map for each soundbite. With phase-related audio tracks, it is possible that the found beats will not be in identical positions in each of the audio tracks. For example, with the multiple drum tracks, the snare will be later in the in the overhead mics than it is in the direct mic.

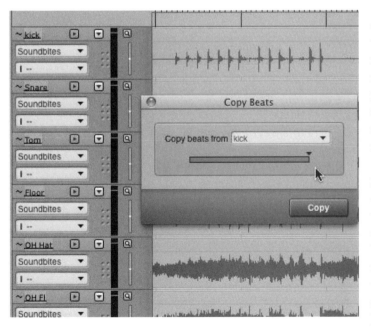

When audio beats are quantized, the quantization is based on the found beats within the soundbite. If DP quantizes the beats in phase-related tracks based on the beat map in each of those soundbites, there is a strong possibility that the tracks will be changed in a way that they are no longer in phase with each other. This can create serious problems in the mix.

The solution for this is to to use a beat map from one soundbite to do the same quantization for every other phase-related track. For example, with the multitrack drums, the snare track could be used as the beat map to quantize all the drums. The beat map from the snare soundbite can be copied to each of the other drum soundbites. Display all the phase-related tracks in the Sequence Editor window. Go to the Audio menu>Audio

Figure 4.103

Beats>Copy Beats... The Copy Beats window will open and will allow selection of the master track.

There is also a sensitivity slider that can vary the density of the copied beats. Drag the slider all the way to the right to copy all beats. Press the Copy button. The beats from the selected track will be copied to the other visible tracks in the Sequence Editor window. Now when audio beat quantization is done to these tracks, it will be done identically to each track, and therefore the tracks will retain their phase alignment.

Groove Quantization

Groove quantization is the process of creating and using a quantize template that is based on a performance, as opposed to the sequence grid. Groove quantization is an excellent way to capture the feel of one track and apply that feel to other tracks.

To create a groove quantize template, select a region of data and choose Create Groove... from the Region menu. The Create Groove window will open to allow naming and saving of the groove. The Create Groove window also allows specification of the beat division of the groove quantize template, as well as the meter. The groove quantize template is still based around the tempo and barlines of the DP sequence.

Once a groove quantize template has been created, it will be available in the Groove Quantize window, as well as the MIDI Groove Quantize plug-in. Select the data to be quantized and choose Groove Quantize... from the Region menu. The Groove Quantize window will open.

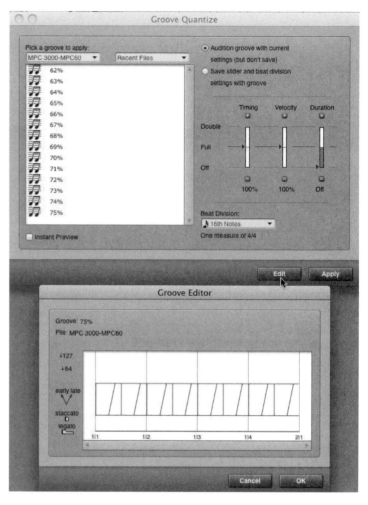

Figure 4.104

The Groove Quantize window allows editing of the selected groove template. The Groove Quantize window has parameters to control the amount of change that is applied to timing, velocities, and note durations.

Working With Loops

A loop is a section of of audio and/or MIDI that plays in a repeating pattern. Digital Performer provides the tools to create and manipulate loops, including tempo matching and beat slicing.

Playback Loops

A playback loop is a timeline selection within a sequence that repeats when in play or record mode. The start and end times in the control panel designate the loop points. The playback loop is engaged with the Memory Cycle button.

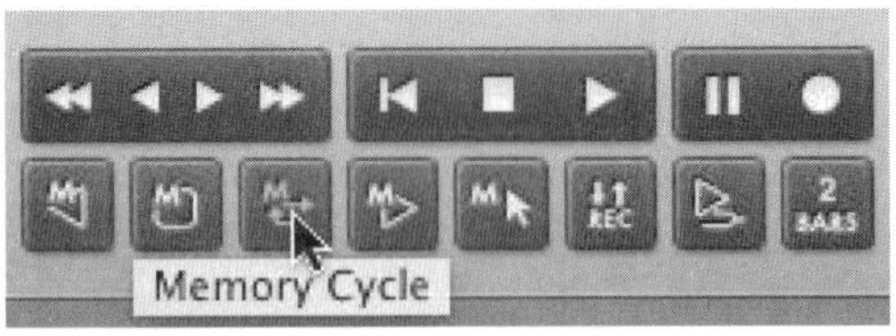

Figure 4.105

Different start and end times can be saved and recalled via the Memory menu in the Control Panel window.

Figure 4.106

The Link Selection to Memory button can be useful for changing loop points by dragging to select in the timeline ruler.

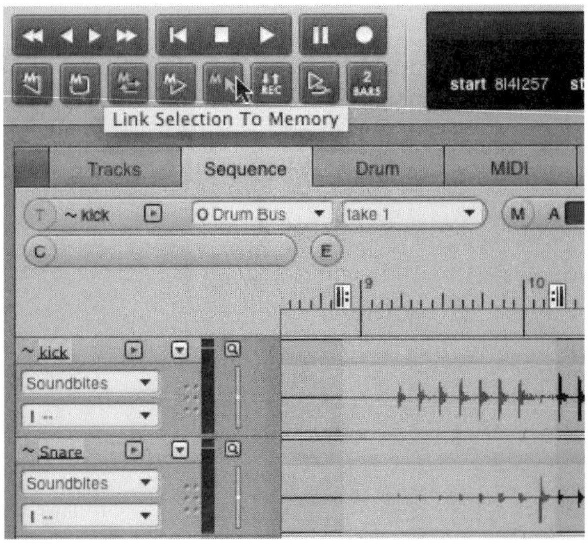

Figure 4.107

Track Loops

A track loop is a section of audio or MIDI data that is repeated in the track. There are two ways to loop data in DP. Digital Performer has a loop tool that allows a region of data to be selected and repeated a specified number of times. MIDI and audio data can also be looped by copying and pasting it back into the track.

The Loop tool works in the Sequence Editor window, MIDI Editor window, and Drum Editor window. Display the track to be looped and choose the Loop tool from the Tool palette. Drag in the track over the data to be looped. To make an exact beat-based selection, enable the Edit Grid button.

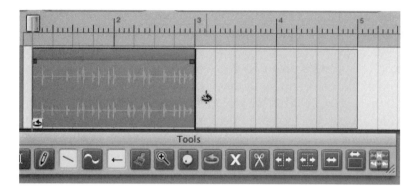

Figure 4.108

Initially, the loop will be set for a single repeat. Click on the loop icon to display the event information about that loop. The number of repeats can then be specified.

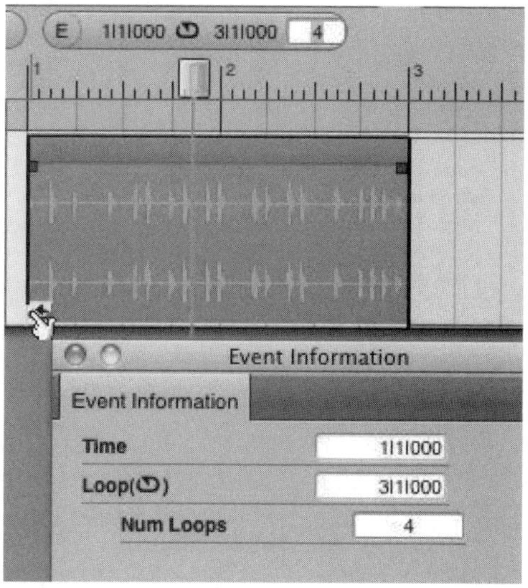

The other method to create track loops is to copy and paste data back into the track by a specified number of times. The difference between this technique and using the loop tool is that copied data can be edited at any point without affecting other portions of the loop.

To copy and loop audio or MIDI data, make a selection in any edit window. Make sure the selection boundaries are exactly where the start and end times of the loop should be. Use the edit grid to make a precise selection. Go to the Edit menu and choose Repeat... The Repeat window will open with choices for how many repeats and whether the repeated data will be pasted, merged, or spliced back into the track.

Choosing the splice option will move any current data in the track further to the right to accommodate the selected and repeated data.

Figure 4.109

Audio Loop Files

It s a common technique to loop audio files within a sequence. The content of the audio file may be rhythmically related to the loop length. Therefore

Figure 4.110

the length of the loop will determine the tempo of the audio. Digital Performer can time-stretch or compress an audio file to change its length. This will change the tempo of the audio loop. DP can automatically match the tempo of audio loops to the current sequence tempo.

Matching Loop Tempo

Digital audio files can contain tempo information. Many commercially available audio loop files include embedded tempo information. Digital Performer can read that tempo information, and can use it to match the audio loop tempo to the sequence tempo.

Drag an audio loop into a track in DP. The loop may have already been edited to exact beat boundaries. If so, and if there is tempo information embedded in the loop, select the soundbite in the track and go to the Audio menu>Adjust Soundbite to Sequence Tempo. If there is embedded tempo information in the original file, DP will make a new audio file that matches the current sequence tempo.

Digital Performer can be set to automatically change the length of audio files to match the current sequence tempo. The preferences are available under Automatic Conversions.

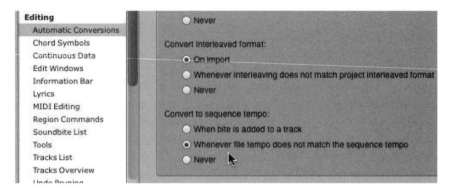

Figure 4.111

It is possible to manually time stretch audio: the left or right edges of a soundbite can be dragged in the Sequence Editor window. To make a grid-based edit, engage the Edit Grid button and hold down the Command button when stretching the audio.

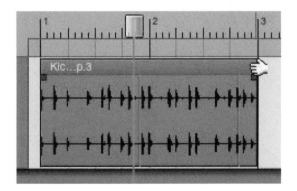

Figure 4.112

Tempo information can be embedded into an audio file by selecting the soundbite and going to the Audio menu>Copy Sequence Tempo to Soundbite. This will embed the current DP sequence tempo, including any tempo changes, into the selected soundbites.

Tempo information can be embedded into audio by selecting soundbites and going to the Audio menu>Soundbite Tempo>Set Soundbite Tempo. The Set Soundbite Tempo window allows tempo to be defined by BPM or beat and bar length.

Creating and Editing Loops

Audio can be cut and edge-edited to define start and end times of a loop. To check that an edit point is correct, Option/Alt+Drag the edited soundbite to create a copy.

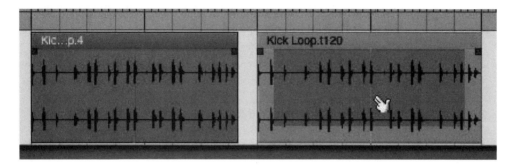

Figure 4.113

Control-Drag the copied soundbite toward the original soundbite. The copied soundbite will be "thrown" to the left and will butt up to the end of the original soundbite.

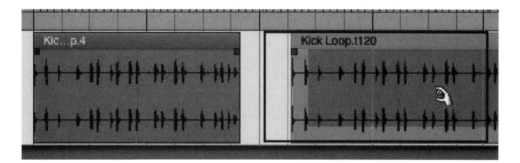

Figure 4.114

Play the sequence and listen to the abutted soundbites. If the edit between the soundbites is smooth, the soundbite is the correct length. If the edit is not smooth, delete the copied soundbite, edge-edit the original soundbite, and make a new copy to check the loop length.

A soundbite can be cut up into smaller soundbites that can be used as loop elements. Cut points can be based on the sequence grid or on audio beats within the soundbite. Select a snap resolution and choose the Scissors tool from the tool palette. Any cut made to the audio will be based on the selected grid resolution. Hold down the Option/Alt key and drag the Scissors tool over the soundbite to create multiple cuts based on the snap resolution.

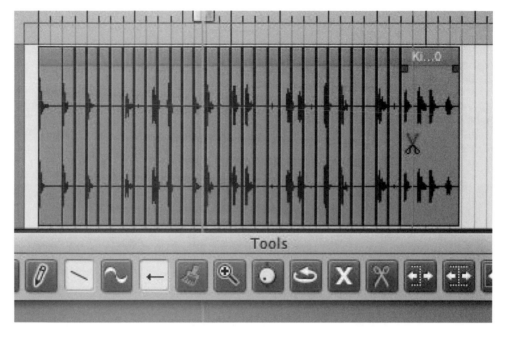

Figure 4.115

The individual beat-based soundbites may now be quantized and edited to create new loops.

Rendering Audio

Digital Performer can create new audio files based the contents of audio tracks and output of virtual instruments. Rendering is an automated process that records the output of audio and instrument tracks. There are several options for rendering audio within DP.

Freeze Selected Tracks

Freeze Selected Tracks is a real-time process that records the output of one or more tracks into a new audio track. Freeze can be used to render the live output of virtual instruments. Freeze can be used to render the output of individual audio tracks, including all edits, automation and plug-ins.

To freeze audio tracks, select one or more audio tracks and choose Freeze Selected Tracks from the Audio menu. The outputs of each selected track will be recorded to new audio tracks. This will print any edits, crossfades, automation, and plug-ins for each track.

To freeze virtual instruments, select the instrument track and any associated MIDI tracks. If multiple instrument tracks are selected, each instrument will be rendered to a separate new audio track. Freeze is a region-based selection, so the time range of the selected tracks is what will get printed as new audio.

Merge Soundbites

Merge soundbites creates new audio based on a selection within an audio track. The new audio will replace any audio in the track within the selection. The merged audio will include any soundbite gain changes, pitch automation, and crossfades. Merge soundbites does not include track automation or plug-ins. Merge soundbites is an efficient way to consolidate audio for multiple tracks for export to another DAW. Multiple tracks can be selected and merged with a single command.

Bounce To Disk

Bounce to disk creates new mono, stereo, or multichannel audio based on a selection of tracks. Bounce to disk can also create a movie file or an audio CD.

Bounce to disk includes edits, crossfades, automation, and plug-ins. Bounce to disk includes live output of VIs.

Bounce to disk can be used to render final mix files. Bounce to disk can also be used to render submixes of tracks. The bounce to disk function provides options to export the bounced file back into the Soundbites window, or even back into a new track in the sequence. Select a region of tracks and choose Bounce to Disk... from the File menu. The Bounce to Disk window will open, providing all the bounce options.

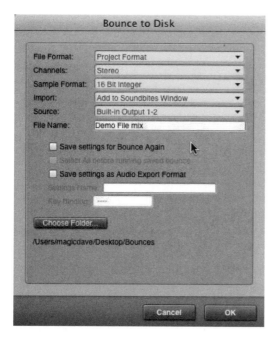

Figure 4.116

Surround Sound

Digital Performer has powerful features for working with surround-sound audio. DP supports Quad, LCRS, 5.1, 6.1, 7.1, and 10.2 channel formats. DP features surround audio tracks, buses, aux tracks, and master faders. DP ships with surround-sound compatible plug-ins.

File Formats

Mono, stereo, and surround audio tracks can all be part of a surround mix. A surround audio track is an audio track with more than two channels of audio. When audio is created in a surround format, the multichannel audio can be contained in a single interleaved audio file, or can be split into separate audio files that represent each channel of the surround configuration.

Digital Performer does not encode or decode DTS or other formats of compressed surround audio. Typically, file compression is done as part of the DVD mastering process.

Monitor Setup

In order to work with multichannel audio, there must be a monitor speaker for each channel. That means for a 5.1 monitoring setup, there will be five standard monitor speakers and a subwoofer. For each speaker in the surround monitor system, there must be an available output on the audio interface. For example, a 7.1 monitor system requires a total of eight discrete outputs from the audio interface.

One of the biggest challenges of mixing surround audio is having an accurate monitor system. Not only must the studio monitor system be set up correctly, but also the listeners' monitors must also be set up correctly. For example, if the horn section is mixed to the back speakers in a 5.1 system, but the listener hasn't hooked up their back speakers, the horns will be missing on playback!

If the mix engineer is confident that the surround mix will be played back on a correctly configured monitor system, they may be more creative and adventurous with the mix. In many cases commercial surround mixes are quite conservative, specifically because of the risk of incorrectly set monitor speakers.

Bundles

Bundles are critical to working with surround sound in DP. Bundles are used for input, output, and internal bussing of surround signals.

In order to monitor surround output from DP, there must be at least one output bundle that is set to the surround format and assigned to corresponding outputs on the audio interface. The individual surround output channels are labeled in the output bundle, and can be dragged to any available outputs on the audio interface. This allows the output of DP to be configured to match the output wiring from the audio interface to the speakers.

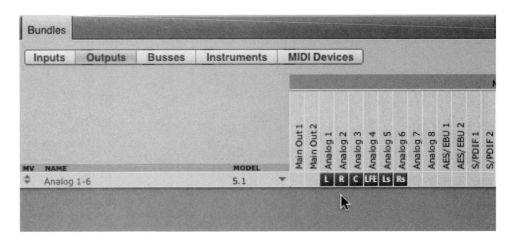

Figure 4.117

Input bundles are required in order to record any audio signal into DP. In order to record into a surround audio track, there must be an available input bundle with the corresponding number of channels. Like output bundles, the channels of an input bundle can be dragged to assign to any available inputs on the audio interface. In this example, a four-channel LCRS input bundle has been created and assigned to the first four inputs of the 896mk3 audio interface.

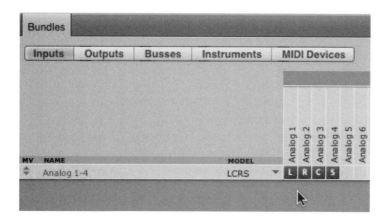

Figure 4.118

Buses are used for internal routing of audio in DP. For example, six mono drum tracks are assigned to a 5.1 bus. The 5.1 bus is assigned to the input of an aux track. The output of the aux track is assigned to a 5.1 output bundle. The aux track now functions as a 5.1 submix of the drum tracks.

Figure 4.119

Tracks

An audio track can be assigned to an output or bus bundle that has the same or a greater number of output channels. For example, a mono audio track can be assigned to a mono, stereo, or surround output or bus. A stereo audio track can be assigned to a stereo or surround output or bus, but it can not be assigned to a mono output. When a mono or stereo track is assigned to a surround output or bus bundle, it then has surround output capability.

It is possible for a surround mix to consist of primarily mono and/or stereo audio tracks that are then mixed to a surround output. Certainly a surround mix may contain any combination of mono, stereo, and surround tracks.

Aux tracks can have surround inputs and outputs. It is possible to have a mono or stereo input to an aux track, and have the output of the aux track set to a surround output.

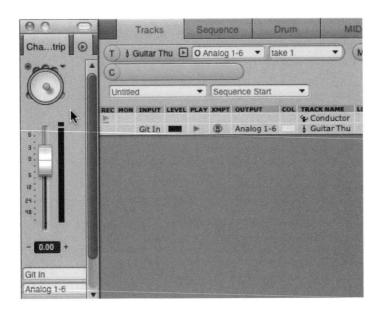

Figure 4.120

Master faders can be assigned to surround outputs or buses. Master faders can be used to downmix a surround mix to mono or stereo. A master fader assigned to a surround bus or output provides a mini mixer to control the individual channels passing through. In the Mixer window click on the button to the upper left of the fold-down menu above the fader.

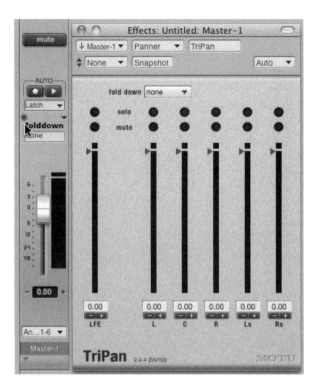

Figure 4.121

Panners

Panners are displayed in the Mixing Board window. Panners can be show or hidden via the Mixing Board window mini menu. Panners can also be controlled via automation in edit windows.

Panners are assigned to audio tracks depending on the output assignment of an audio track. If a mono audio track is assigned to a mono output, no panner is displayed in the mixer. If a mono or stereo audio track is assigned to a stereo output, a stereo panner appears in the mixer. If an audio track is assigned to a surround output or bus, a surround panner is automatically created for that track in the mixer. In the following graphic, three mono audio tracks are assigned to a mono, stereo, and surround output.

Surround panners are more sophisticated than mono or stereo panners. Therefore basic pan controls are displayed in the mixer, but additional controls are available in an expanded panner window. To open the panner window, click on the small dot in the upper left of the mixer panner.

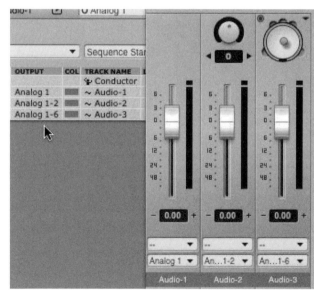

Figure 4.122

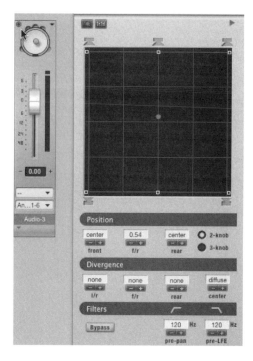

Figure 4.123

The red dot in the panner window represents the source signal in the surround mix.
There is an additional arrow button that further opens the panner window to reveal
VU meters and additional controls. Note that LFE (sub-woofer) volume is controlled
with a slider next to the output VU.

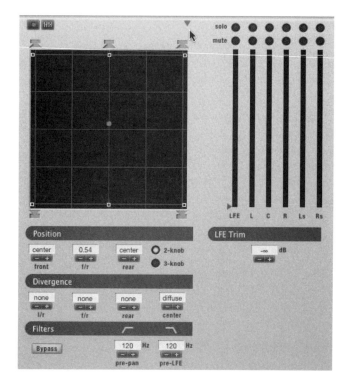

Figure 4.124

Output channels can be soloed or muted. For example, the center speaker output may be muted for music tracks in a 5.1 movie soundtrack. This leaves the center speaker open for dialog.

There are crossover controls for the LFE channel. There are controls for diffusion to adjacent channels. For example, in a 5.1 panner, setting center divergence to diffuse will allow a center panned signal to output to left, center, and right speakers. If the center divergence parameter is set to "Sharp," a center panned signal will only output through the center speaker.

In the upper left-hand corner of the panner window are two buttons. The right-hand button changes the panner view to a simple output mixer.

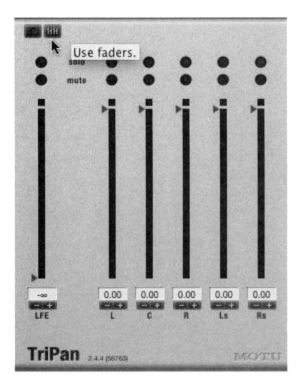

Figure 4.125

When a stereo source signal is assigned to a surround output, the panner provides five separate modes for handling the stereo signal within the surround output. The five modes are Balance, Mirror, Asymmetric, Parallel, and Mono. The modes are selectable via a pop-up menu in the bottom of the panner window.

Here are the five methods available to handle stereo signals in a surround output:

- Balance: When Balance mode is selected, moving the panner to the left attenuates the right side of the stereo input. Moving the panner to the right attenuates the left side of the stereo input. Left input is assigned to left output. Right input is assigned to right output.

- Mirror: In mirror mode, left and right signals are represented with separate panner icons.

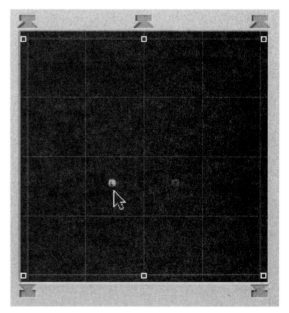

Figure 4.126

Left and right signals can be dragged closer together or further apart. Left and right can be reversed. The overall stereo input is always centered and can be brought to a center mono.

- Asymmetric: Three icons are displayed, representing left, right, and mix center of the stereo input. The stereo mix can be collapsed to the left or right of the surround output.

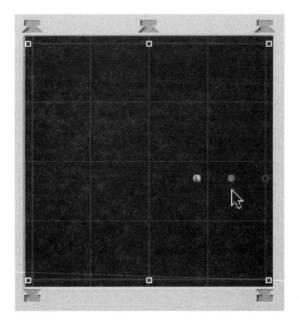

Figure 4.127

- Parallel: Three panner icons are displayed, representing left, right and center. The stereo mix can be moved left or right in the stereo mix. Left and right separation are always maintained.

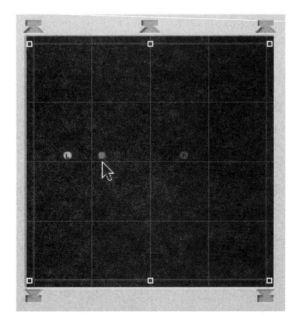

Figure 4.128

- Mono: In mono mode, the left and right input signals are combined and treated as a mono source into the surround output.

Digital Performer features four different types of surround panners. To change the surround panner type, click on the triangle pop-up menu in the upper right-hand corner of the panner in the mixer. It is also possible to change panner types by clicking on the pop-up menu in the panner window.

The default TriPan panner provides spatial control with divergence control over individual speakers.

In addition to the TriPanner, DP includes three other surround panner types:Arc Panner. This panner provides a radial grid for pan control.

Figure 4.129

n-Panner. This is similar to the TriPan, but without divergence controls.

Auralizer. The Auralizer provides doppler shift and relative ambience as part of the panner function

The surround panners in DP can be controlled via external joysticks. Digital Performer supports the standard USB Joystick controllers typically used for Mac and PC game control.

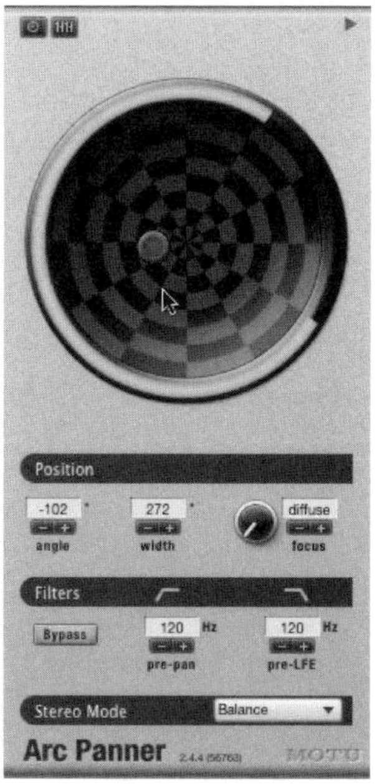

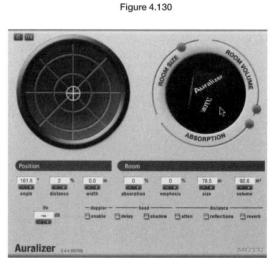

Figure 4.130

Mixing

As with stereo mixing, it is always a good idea to use a master fader on the final output of the mix. The master fader provides a way to monitor and control the overall mix volume. It is also possible to use specific surround effect plug-ins on the final output master fader.

Surround automation can be done from effects and panner windows, the Mixing Board window, and via graphic editor windows. It is possible to use a standard USB joystick controller for external control of the surround panners.

A surround mix may consist of mono, stereo, and surround source signals. Mono and stereo tracks can be placed in the surround field. Typically, an audio track recorded as a surround signal will be played back the same way it was recorded.

Figure 4.131

A properly set-up surround monitor system uses full-range speakers, and depending on the format, one or more low frequency speakers (subwoofers). In other words, the surround speakers should be able to handle a full frequency signal. The LFE channel is a special effects channel for specifically assigned low frequency signals. Each sound source in a surround mix has its own LFE send level. LFE output can be further handled with a master fader and Bass Manager plug-in.

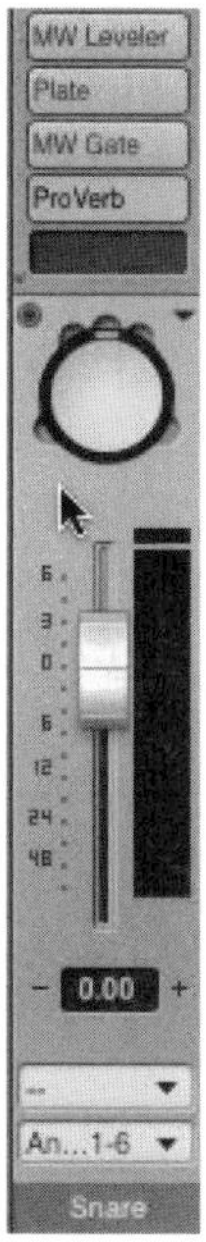

Figure 4.132

There are traditional techniques of mixing for surround, especially for movies. In a typical movie surround mix, the center speaker is reserved for dialog.

Surround Plug-Ins

When mono and stereo signals are mixed in surround, it is possible to use mono, stereo, or surround plug-in effects. For example, if a mono snare drum track is mixed into a surround output, the effect chain could be a mono to mono compressor, followed by a mono to stereo gated reverb, which is then further processed with a stereo to 5.1 reverb.

The Effects Chooser window displays the available channel format plug-ins for an insert.

The master fader can be an efficient place to manage the LFE channel and low frequency signal in a surround mix. The Bass Manager plug-in is a powerful tool for this job. Signals assigned to LFE channels from individual tracks can be redirected back into the surround speakers. Low frequency content from the general surround mix can be extended to the LFE channels. Individual signals can be muted or soloed. High-pass and low-pass crossover filter points can be set.

It is always a good idea to use a mastering limiter on the final insert of a master fader. The MW Limiter adapts to the number of channels assigned to the master fader. For example, on a 7.1 master fader, the MW Limiter provides separate level control for eight channels of output, including the LFE channel. LFE limiting can be linked or separated from the surround channel limiting. The MW Limiter also provides available bit quantization, dither, and noise shaping for final output mastering.

The Calibration plug-in is used to check speaker levels in a surround monitor system. The Calibration plug-in is typically placed on a master fader. The plug-in can generate noise, and has a mic input. The mic input can be use to check levels for each speaker. It is also possible to autocalibrate the outputs to compensate for speakers that cannot otherwise be externally calibrated. Ideally, the levels will match for each output channel when the noise signal is sent from the Calibration plug-in, through the monitor speakers, into a mic, and back into the plug-in.

Some effect plug-ins have multi-channel outputs for surround mixes. For example, the Delay plug-in provides a separate delay tap for each surround channel. A mono or stereo signal sent into a surround delay can be a dramatic effect. Be sure to check out the tempo synched delay presets.

Figure 4.133

Figure 4.134

Figure 4.135

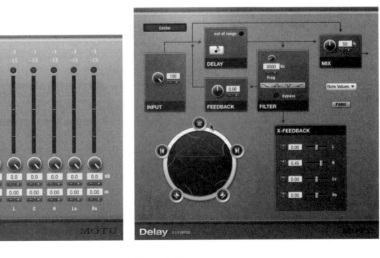

Figure 4.136

The ProVerb can provide surround output when multichannel impulse responses are used. The ProVerb ships with stock impulse response reverbs for multichannel output. With the stock multichannel reverb samples, it is possible to position the source signal within the surround reverb field. This can provide the most realistic surround ambience.

Modulation plug-ins such as Flanger, Tremolo, or Autopan can provide movement and spatial depth to any mono or stereo signal within a surround mix.

Some virtual instruments have the option to provide multichannel surround outputs. For example, the MOTU MachFive 3 sampler can provide mono, stereo, quad, 5.1, 6.1, or 7.1 output.

If a surround output instrument track is created, the output of the instrument track must be assigned to a surround bus or output. It is up to the instrument to route signal to its output channels. Some instrument sounds are designed specifically for surround output. Other "surround" sounds may include mono or stereo instruments that have some sort of multichannel effects processing on output.

One interesting use of a surround instrument output could be for live triggering of a surround mix playback from a sampler. A complete mixed section of surround audio is loaded into a sampler, and can then be triggered on the fly via MIDI input trigger. This can be useful in a live theatre production.

Bounce to Disk in Surround

When a surround mix is selected for bounce to disk, the bounce options include interleaved or de-interleaved surround, stereo, or mono. The choice of which option to use is based on where the mix will go next. For example, DVD Studio Pro from Apple is used for DVD mastering. DVD Studio Pro includes a utility called APAC, which is used to create encoded surround audio tracks for DVDs. APAC is set up to accept separate stems for each channel of the surround mix. If the purpose of the surround bounce in DP is to export the mix to APAC, the best choice for bouncing is to de-interleaved AIFF. This will create separate audio files for each channel of the mix, which can then be imported into the APAC utility.

It is possible to bounce a surround audio track into a movie file. If there is a movie in DP, the surround mix will be embedded when the movie and mix are selected and bounced. The surround mix will not be an encoded DTS signal. It will be a multichannel audio track which can play back through a properly configured computer system.

Mastering

Mastering is the process of creating a finished audio recording that is ready for delivery in different formats. Individual recordings may be mastered. A collection of recordings can be assembled as a compilation or album. Mastered audio mixes can be distributed in many formats, including digital audio files, vinyl records, CDs, and DVDs.

Audio mastering, like songwriting or playing an instrument, is a craft. A mastering engineer requires some basic tools to do the job, but there is no substitute for skill and experience. Most artists and engineers will admit that the learning never stops.

Digital Performer has a complete set of tools for audio mastering. DP can create a variety of digital audio formats, including burning CDs and exporting as a movie file. There are many techniques that can be used in the mastering process. DP provides many options.

Bounce to Disk Versus Real-time Recording

There are two basic ways to render a mastered audio file from DP. A mastered file can be generated via Bounce to disk, or doing a real-time recording. Digital Performer can also generate audio files via export or merging soundbites. The difference is that exporting and merging do not include any plug-ins or automation. Bounce to disk and real-time recording can create finished audio files that include edits, crossfades, plug-ins, and automation.

To bounce a multitrack sequence to a single audio file, select the tracks and duration desired and choose Bounce to Disk from the DP File menu. The Bounce to Disk window will open, providing all the various file output options. If the bit depth of the multitrack sequence is set to 24- or 32-bit resolution, the Bounce to Disk window provides a convenient way to create a 16-bit audio file with no further conversion. The Bounce to Disk window does not offer any type of sample rate conversion. If the final mastered audio file needs to be at a different sample rate than the multitrack sequence, the sample rate conversion will have to be done as a secondary step after the bounce.

Bounce to disk can include live virtual instruments. In other words, if there are virtual instruments in the project, they do not need to be recorded to audio tracks before the bounce process. The virtual instrument playback will be included in the bounce.

Bounce to disk is a faster than real-time process. If a sequence is four minutes long, it won't take four minutes to create a bounce file. How long the bounce takes is based on the power of the computer and complexity of the sequence. Digital Performer will take as long as it needs to render all of the mix data into the bounce file. In many situations, the bounce can happen quickly.

Real-time recording produces the same result as bounce to disk. Real-time recording is the process of setting up a stereo or surround mix track, and recording the multitrack playback into that track. Because this is a real-time process, a four-minute mix will take four minutes to record. The most common reason for doing a real-time recording is that the recording includes elements that are outside the DP sequence. For example, if the DP sequence playback is sent out through the audio interface, through external processing gear, and then back into the computer for re-recording, that will require a real-time recording of the final mix file.

Here is a sequence set up for bounce to disk. The tracks are assigned to the main monitor output and there is a master fader assigned to that output.

INPUT	LEVEL	PLAY	XMPT	OUTPUT	TAKE	COL	TRACK NAME	E
					1		Conductor	
	▬	►	Ⓢ	Main Out 1-2	1	▬	Master	
Verb Bus	▬	►	Ⓢ	Main Out 1-2	1		Verb Ret	
Echo Bus	▬	►	Ⓢ	Main Out 1-2	1		Echo Ret	
Drum Bus	▬	►	Ⓢ	Main Out 1-2	1	▬	Drum Sub	
--	▬	►		Drum Bus	1		kick	
--	▬	►		Drum Bus	1		Snare	
--	▬	►		Drum Bus	1		Tom	
--	▬	►		Drum Bus	1		Floor	
--	▬	►		Drum Bus	1		OH Hat	
--	▬	►		Drum Bus	1		OH Fl	
--	▬	►		Main Out 1-2	1	▬	Bass	
--	▬	►		Main Out 1-2	1		Git	

Figure 4.137

Here is the same sequence set up for real-time recording. Note that the track outputs have been assigned to a bus pair, and the bus is assigned to the input of the mix record track. The master fader has been reassigned to the bus pair.

K	REC	MON	INPUT	LEVEL	PLAY	XMPT	OUTPUT	TAKE	COL	TRACK NAME	ENA	PAT
	▶							1		🐝 Conductor		
	▶	◀	bus 1-2	▬	▶		Main Out 1-2	1	▬	≈ Mix Track	●	
				▬	▶	Ⓢ	bus 1-2	1	▬	⊣ Master		
			Verb Bus	▬	▶	Ⓢ	bus 1-2	1		◊ Verb Ret	●	
			Echo Bus	▬	▶	Ⓢ	bus 1-2	1		◊ Echo Ret	●	
			Drum Bus	▬	▶	Ⓢ	bus 1-2	1	▬	◊ Drum Sub	●	
			··	▬	▶		Drum Bus	1		~ kick	●	
			··	▬	▶		Drum Bus	1		~ Snare	●	
			··	▬	▶		Drum Bus	1		~ Tom	●	
			··	▬	▶		Drum Bus	1		~ Floor	●	
			··	▬	▶		Drum Bus	1		~ OH Hat	●	
			··	▬	▶		Drum Bus	1		~ OH Fl	●	
			··	▬	▶		bus 1-2	1	▬	~ Bass	●	
			··	▬	▶		bus 1-2	1	▬	~ Git	●	

Figure 4.138

Here is a sequence that is set up to do a real-time record based on sending the audio out through external processing gear and back into the computer. Note that the sequence is set up as if doing a bounce to disk, but a mix record track has been created to capture the returning signal. It is important to make sure that the output of the mix track does not patch back through to the output while recording. This will cause a feedback loop. In this example, the sequence tracks are assigned to outputs 3 and 4 on the audio interface. Outputs 3 and 4 go to the input of the external effects processor. The effects processor returns its signals to inputs 3 and 4 on the interface. The final mix track records the externally processed signal from inputs 3 and 4, and its output assignment is the main monitor outputs.

K	REC	MON	INPUT	LEVEL	PLAY	XMPT	OUTPUT	TAKE	COL	TRACK NAME	
	▶							1		🐝 Conductor	
	▶	◀	Analog 3-4	▬	▶		Main Out 1-2	1	▬	≈ Mix Track	
				▬	▶	Ⓢ	Analog 3-4	1	▬	⊣ Master	
			Verb Bus	▬	▶	Ⓢ	Analog 3-4	1		◊ Verb Ret	
			Echo Bus	▬	▶	Ⓢ	Analog 3-4	1		◊ Echo Ret	
			Drum Bus	▬	▶	Ⓢ	Analog 3-4	1	▬	◊ Drum Sub	
			··	▬	▶		Drum Bus	1		~ kick	
			··	▬	▶		Drum Bus	1		~ Snare	
			··	▬	▶		Drum Bus	1		~ Tom	
			··	▬	▶		Drum Bus	1		~ Floor	
			··	▬	▶		Drum Bus	1		~ OH Hat	
			··	▬	▶		Drum Bus	1		~ OH Fl	
			··	▬	▶		Analog 3-4	1	▬	~ Bass	
			··	▬	▶		Analog 3-4	1	▬	~ Git	

Figure 4.139

Mastering Directly from Multitrack Sequences
A typical workflow is that a multitrack mix is bounced or recorded to a two-track (or surround) audio file, and that file is then further processed in a final mastering stage. It is also possible to create a completely mastered audio file directly from the multitrack sequence.

There are advantages and disadvantages to mastering directly from the multitrack sequence. Part of the mastering process may involve comparing different recordings that belong to the same project. When a project is mastered, it is simple to line up the separate recordings and quickly switch between them to compare tone and volume. Part of the mastering process may include setting the space between recordings, including creating crossfades. In these situations it is usually more efficient to work with stereo or surround audio files as opposed to multitrack sequences.

If master files are created from multitrack sequences, any changes to the master are made directly in the sequence. For example, if during the final mastering of the mix it turns out that a kick drum is too loud, it is a simple thing to turn the kick drum down in the mix, and then continue with the mastering process. The two primary advantages of mastering directly from the multitrack sequence are the time saved and the ability to make mix changes during the mastering process.

Mastering Mix Files

The most common technique for mastering is to work with mono, stereo, or surround mix files that have been delivered from the mix engineer. The raw mix file may be processed with plug-ins and automation during the mastering process. Edits and fades may be applied. If the mastering project includes multiple recordings, the raw mix files can be aligned for proper spacing between tracks on a CD or vinyl record. Digital Performer makes it easy to set up a mastering template for mix files.

It is common for raw mix files to be a higher resolution than the final mastered output. A typical work flow is to create 24-bit mix files, which are converted to 16-bit files during the mastering process. The mastering process may also include sample rate conversion. To maintain maximum fidelity, it is useful to keep the project at high resolution right up to the final mastering stage. For example, a mix may be rendered at 96 kHz, 24-bit resolution. That high-resolution file may then be mastered to a 44.1 kHz, 16-bit file for CD output. The mix could also be rendered to compressed file formats such as MP3 or AAC. Digital Performer can work with high-resolution source files, and output to a wide range of file formats and resolutions.

Some record labels actually require that final masters are delivered at high-resolution formats. This preserves the master at the higher resolution, while providing the option to reduce the master to lower resolutions as required.

Mastering Template

The purpose of the mastering template is to provide a layout within DP that allows the engineer to assemble a mix or multiple mixes into a final product. A mastering template may contain a single audio track, or it may consist of multiple audio tracks and a master fader. The DP sequence timeline can be used to create a layout for separate mixes for assembly to a CD or movie soundtrack.

There are two basic ways to set up DP for mastering audio mix files. Mix files can be placed on separate audio tracks in a DP sequence. The alternative is to use a single audio track for all mixes. The advantage of working with multiple audio tracks is that edits and plug-in changes made in one track do not disturb other tracks. In other situations, it may make more sense to have a single audio track that represents the final master, with automation used for any changes. The choice may end up being a personal preference of the engineer.

If multiple audio tracks are used to create a master, it is usually a good idea to use a master fader. The master fader provides a single point to check levels and and overall tone. Common processing effects can be applied to multiple tracks via a single master fader. For example, separate EQs may be applied to individual mixes, and a common mastering limiter may be applied via a master fader.

Automation can be used to change settings between or within mixes. Automation can be used for mix levels, as well as for plug-in parameters.

In this graphic, DP is set up for mastering with a single stereo audio track:

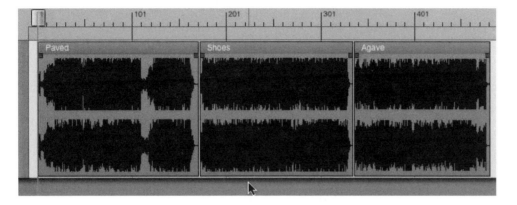

Figure 4.140

In this graphic, DP is set up for mastering with multiple audio tracks and a master fader:

Figure 4.141

CD Layout

The process of creating a mastered audio CD involves setting the space between tracks, including any fades or crossfades. It is possible to create CD track index points within a piece of music. This is a common technique with classical music as well as live recordings. Track index points may be created for different movements within a piece of music. Track index points may be created in live recordings, without interrupting the crowd sounds between songs.

- Start by placing each mix file in the appropriate position on the DP timeline. This can be done with a single audio track or multiple audio tracks. Mix files can be dragged from the desktop or Soundbites window into any audio track editing window. If the mix files are dragged into the Sequence Editor window, they can be manually placed in position. If mix files are dragged into the Event Edit list, they will automatically be placed one after another, with no space between the files. Dragging mix files into the Event Edit list can be a fast way of getting all the mix files into a single track, in order, and butted up against each other.

Figure 4.142

- The first mix file will start exactly at the beginning of the sequence. If there is any empty space at the beginning of the mix file, this can be trimmed. If there is any ambient noise at the start of the mix file, it may be desirable to create a fade-in for the mix. This can be done with track automation or a soundbite fade.
- At the end of the first mix file, it may be desirable to create a fade-out, or even a crossfade. After the end of the first track, position the next audio file on the sequence timeline so the desired space exists between the end of track 1 and the beginning of track 2. When the CD is created, the correct amount of space will be part of the end of track 1. This allows the correct spacing between the tracks when they are listened to in sequence. If track 2 is called up, it will start exactly at the beginning of its audio.
- Markers can be placed to indicate track index points within mixes.
- Once the correct spacing and fades are created, the sequence should represent what will happen when the CD is played from beginning to end. Any required processing or automation is also done, so that when listening to the sequence, what is played back is exactly what the final CD will sound like.
- Individual tracks can now be bounced to finished audio files. The mastered audio files can be archived, re-rendered to compressed file formats, or burned to an audio CD using any software that has that capability.
- It is also possible to select the entire sequence and burn directly to an audio CD from within DP. Burn Audio CD is a file format option in the Bounce to Disk window. Because audio CDs are 44.1 KHz sample rate, Burn Audio CD will only be available if the project format sample rate is set to 44.1 KHz. Burn Audio CD provides the option for CD track index points to be created based on soundbite start times, markers, or both.

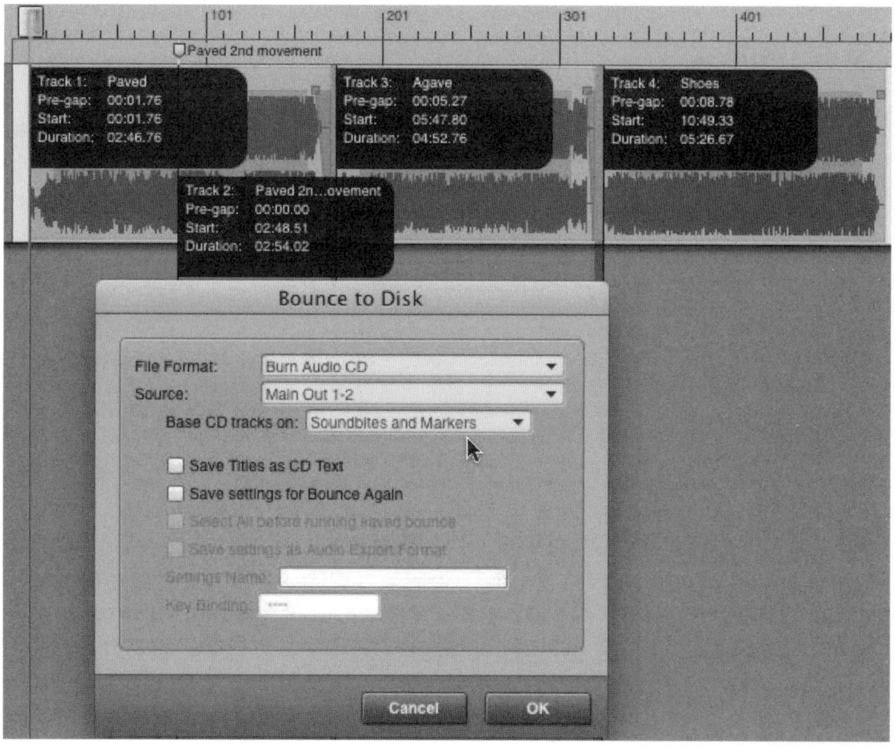

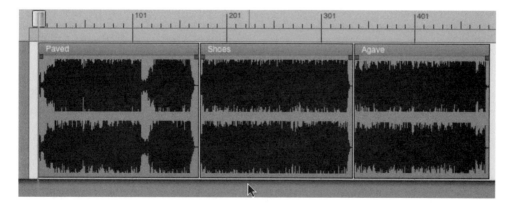

Figure 4.143

- A third technique is to select the entire sequence, including all tracks, and do a single bounce to disk. This will create a single audio file that contains all the tracks, including the spacing between the tracks. In the Bounce to disk window, choose the Import option to Add to Sequence. The bounced file will now show up in a new track in the sequence, along with the original mix files.

Figure 4.144

- Use the Scissors tool to make cuts exactly where the CD track index points will be. Rename each newly created soundbite to represent the track name.

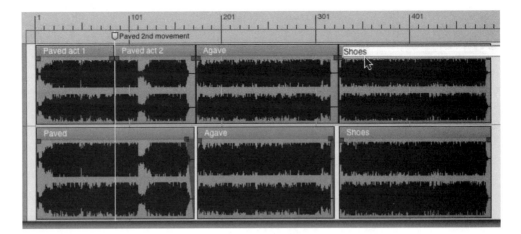

Figure 4.145

- Go to the Soundbites window. The newly created and named soundbites will be listed. These soundbites can now be selected and exported as separate audio files. One advantage of this technique is that if the original mixes are not at a 44.1 kHz sample rate, the export process is a convenient place to convert the files to 44.1 kHz for burning to an audio CD.

Audio Processing

The most common processes done in mastering include EQ, dynamics control, bit quantization, and dithering. Additional processing may be done with multiband compressors, mid-side processors, reverbs, or any other sonic tool required to get the finished sound of the master.

The bottom line of mastering is that the finished product must be high-enough quality for delivery. That means the audio must sound good on different monitor speakers. The levels of the mastered audio must be competitive with other mastered audio in the same genre. For example, when mastering a hip hop track, the final master must be able to played before or after other commercial hip hop tracks and have similar level, frequency response, and dynamics.

Bit Depth Quantization, Dithering, and Noise-Shaping

An audio sample is described by a number of binary bits. The number of bits in the sample is referred to as the Bit Depth. The more bits that are in a sample, the higher the resolution of the available dynamic range. For example, a 16-bit sample can describe a dynamic range of 96 dB. A 24-bit sample can describe a theoretical dynamic range of 144 dB. Internally, DP uses 32 and 64-bit floating-point resolution, which provides a theoretical dynamic range of over 1500 dB. Floating-point resolution means that the number represented by the sample can have a movable decimal point. Fixed-integer resolution means there is no available decimal point in the number represented by the sample.

It is generally accepted that a healthy human ear has an effective dynamic range of around 120 dB. For adults, and anybody with hearing damage, that number can be significantly lower. Mastered audio can have a great deal of dynamic range, such as a movie soundtrack. Mastered audio may also have relatively little dynamic range, such as pop music that is created specifically to sound as loud as possible compared with other mixes.

Typically audio production is done at higher resolutions than what the finished product needs to be. This preserves fidelity through the production process and provides a better quality final output, even at the lower resolution.

Therefore a common part of the mastering process is bit-depth reduction. Bit depth is reduced from the 32- and 64-bit floating point resolution in DP, to 24- or 16-bit fixed integer resolution. The process of bit-depth reduction discards audio information, so this process must be done in a way that does as little damage to the audio as possible.

The first step of bit-depth reduction is quantization. Quantization is the rounding up of a larger number to a smaller number. For example, the three-digit number 7.99 can be rounded up to the single-digit number 8. When a 24-bit sample is quantized to become a 16-bit sample, the last 8 bits of the 24-bit sample are rounded up into the bottom bits of the remaining 16-bit sample. The content of the resulting smaller sample is very close to the original content of the larger sample. However, there is a certain amount of inaccuracy in the bottom bits of the smaller sample. This is called quantization error. The sonic result of quantization error is a metallic sounding distortion at low signal levels.

In order to reduce the quantization error distortion, engineers have developed a process called dithering. Dithering is the randomization of the bottom bits of the sample. By randomizing the bottom bits of the sample, noise is created that masks the quantization distortion.

The final step of quantization and dithering is noise shaping. Noise shaping is an option within the dither process. Noise shaping biases the randomization of the bottom bits so that the resulting noise has a frequency bias. The application of noise shaping to dithering is a preference of the mastering engineer, and is typically based on the frequency content of the actual audio. For example, if a piece of music fades out with a high-pitched signal such as a flute, it is desirable to bias the dither noise to be in roughly the same range as the flute. Therefore the flute will mask the dither noise. Conversely, if the audio fades out with a low frequency signal, it may be desirable to have a dither noise that is bias towards lower frequencies.

It is important to note that quantization, dither, and noise shaping should only be applied once, at the very end of the signal chain in the master process.

Sample Rate Conversion

Sample rate is the number of audio samples per second. The sample rate represents double the audio frequency that can be represented with the digital audio file. For example, a sample rate of 44.1 kHz can describe up to 22 kHz of actual audio signal. Although it is generally recognized that the upper limit of human hearing is around 20 kHz, many audio engineers prefer to do production work at higher sample rates. There is a fair amount of controversy about how much sonic difference higher sample rates actually make. It is reasonable to say that the higher sample rates do provide more raw material for the production process, and many engineers feel that it does make a difference in the final output. If an artist or engineer is curious about the sonic difference of different sample rates, it's not difficult to do test recordings at different resolutions, and compare any perceived differences.

If the sample rate of the digital audio needs to be changed, this is done with a process called sample rate conversion. Sample rate conversion has nothing to do with bit depth, quantization, or dithering. Those are completely separate from the sample rate of the audio. Sample rate conversion is a DSP process where the software rebuilds the digital audio to represent the same sonic content at the lower rate. Sample rate conversion should not have any audible effect on the signal as long as the rate is not converted to below 44.1 kHz. If the sample rate is converted to lower than 44.1 kHz, that will begin to diminish the high frequency content of the audio. For example, audio with a sample rate of 20 kHz can not represent any frequency over 10 kHz.

It is a common misconception that sample rate conversion works better with even-numbered conversion. For example, audio can be recorded at 88.2 Hz, which is exactly double the sample rate of 44.1 kHz. However, if the sample rate conversion is done properly, there is no difference if the source material is 88.2 kHz or 96 kHz. The resulting 44.1 kHz file will be the same.

Digital Performer provides sample rate conversion as an export option. Audio export is available from the File menu and from the mini menu in the Soundbites window. One or more soundbites can be selected and exported, and during this process, they can be sample rate converted. The Export Selected Soundbites... item in the Soundbites window mini menu offers a series of options for the sample rate conversion.

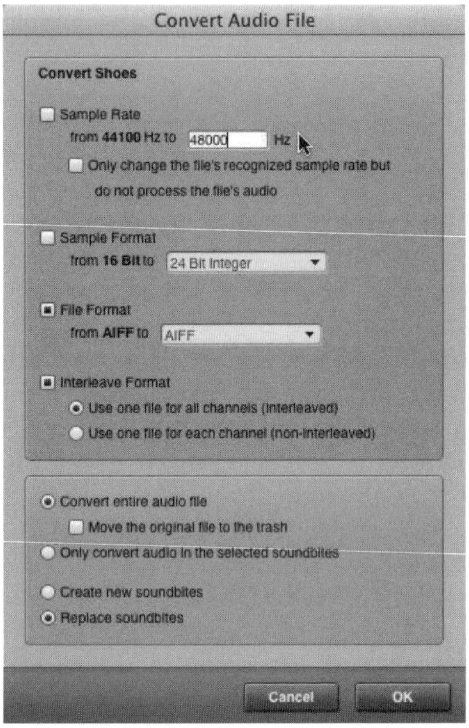

Figure 4.146

Sample rate conversion, if required, is usually done as the very last step in the mastering process.

MW Limiter Plug-In

Digital Performer includes the MW Limiter, which is a high-resolution mastering limiter. The MW Limiter provides dynamics control, precise metering, and functions for bit quantization, dithering, and noise shaping.

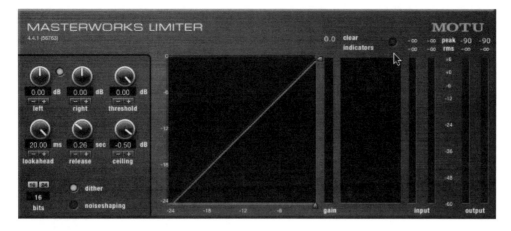

Figure 4.147

Figure 4.148

One of the most important plug-ins in the mastering process is the mastering limiter. The mastering limiter is used to ensure there will be no peaks that exceed maximum level and cause clipping. The mastering limiter is often used to raise the apparent gain of a mix. It is not uncommon to apply bit-depth quantization, dithering, and noise shaping with a mastering limiter as the final step of the audio mastering process.

Typically the mastering limiter is the last plug-in in the mastering effects chain. The mastering limiter may be placed on the bottom (last) insert of a master fader. No additional gain should be added after the mastering limiter. Therefore the master fader should either be set to unity gain, or the mastering limiter should be placed on a post-fader insert. By default, the inserts for a DP audio track are pre-fader. To make an insert post-fader, drag the handle up from the bottom of the insert list. A divider line will appear to indicate that any inserts below that point are post-fader.

One of the most important aspects of the MW Limiter are the meters on the right side of the plug-in window. There is a large graphic representation of playback level, with a handle to adjust the output ceiling. The MW Limiter is a "brick-wall limiter." That means it will absolutely not let an output signal exceed the specified ceiling. This is a form of insurance. The MW Limiter guarantees that the final output will not clip and therefore distort.

If playback exceeds the set ceiling, the next meter shows how much gain reduction had to be applied to keep the signal from exceeding the ceiling. There is a peak/hold indicator at the top of the gain reduction meter. This allows a mix to be played from start to finish, and the peak hold meter will indicate the largest amount of gain reduction that had to be done during playback. The peak indicator can be cleared by clicking the button to the right.

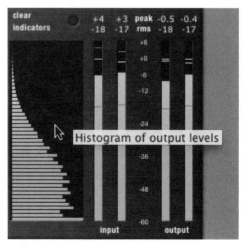

Figure 4.149

The next large graphic meter is a histogram. The histogram shows average signal level over time (since the last time the Clear Indicators button was pressed). For example, if the histogram shows a bias towards the bottom of the graph, that indicates a relatively low level of the mix over time.

To the right of the histogram are the input and output meters. Input level can be controlled with the knobs on the far left. The output meters represent the final output from the limiter. There are two sets of numbers above these meters. The peak indicator shows the highest amount of signal gain played back since the Clear Indicators button was last pressed. The RMS indicator describes the average signal level. This is a critical measurement.

The human ear perceives the volume of a mix based on average signal level, not transient peaks. A mix may have a great deal of dynamic range, with transients that do hit the maximum output gain of the limiter. However, if the average gain of the signal is low, the overall mix will not sound apparently loud.

It is possible to raise the average gain of a mix to increase the perceived loudness. If there are loud transients in the mix, increasing the average gain may require that the limiter attenuate the transient peaks. Dynamic range and perceived loudness are a preference of the artist and engineer. Some pop mixes are limited to the point of having little dynamic range so they sound loud. In some cases, it is not appropriate to squash the dynamic range of the audio. An overly limited recording can sound harsh and unnatural.

It can be educational to check the average levels of different commercially produced mixes. Drag an audio track from a commercial CD into a track in DP. Set up the MW Limiter on the track and play back. Because the mix is already mastered, the MW Limiter will not do any additional gain reduction. However, the MW Limiter will show the average signal level of the track. In order for a mix mastered in DP to have the same apparent loudness as the commercial mix, it will need to have the same average signal level.

In the process of raising the average level of the mix, it may be required that the limiter do significant attenuation to the signal. This can be a problem. For example, if the kick drum is too loud in the mix, compressing the dynamic range of the mix will cause the limiter to react to the kick drum. This will attenuate the entire mix, and can result in an undesirable artifact known as "hole punching." In this case, the fix would be to go back to the original mix and turn down or compress the kick drum. Excessive limiting generally does not produce pleasant sonic results.

There is a great skill involved in creating a mix that sounds reasonably dynamic, but can be compressed to commercially acceptable average levels. In some cases a mastering engineer will send a mix back to the mix engineer with instructions for certain fixes. Some mastering engineers consider that if more than 4 dB or so of limiting or EQ is required in the mastering stage, the mix should be sent back reworked before the master is attempted again.

On the left side of the MW Limiter are controls for input gain, threshold, lookahead, release, and ceiling.

The input level knobs can be linked or unlinked for separate left and right volume control. Raising the input level is similar to lowering the threshold control. Both actions will cause the gain of the signal to increase.

The lookahead control delays the signal going into the limiter. This allows the limiter to detect a peak before it actually happens. The limiter can then begin to attenuate the signal before the actual peak occurs. This provides for a smoother limiting effect. In most cases, the lookahead control will be set at its maximum of 20ms.

The release control determines how long the limiter will take to recover from any peak attenuation. A slower release time will create a much slower response for the limiter and provides a gentle leveling effect. A faster release time preserves the dynamics of the mix when .the limiter recovers quickly from peaks. The release control is set according to the content of the audio and the preference of the mastering engineer. A good general place to start with the release control is around .20 seconds.

The ceiling control determines the maximum output of the plug-in. If dithering is applied, it is applied after the limiter section. Therefore it is typical to set the ceiling at .05 dB when using dithering.

Lastly, there are controls for bit quantizing, dithering, and noise shaping. Bit quantizing is used to round samples to lower bit depth resolution. Dithering should only be applied if the limiter is being used as the very last step of the mastering process. Noise shaping is added based on the preference of the mastering engineer. One way to get a good idea of what dithering and noise shaping do is to set the bit quantization to a low number such as 4. When dithering is then turned on, the dither noise will be obvious. When noise shaping is then applied, the difference in the dither noise will also be obvious.

Dynamic Equalizer Plug-In

It can be desirable to apply frequency boost or cut during the mastering process. The Dynamic Equalizer is a specialized plug-in that provides five bands of parametric EQ, while also providing separate dynamic control for each of the frequency bands.

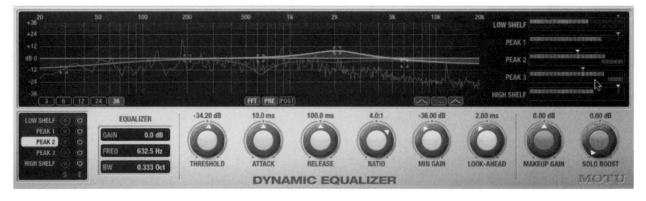

Figure 4.150

By combining EQ control with frequency-specific dynamics control, the Dynamic Equalizer is a powerful tool for controlling specific frequency levels in a mix. For example, if the kick drum is too loud in the mix, it will cause "hole punching" if controlled by a broadband compressor or limiter. A broadband compressor or limiter doesn't care which frequency is too loud. If the compressor or limiter sees any signal that exceeds the threshold, it will attenuate the entire frequency spectrum of the signal. The Dynamic Equalizer solves this problem by applying compression (or expansion) to specific frequency ranges. In the example of the kick drum, a frequency band can be used to isolate the low frequency of the kick drum. That frequency band can then be compressed. If the compression attenuates too much of the kick drum from the mix, the EQ gain can then be used to restore that frequency.

Each of the frequency bands can be muted or soloed. This is an effective way to isolate the specific frequency bands and signals that need to be controlled.

The Dynamic Equalizer can show an FFT display of the frequency content of the signal. The FFT display can be set to show the signal before or after the EQ and compression.

Spatial Enhancer Plug-In

The Spatial Maximizer plug-in is designed to work specifically on stereo mixes or stereo submixes. A stereo mix contains information that is common to both left and right channels, and information that exists only in the left or right channels. The Spatial Maximizer works by using a process called mid-side encoding. Mid-side encoding means that the plug-in separates the mono content of the mix (mid band) from the left and right content of the mix (side band). Those elements of the stereo mix can then be processed separately. This can be a powerful tool in the mastering process.

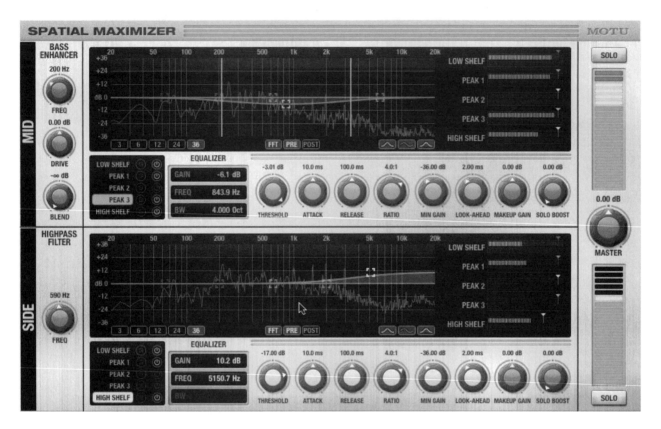

Figure 4.151

For example, in a typical pop mix, the lead vocal track is placed in the center of the mix as a mono signal. Stereo effects may be used on the lead vocal, but the primary signal is typically mono to provide focus and clarity. Therefore if the mid band of the mix is muted, the lead vocal could well be gone from the remaining left and right signal.

The Spatial Maximizer provides a five band parametric EQ for the mid band, and another five band EQ for the side band. Each band of EQ also has dynamics controls for compression or expansion. Individual EQ bands can be soloed or muted. Therefore it is possible to precisely control frequency response and dynamics of the mono content, independent of the stereo content. Using the example of the mono lead vocal, it is possible to use an EQ in the mid band to raise or attenuate that portion of the mix. This allows a mastering engineer to bring up or down the lead vocal within a finished stereo mix.

The mid band also includes bass enhancement controls. Bass enhancement works by adding low frequency harmonic distortion. The result is that bass becomes more apparent on headphones or small speakers.

Working with EQ and dynamics with the side band will have a dramatic affect on the apparent stereo width of the signal. For example, raising the high frequency of the side band with a high-shelf filter, will enhance the detail that is specific to the left and right content. Attenuating frequencies in the side band will make the mono content of the mix more dominant.

One last control that is important is the high-pass filter on the side band. The high-pass filter removes bass content that is exclusive to just the left or right sides of the mix. Typically, bass content is mixed to the center of the mix. Besides sonic focus, there are specific engineering reasons to attenuate bass frequencies that are found only on the left or right side of the mix. When mastering for vinyl, mid-side encoding is used to press the actual record. The up and down movement of the of the needle in the groove represents the mid band. The side to side movement of the needle represents the side band. If there is excessive bass content in the side band, the needle is liable to jump out of the groove. Therefore it is common practice to place a high-pass filter on the side band when mastering for vinyl. A similar situation exists with digital file compression. When a digital audio file is compressed using a format such as AAC or MP3, the compression format looks for signal that is common to left and right. If the compression format detects a great deal of difference in left and right channels, it does its best to represent that difference. However, if that different left and right content is low frequency, the file compression works to preserve that low frequency as much as it works to preserve higher frequency content. The high frequency content will then be compromised with little or no apparent sonic advantage. Therefore, it is a good idea to clean up the low frequency content of the side band if the mix is intended to be run through some sort of file compression format.

Waveform Editor

The Waveform Editor window can display and edit mono, stereo, or multichannel audio files. The difference between the Waveform Editor window and other edit windows in DP is that edits done in this window are destructive. That means they actually change the content of the audio file on the hard drive. This can be useful in the mastering process. The Waveform Editor can be used to snip blank audio from the beginning or ending of an audio file. The Waveform Editor can be used to create fade-ins or fade-outs.

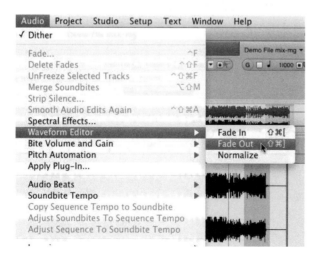

Figure 4.152

One type of mastering job is audio or tape restoration or remastering. For example, music that exists only on vinyl or magnetic tape can be recorded into DP and "cleaned up" for re-release in a digital format.

In the case of audio transferred from vinyl, it could be possible that there are ticks and pops as a result of scratches or an old record. The pencil tool in the Waveform editor can be used to draw out those artifacts.

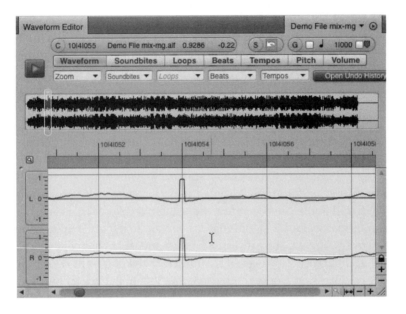

Figure 4.153

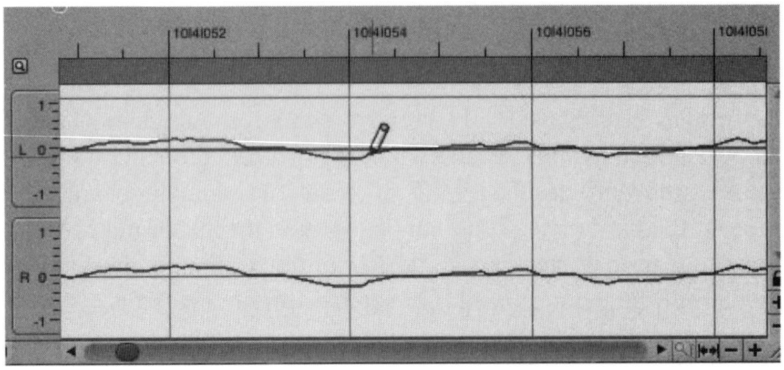

Figure 4.154

APPENDIX: ABOUT THE DVD-ROM

The included DVD contains DP projects with audio, as well as movie files. Files should be copied from the DVD to a local hard drive in order to be viewed and played.

The movie files describe specific procedures in DP. The project files are the files that are used in the movies. This allows the reader to work with the example files in DP while watching the accompanying movies.

Example Projects

The DVD contains three separate DP projects. Each project folder contains a DP session file and associated audio files. The project folder must be copied from the DVD to a local hard drive before it can be opened in Digital Performer. A complete install of DP8 is required in order to open the example projects. Each project is described in detail by an accompanying movie.

Live Virtual Instrument and Guitar Processing Template

This session file is an example of using DP for live virtual instrument triggering and guitar processing on stage. Stock DP VIs are used, along with stock DP effect plug-ins.

Film Scoring Template

This project includes a DP session file and an example movie file for a scoring session. A sequence offset time has been set for the movie. Markers have been created that reference movie hits. A tempo map has been created using the markers. Streamers have been added as visual cues.

Multitrack File and Mastering Template

This file is set up for a multitrack recording session. There are audio tracks, as well as subgroups and a master fader.

The session contains a multitrack recording of drums, bass, and guitar. There are several recorded takes in a single sequence. Those takes have been separated into individual sequence chunks. A tempo map has been created for the first separated sequence. The first separated sequence has been set up for a mixdown. There is a sequence chunk set up as a mastering template.

Movies

Each of the included movies describe a specific function or workflow in DP. The session files referenced by the movies are included on the DVD. This allows the reader to work with DP while watching the movies.

Exploring a Live Playback Session File

This movie includes a detailed description of DP and can be set up for live playback use. This includes audio and MIDI playback, SMPTE time code output, and multiple sequence chunks for set lists.

Virtual Instrument and Guitar Processing On Stage

In this movie, DP is set up with an audio interface, guitar input, and external MIDI keyboard input. Signal path, effects processing, and real-time control are described.

Film Scoring in DP

This movie describes importing a movie file into DP and setting a sequence start time. Markers are created and a tempo map is created based on the markers.

Demo Movie for Film Scoring

This movie is found in the Film Scoring Template project folder. This movie is used as the example movie for the scoring session.

Exploring the Multitrack Recording Template

In this movie, DP is configured with a multichannel audio interface for a live recording session. Once multiple takes are recorded into a single sequence, that sequence is then divided into separate sequences for each take.

Creating a Tempo Map Based on Live Performance

In this movie, a tempo map is created based on a live recording that was done without a click track. The tempo of the recording is then changed. A section of the recording is then quantized based on audio beats.

Exploring a DP Mixdown

The multitrack sequence is set up for final mixdown. This includes subgroups, effects send and returns, and master faders. Automation techniques are described. Stock plug-ins and presets are used in the mix.

Mastering in DP

The stereo mixdown of the multitrack session is set up for final mastering. Mastering plug-ins are discussed. The final master file is created and exported to different formats.

INDEX

quick PRO

guides *series*

Producing Music with Ableton Live
by Jake Perrine
Softcover w/DVD-ROM •
978-1-4584-0036-9 • $16.99

Sound Design, Mixing, and Mastering with Ableton Live
by Jake Perrine
Softcover w/DVD-ROM •
978-1-4584-0037-6 • $16.99

Mixing and Mastering with Cubase
by Matthew Loel T. Hepworth
Softcover w/DVD-ROM •
978-1-4584-1367-3 • $16.99

The Power in Cubase: Tracking Audio, MIDI, and Virtual Instruments
by Matthew Loel T. Hepworth
Softcover w/DVD-ROM •
978-1-4584-1366-6 • $16.99

The Power in Digital Performer
by David E. Roberts
Softcover w/DVD-ROM •
978-1-4768-1514-5 • $16.99

Logic Pro for Recording Engineers and Producers
by Dot Bustelo
Softcover w/DVD-ROM •
978-1-4584-1420-5 • $16.99

The Power in Logic Pro: Songwriting, Composing, Remixing, and Making Beats
by Dot Bustelo
Softcover w/DVD-ROM •
978-1-4584-1419-9 • $16.99

Mixing and Mastering with Pro Tools
by Glenn Lorbecki
Softcover w/DVD-ROM •
978-1-4584-0033-8 •$16.99

Tracking Instruments and Vocals with Pro Tools
by Glenn Lorbecki
Softcover w/DVD-ROM •
978-1-4584-0034-5 •$16.99

The Power in Reason
by Andrew Eisele
Softcover w/DVD-ROM •
978-1-4584-0228-8 • $16.99

Sound Design and Mixing in Reason
by Andrew Eisele
Softcover w/DVD-ROM •
978-1-4584-0229-5 • $16.99

Studio One for Engineers and Producers
by William Edstrom, Jr.
Softcover w/DVD-ROM •
978-1-4768-0602-0 • $16.99

quickproguides.halleonardbooks.com
Prices, contents, and availability subject to change without notice.

0113